HOW TO PARENT ALONE

BY JOAN BEL GEDDES

Small World
To Barbara With Love
How to Parent Alone

WITHDRAWN

Kirtley Library
Columbia College
8th and Rogers
Columbia, MO. 65201

HOW TO PARENT ALONE

A Guide for Single Parents

Joan Bel Geddes

A Continuum Book
THE SEABURY PRESS · *NEW YORK*

DEDICATION

To Anne, Nicholas, and Katie, who are still trying
to teach me how to be a good single parent,
to whom I apologize for not always being able
to practice what I preach except in one respect:
they *always* have my very, very great love.

The Seabury Press
815 Second Avenue
New York, N. Y. 10017

Copyright © 1974 by Joan Bel Geddes

Printed in the United States of America

Designed by Paula Wiener

All rights reserved. No part of this book may be reproduced in any form, except for brief reviews, without the written permission of the publisher.

Library of Congress Cataloging in Publication Data

Bel Geddes, Joan.
   How to parent alone.

   (A Continuum book)
   1. Single-parent family.   2. Single people.
I. Title.
HQ734.B514   301.42'7   74–8241
ISBN 0–8164–9243–3

CONTENTS

Dedication	v
Introduction	1
1: ACCEPTING YOURSELF *How to replace wishful thinking with realistic hopes and goals*	7
2: KNOWING YOURSELF *How to become happier through increased self-awareness*	21
3: EXPLAINING YOURSELF *How to answer difficult questions sensibly and helpfully*	37
4: ADJUSTING YOURSELF *How to make the transition from grief to peace*	57
5: COMFORTING YOURSELF *How to get rid of self-pity through increased understanding*	71
6: RESPECTING YOURSELF *How to conquer guilt and self-hatred and achieve self-esteem*	91

CONTENTS

7: CHANGING YOURSELF   109
*How to break harmful old habits
and build useful new ones*

8: RELYING ON YOURSELF   125
*How to emerge from overdependence
into self-confident independence*

9: ASSERTING YOURSELF   149
*How to avoid timidity and vacillation
to become decisive*

10: ENJOYING YOURSELF   169
*How to overcome loneliness through
an active social life*

11: INVOLVING YOURSELF   193
*How to eliminate boredom by
developing strong new interests*

12: PROTECTING YOURSELF   211
*How to handle financial problems
and stretch your money*

13: SUPPORTING YOURSELF   231
*How to find and get a job and
combine it with parenthood*

14: EXTENDING YOURSELF   251
*How to bridge the generation gap
by empathy and communication*

15: OPENING YOURSELF   269
*How to face the unknown future
with eagerness instead of fear*

INTRODUCTION

Many books have been written (some people think too many) on child care, but surprisingly few of them have very much to say about *parent care*. This is a little as if architects were to write detailed instructions for builders on how to erect a skyscraper without paying attention to the need for a sound, strong basement and ground floor. For beautiful music such as Bach's to exist, there must first be a Bach. And you wouldn't be able to achieve very good or durable results if you tried to paint an exquisite picture on a background of torn or moldy canvas.

This book is primarily about parent care.

It is for a particular type of parent who is in extra need of care: the parent who has no full-time collaborator to help with the job of parenting and who therefore needs to develop above-average independence, self-confidence, resilience—and wisdom.

In addition to the many problems which concern all parents, the parent operating on his or her own carries a double load. No one else is there to share daily tasks and worries. No one is reliably, consistently, at hand to consult on important decisions, to back one up when firmness is needed, or to counteract it when firmness has gone too far, or to give special comfort and support in times of emergency or hardship. No one is there to provide a salutary balance that will compensate for personal limitations in regard to temperament, judgment, knowledge, aptitudes, and attitudes.

Single parents, even if they are blessed with cheerful dispositions, are apt to worry a lot more than other parents, because they know they have imperfections and problems and yet they and they alone are responsible for the welfare of people they love.

Instead of pretending that one doesn't have defects, trying to ignore them and hoping that "what I don't know won't hurt me," the best way to reduce imperfections and problems is to face them frankly, so that one can learn *from* them and *through* them. This book therefore deals with a lot of unpleasant subjects, because dealing with them can make life more pleasant—for both parents and children.

If you are a single parent it isn't wise, or even possible, to pester and exploit your friends continually, expecting them to take the constantly deep interest in you and in your children which a loving fellow-parent would normally take. No matter how many or how intelligent or how kind your friends may be, you must learn to rely on and trust yourself more than anyone else. And you must develop the qualities you need if your trust, and your children's trust, is to be justified instead of fatally misplaced.

For most of us, this means we have a lot of work to do on ourselves. Sometimes pretty hard work. Especially in the beginning. The onset of single parenthood is usually a rather traumatic period when we are particularly bewildered and encumbered by acute problems, with enormous adjustments to be made both emotionally and financially.

We must learn to accept ourselves, our situation and its responsiblities—not fatalistically, resentfully, or fearfully, but realistically.

We must learn to adjust to a new life style, to adapt to one which has definite drawbacks—and certain advantages. We should learn what these are and take full advantage of all possible advantages.

We cannot afford to continue habits and attitudes which may have been appropriate and helpful once but which are now useless or even harmful. Therefore, in many ways, whether we want to or not, we will almost certainly have to change ourselves. Some changes must be made promptly, others can be made gradually. Some will be temporary, others permanent. Some major, some minor. Some relatively easy to accomplish, some extremely painful.

In order to change constructively and intelligently and peacefully, we will have to get to understand ourselves and our situation and our children's needs.

This means we must get to know ourselves—with neither self-pity nor self-hatred on the one hand nor with exaggerated conceit and over-optimistic expectations on the other. Some people think they know themselves but honestly don't like themselves very much. Others think they know themselves but nonetheless expect too much (or too little) of themselves. Both types are in danger of chronic disappointment, unless they change. But in order to change they must learn not only *why* and *what*, but *how*.

There cannot be a neat chronological or logical progression in discussing these personal needs and attitudes, which are the principal subject matter of this book, because emotions refuse to live in tiny, tidy compartments uninfluenced by each other. So do problems. Problem *B* does not wait politely and patiently in the wings while Problem *A* has its moment in the spotlight. They converge and clash, interrupt each other and compete.

Real life defies abstract, clear-cut categories, and the simultaneity of problems and duties makes life even harder to cope with than their multiplicity does. We do not *first* get to know ourselves and *then* understand ourselves and *then* learn to accept and/or change ourselves and *then*, finally, to like ourselves and enjoy ourselves. All of these processes intermingle and overlap, sometimes reinforcing each other and sometimes interfering with each other.

Yet they must be examined and discussed as if they were

separate processes, since one cannot talk intelligibly about everything at once. So we have to look at the same problem from different angles at different times, in relation to different factors, and a certain amount of back-and-forth repetition is unavoidable.

Please, therefore, dip and skim freely as you read this book. One day (or month or year) one part may suit your current mood or need. At another time a different point, or a different way of examining the same point, will be more relevant.

Typical problems frequently repeat themselves, but with an infinity of variations because no single parent is really "typical." The only thing they all have in common is the single fact that they are single parents, trying to raise children without the aid (and/or interference) of a full-time collaborator or co-pilot. A desperately unhappy young widow has very different woes and worries from those of a bitter (or gay) divorcee. A parent alone with an only child faces a very different set of problems from one who is presiding over a large gang. A frightened and naive young girl who has had a baby out of wedlock has different needs from a daring counter-culture rebel who glories in defying convention. And all of these single parents have different concerns and questions from a husband who is struggling to be father-mother to the children of an alcoholic or invalid wife.

To discuss and deal adequately with all of these problems would require the combined resources of teams of psychologists, sociologists, home economists, financial advisers, lawyers, clergymen, gynecologists, pediatricians, social workers, fashion and beauty consultants, vocational guidance counselors, and probably several other people I haven't thought of—not to mention a few close and loving personal friends. Since so many diversified problems cannot possibly be dealt with in one book, I am going to have to generalize, and not everything I say will be equally pertinent to every reader.

Whoever you are, whether you are single by choice or by chance, whether you love or loathe your children's other and now-absent parent, whether you gave birth to your children or

INTRODUCTION | 5

adopted them, I am going to have to make a few basic assumptions about you. I am going to assume, for one thing, that you did not arrive at this point in your life reclining on a velvet cushion, in a shiny Cadillac, chauffeured over a smooth highway. I imagine, rather, that you have been through a rather bumpy, sometimes scary, ride and that you have picked up a trauma or two along the way. And I suspect that some of the adjustments and new demands you are being required to make and meet are exceedingly difficult. If they are not, you are either remarkably unobservant or remarkably free of hang-ups and remarkably lucky.

I may refer to you fairly often as "she" or "a mother." If you are a father I apologize—but you are a statistical minority and it is the fate of all minorities to be neglected and unjustly treated at times! (You are a growing minority, however—the number of children living with divorced fathers jumped 50 percent between 1970 and 1972.)

Statistics tell me that the average single parent is in the late twenties with small children, is an urbanite, and will get remarried someday. If you happen to be in your forties, instead, with teen-age children, and you live on a farm and have no marital prospects or intentions, some of the comments I make will not apply to you, at least not without alterations. This cannot be helped. Family situations, life styles, individual personalities, needs, opportunities, convictions, and tastes vary so enormously that you must pick and choose carefully in these pages, tasting and digesting only what you think is good for you.

Be selective. Translate or modify my suggestions to fit your own conditions. Ignore them altogether if they don't seem relevant. Before discarding any idea, examine it with an open mind, but examine it with *your* mind, not with mine. Judge it by your own values and standards and needs, not by those of anyone else. I may not know who you are or what is good for you, but it is extremely vital that *you* know.

It is my hope that the day will come—and long before you think it will—when you consider all this discussion of problems and needs unnecessary, even melodramatic, because you will have succeeded in discovering your real assets and opportunities, breaking destructive habits, developing strong new interests, achieving financial security, and establishing such warm rapport with good friends and with your children that you have none of the problems discussed on these pages. You will have overcome confusion, embarrassment, grief, anger, self-pity, self-doubt, self-hatred, guilt, indecision, boredom, loneliness, shyness, anxiety, and fear so completely that you can hardly remember what these unpleasant, crippling emotions felt like.

When this happens—and it will if you make it happen—then your only big problem will be to avoid becoming smug and unsympathetic with other people to whom it hasn't happened yet!

Being a single parent is never going to be easy. But if you don't let that scare you too much, you will find that doing the best you can for yourself and for the little people you live with is a great deal of fun, and it brings huge rewards, immeasurably greater than any of your problems.

1

ACCEPTING YOURSELF:
Being realistic

If you are somewhat sad about or resentful of the fact that you are a single parent and find this status hard to accept, it may help you to know that you are part of a very large, increasingly fashionable group. In America today more than eight million children are being raised in one-parent households.

Once upon a time divorce was very rare. Even after it became less so it remained rare among parents. People who got divorced tended to do so, as a general rule, in the first few years of marriage before any children were born, or else they stayed together "for the sake of the children" until their children were grown and out of the house. But today the story is very different. The divorce rate in the United States increased 80 percent between 1960 and 1972. Almost half of all American marriages now end in separation or divorce. And twice as many children were involved in divorce actions during the past year as were fifteen years ago. The U.S. Census Bureau says most divorces now take place among young couples who have several children.

Furthermore, refugees from broken marriages are by no means the whole story. Under the heading of "single parents" there are many types of people. Widows and widowers. Unwed mothers who have decided to keep their babies (these days more than half of them do). Anyone whose husband or wife, because of chronic illness, or war, or a job requiring constant travel, is away from home for very extended periods.

In our era there are, in addition, growing numbers of voluntarily single parents. Many people, though not married, have chosen to adopt children, either temporarily as foster parents or on a permanent basis. Until recently child welfare agencies and laws did not permit adoption by a single person, but nowadays they often do and at times even actively encourage it, having discovered that children are far, far better off with one good parent than with none (or even with one good parent rather than with two not-so-good ones).

Both GIs and civilians, at an increasing rate, have befriended and then adopted war orphans. Many idealistic young women—and men—are finding an inspiring vocation in the parenting of "unadoptable" children, racially mixed children or those with physical, mental, or emotional handicaps. The patience, sweetness, creativity, hopefulness, cheerfulness, lovingness, and tireless energy of some of these parents, who have performed miracles of healing—curing supposedly incurable schizophrenia with love, turning delinquent children into happy and lovable ones, and spending years and fortunes on operations to correct physical defects—make me feel that the twentieth century is a wonderful time to be alive, no matter how many terrible problems it has. These parents are living reminders of how foolish it is to complain about trivial problems and of how powerful love is when it is applied to big problems. These are great people, greater than more famous ones—but one of the great things about them is that they don't do what they do in order to become famous and to be considered important or wonderful but just because they see an individual child in need and their hearts respond.

There is also beginning to appear, in the younger generation, another new type of single parent. An increasing number of young people are so disillusioned by traditional marriage as they have seen it function (or rather, fail to function) that they have made up their minds never to marry, even if they fall in love, and yet they have or plan to have children. They consider lifelong fidelity an unlikely possibility—understandably so, from the examples they have seen around them, and also because of the greatly lengthened life span and increased mobility which nowadays introduce so many people to each other and make families so much more unsettled than they were in earlier generations. Some of these young people consider lifelong marriage not merely an unlikely but even an undesirable goal, viewing domesticity as a trap that exploits and frustrates women and inhibits and overburdens men. In any case, rightly or wrongly, they have deliberately decided to have children outside of the conventional two-parent family setting.

Therefore, if being a single parent makes you feel peculiar, not quite respectable, or a marital "has-been," someone for whom the most important part of life—marriage—is over, try to modernize your attitude. The most important and challenging part of your life is just beginning. Try thinking of yourself not as deprived but as part of a growing group of imaginative social experimenters, innovators, pioneers developing a new life style. Even if you don't personally feel very adventurous, realizing that you are being called upon to join people who are may stimulate you to extend and surpass yourself. This is what's called making a virtue of necessity!

To cope effectively with problems, or to rise triumphantly to challenges, may require courage, patience, sustained energy, and imagination, but it also requires something even more basic: *realism*.

When a situation is unavoidable, no matter how difficult or unpleasant it is, it doesn't help to rail and rage against it. The quickest way to improve the situation is to accept it serenely. Margaret Fuller, a wise lady, once said after a period of deep meditation on the mysteries of good and evil, "I accept the universe." Thomas Carlyle's comment on her comment was, "Egad, she'd better!" The point is that this universe is the only one we have, and the only way to enjoy our brief stay in it as thoroughly as possible is to accept both the restrictions and opportunities it gives us, learning to function as well as we can within the boundaries these establish.

Refusing to accept the limitations imposed on us by the law of gravity, for instance, setting off to fly without wings, might make you feel exhilarated, like a conquering angel—but only for one split second. The concussion or broken limbs you would promptly get as a result of your declaration of independence would restrict you far more than realistic observance of the law would have. Walking gets us around more slowly than flying, but it's a lot faster and easier than hobbling on crutches.

Not only is this universe—and our small part of it, the Earth, with all the inconveniences, disappointments, injustices, and other limitations it contains—the only universe we have, but *you* are the only *you* you've got. Perhaps you would like to be a queen or a king or a millionaire or next year's Nobel Prize winner or this year's Miss Universe, but (unless you are) that's out. In some ways it would be very nice indeed to be a great beauty with an adoring and wealthy husband or a world-famous genius with a devoted and helpful wife (though not even great beauties, geniuses, millionaires, and happily married people are immune from problems), but you happen in fact to be You, so *your* possibilities are all you have to work with.

"For richer for poorer, for better for worse, in sickness and in health, till death . . ." These words are not merely part of the traditional marriage vows. They are the conditions of our own lives, even when someone is single, because one cannot get unmarried from oneself.

No matter how much you may admire or envy someone luckier or smarter than you are, since you can never change places with anybody else it is childish to fret and daydream endlessly, comparing and complaining, wishing you were what you will never be, yearning for perfection that doesn't exist. "When I was a child I thought as a child, I spoke as a child, I played as a child, but when I became a man I put away childish things,"

Saint Paul once said—and so should we. Childishness is appropriate to children, not to parents. Grown-ups must grow out of juvenile fantasies and learn to accept themselves with whatever real assets and liabilities they possess and with whatever heartaches and headaches they have acquired while arriving where they are.

"Accept" doesn't mean just "tolerate" or "endure" or "put up with." That minimum type of acceptance is required even of childish nonrealists, whether they like it or not. Even Houdini, the world's greatest escape artist, was unable to escape from illness and death. By *accept* I mean something much more positive: *welcome reality* with an open, receptive mind, with curiosity, with eagerness to find out what its possibilities are. Realize that inextricably entangled with real life's real problems there are real joys, of which you will deprive yourself if you withdraw from life. Weeds and flowers, tares and wheat, grow from the same soil.

Don't be afraid to look reality straight in the face. Unrealistic fears and exaggerated worries are, by definition, unrealistic and exaggerated, and therefore always worse than real problems. And the greatest imaginary achievement is far less gratifying than the smallest actual one. It is therefore very foolish to try to fool yourself into thinking you (or things) are better than you (or they) are, just as it is also silly to make yourself unnecessarily wretched by regarding them as worse than they are.

What really *is* is almost always, when we really think about it and really understand it and really face it, much more interesting than fantasies. God is more inventive than the cleverest human being, and the real world is full of far more fascinating things to do and to see than our limited imaginations could ever dream up to entertain and help us. We can have more enjoyment with any living person whom we really understand than from any imaginary dream man or woman. We can learn more from any real experience (even an unhappy one) which we really understand than from any abstract hypothesis or daydream—and learning from experience, so that we know more and more and can do more and more and see more and more and enjoy more and more is what life is all about.

It isn't enough to accept reality in a theoretical, philosophical, general way while still getting unduly upset over daily trifles. That's like Charlie Brown saying, "I love mankind, it's people I can't stand." To function well we must learn to put up peacefully with this delay or that foible, this pest and that frustration. Never mind if yesterday was happier; today my job is to meet the situation I find myself in today. I may think (probably mistakenly) that I would have been edifyingly brave if I were about to be burned at the stake back in the middle ages, but that is not what life is demanding of me at this moment. I must achieve enough patience and courage and wisdom to cope with my current loneliness and to do this week's laundry or take care of my son's mumps or help my daughter memorize a French vocabulary list, *now*.

Some of us find it far easier to be heroic on a grand scale about a tremendous tragedy than to put up with small, hardly noticeable, normal nuisances or drudgery. Serious difficulties bring out the best in us while petty irritations turn us into nags and gripers. When called upon to make great sacrifices we manage somehow to rise to the occasion (perhaps because the drama of the situation appeals to the show-off in us, or perhaps because we make a greater effort), while a repetitious collection of uninteresting, minor, unappreciated, unnoticed-by-anyone sacrifices seems more than we can bear and makes us irritable rather than noble.

These characteristics of human nature are complicating factors in life, troubles that add to our troubles. But they are part of the reality about ourselves which we have to accept. They are only unbearable when we let them throw us completely. With the help of three senses—common sense, a sense of proportion, and a sense of humor—we can cope with the vast majority of daily problems even when we wish we didn't have to.

Acceptance of reality does not mean becoming fatalistic. It doesn't mean convincing ourselves that we are stuck in an unpleasant situation with no way out. It is definitely *not* realistic to accept one's fate as inexorable and permanent. Everything changes, sooner or later. And we ourselves are among the agents that produce change. It is in our power to make our lives better, just as it is also, unfortunately, in our power to make them worse.

To be fatalistic means to feel helpless, like a pawn, trapped in a situation not of our own making and powerless to affect our own destiny. But *real* acceptance of reality is quite different. It means accepting not only what has happened to us but also accepting our responsibility to improve ourselves and to take the measures required to improve our situation when we can and should.

Hopeless submissiveness, far from being true acceptance of reality, is an evasion and denial of one of the most important aspects of reality: our freedom to be creative and to work toward goals—in other words, to alter our "fate."

For instance, I may feel bitter about my fate because I wish I were a great artist and I'm not. Well, if I really love art I can do several things about it. First of all, I can set about equipping myself. A person who wants to paint but has no paint will have to get off the bed on which he is daydreaming and get himself some paint. If none is available, he'll have to satisfy his creative urge with another medium. The greatest artist in the world cannot paint without paint.

And of course, though that is an essential step, it is only one of many. As the Chinese proverb says, "The journey of a thousand miles begins with a single step." But no great ambition can be realized until *many* steps have been taken—and a lot of them uphill.

If I want to be a good artist (a good anything) I must be willing to work at it. As moral theologians say, "If you will the end you must also will the means." So I must study art and I must practice. It may turn out that I don't have enough talent to be really great, but if I work very hard I can probably at least become skillful enough to enjoy myself. Unless I have no hands! Though even then I still don't have to sit around idly, bemoaning my cruel fate. I can find something else interesting to do, related to art, that doesn't require using hands. (In fact, if I really want to paint enough I may still be able to. I know of a professional greeting card artist whose hands are deformed; she paints with the brush held between her teeth. I also know of another good painter without arms who holds the brush with his toes. You may think I'm making those cases up to prove a point, but I'm not; they're real.)

Both my goals and the means I take to reach them must be rooted in reality—but reality may contain more amazing possibilities than I at first realize.

Three things are always required when a person wants to find out if he or she has a religious vocation: (1) desire, (2) opportunity, (3) ability. No one or even two will suffice. And those are three very good norms to apply when testing the sincerity and practicality of any ambition.

Accepting reality means acknowledging and intelligently analyzing the actual conditions under which we must work as well as the equipment we have available with which to work, and realizing that within those circumscribed limits we can be imaginative and active and productive and free.

Another example: If you are husbandless or wifeless but wish that this were not true, it is true just the same. So it's a sheer waste of time to bemoan the fact indefinitely. It's far more sensible and peace-and-happiness-inducing to accept the fact as a fact and promptly set about discovering, quite factually, all the things there are that you can do and enjoy without a spouse. . . . and there actually are a great many.

Look over your present circumstances objectively. Calmly. Unevasively. Not through a mist of tears, fears, prejudices, preconceptions, pet theories and idle dreams. You will discover that you really do have certain definite advantages as well as disadvantages. The disadvantages may be all too obvious: your life contains a degree of loneliness, tedium, disappointment and problems, some large and some little, that cannot go away completely—but that can be borne and even reduced. Going after them can be interesting, enjoyable, exciting—like learning to knock down pins in a bowling alley. Conquering an actual problem, when you have made up your mind to do it and started going about it, is intriguing and satisfying, while yearning vainly for magical solutions that never materialize simply produces an ever-increasing sense of impotence.

It would be extremely foolish to fail to enjoy a gift of fifty dollars because you would rather have been given a hundred. So work with what you have, and enjoy it as much as possible, instead of thinking about all the things you don't and can't have. G. K. Chesterton once said that if a thing is really worth doing it's worth doing badly; I agree and would add that if a thing is really worth having it's worth having incompletely. A partial pleasure, a temporary bit of happiness, a few delightful qualities which co-exist with defects—these are all very much worth having, as long as we accept them for what they are. Concentrate on what they *are,* not on what they are *not.*

Never confuse "acceptance" with passivity or cynicism. Passivity is fatalism's lazy twin brother, and cynicism is fatalism's sophisticated brother.

People sometimes consider themselves realists when they are willing to accept injustice without protest. They think they are being practical and patient and, furthermore, noble, when they are really just being too indolent or cowardly or too corrupt to battle against evil. *Genuine* acceptance of reality has nothing in common with masochism or listlessness. It is, like genuine tolerance or genuine faith, an *active* attitude involving alertness and awareness and responsiveness. It doesn't mean putting up with bad situations supinely; it means analyzing them intelligently, so that you can improve them, and it also means not letting a lucky break slip by unobserved, not letting a small handicap stay in the way of an attainable advantage, being able to see the woods as well as the trees *and* the trees as well as the woods.

Instead of being helpless and inert—"this is the way things are (frown) and I've always been this way (sigh) and I just have to accept it whether I like it or not (groan) because there's nothing anyone can do about it (sob) or it's too much trouble to do anything about it (yawn)"—acknowledge facts honestly, fearlessly, observantly, both the bitter and the better, and then do something about them. Realize that *here* is your present situation and *there* is where you wish you were and *these* are the steps that may lead you from here to there. Accept the size and shape of the framework within which you *can* do something, and then *do* it, instead of complaining about the smallness of the frame and wishing you could burst out of it and run away to never-never land.

There are two other things that accepting ourselves and the reality of the situations in which we find ourselves does not mean. *Acceptance doesn't mean defeatism. And it doesn't mean complacency.* It does mean striving toward realizable goals by practical means. It means acknowledging our strength (without conceit) and our weakness (without despair). It means avoiding exaggeration, choosing facts over fantasy.

Some people are so deeply embarrassed or angry or discouraged over their own and life's and their children's imperfections that they are permanently disgruntled. They may demand too much of themselves or of other people or of life as a whole, while other people expect too little. Both attitudes are self-defeating, because both are equally unrealistic.

Judgments and expectations should be built on a solid bedrock of *fact*. When we demand more of ourselves or of life or of other people than can possibly be delivered we assure ourselves of perpetual disappointment. But it is equally ridiculous to try to protect ourselves from "inevitable" disappointments by never expecting anything to go right and by demanding *less* of ourselves or of life or of other people than we or it or they can give. When we do that we short-change ourselves, guaranteeing in advance the less-than-best existence we are trying to steel ourselves against, becoming permanently a little sad. Does it make sense to try to protect yourself from occasional sadness by cultivating an attitude that makes you permanently sad?

To say that goals should be realistic does not imply that they cannot be high. It is no more realistic to think you must always settle for the minimum than to insist always on the maximum. The middle of the target is where the bullseye is—and an archer who wants to be sure to hit the bullseye must always aim slightly above dead center.

Hope is the balance between, and the corrective for, the two opposite extremes of presumption and despair. And genuine hope is practical. Don't confuse it with the phony variation on it known as wishful thinking. To be hopeful does not mean indulging in impossible dreams; it means making use of the spiritual energy which often makes dreams that *seem* impossible come true.

Any infant who was firmly convinced that he could never learn to walk would be quite right. He wouldn't try, and therefore he would fulfill his prophecy. On the other hand, if he was firmly convinced that he already knew how to walk when he didn't, he would never learn either. In either case his delusion would deprive him of the incentive he needs to exercise in order to fulfill his hope of walking. A baby learns to do what he cannot yet do by *wanting* to do it very much and by *determining* to do it and by patiently *practicing* doing it again and again and again, refusing to be discouraged to the point of defeat by the fact that he fails a thousand times. He responds actively to the creative urge inside him, and he is willing to risk the humiliation of repeated failure in order to achieve success.

It may be natural to wish we had no faults and no problems, but wishing will never make that so. That is a perfect example of an unrealistic, and therefore futile, wish—an "impossible dream"—as against the realistic hope that if we try we can steadily improve, even though never becoming entirely perfect. The only person who has no faults and no problems is a corpse.

There is one more point that is important: *Acceptance doesn't mean grim stoicism. Acceptance means contentment*—i.e., happiness. So don't overlook the opportunities for sheer fun that come your way because you're too preoccupied with problems.

Just as there are Three Rs which every child should learn how to apply in order to get along well in life, there are three which every adult should learn how to apply: Realism, Resolution, and Recreation. And there are also three which should be renounced forever: Recriminations, Rage, and Regrets.

Realistically resolve to re-create yourself and your circumstances (realize that the word *recreation* means "re-creation") and enjoy the process as well as the results. Remember the tourists' slogan: "Getting there is half the fun."

An eloquent inscription on one of the walls of an old church in Baltimore, under the general heading of *Desiderata*, he describes a few of the attitudes which are to be desired in human beings. Some of them apply directly to the subject of accepting reality, and I suggest reading them and thinking about them, even memorizing them:

As far as possible without surrender be on good terms with all persons. Speak your truth quietly and clearly—and listen to others, even the dull and ignorant; they too have their story. Avoid loud and aggressive persons—they are vexatious to the spirit.

If you compare yourself with others you may become vain and bitter, for always there will be greater and lesser persons than yourself.

Enjoy your achievements as well as your plans. Keep interested in your own career, however humble; it is a real possession in the changing fortunes of time.

Exercise caution in your business affairs, for the world is full of treachery—but let this not blind you to what virtue there is; many persons strive for high ideals, and everywhere life is full of heroism.

Be yourself. Neither be cynical about love, for in the face of all aridity and disenchantment it is as perennial as the grass. . . .

Nurture strength of spirit to shield you in sudden misfortune. But do not distress yourself with imaginings. Many fears are born of fatigue and loneliness. Beyond a wholesome discipline, be gentle with yourself.

You are a child of the universe, no less than the trees and the stars; you have a right to be here. And whether or not it is clear to you, no doubt the universe is unfolding as it should.

Therefore be at peace with God, whatever you conceive him to be, and whatever your labors and aspirations, in the noisy confusion of life keep peace with your soul.

With all its sham, drudgery, and broken dreams, it is still a beautiful world. Be careful. Strive to be happy.

2

KNOWING YOURSELF:
Increasing self-awareness

Who are you and what are you like?

If your first instinctive answer to that question is, "I'm ME!" and you have a very clear idea of Me's value and individuality, great! But if it was, "Oh, I'm nobody special—just an average person," you're wrong.

There is no such thing as an average person in the whole wide world. The only place averages exist is on paper and in mathematicians' heads. If you were an "average" person you would be living in a country where the annual per capita income is less than seven hundred dollars a year and you would have something like two and seven-eighths children—a neat trick.

Everyone on earth is special, one of a kind, unique from his soul to his fingerprints. But people who are newly widowed or divorced often feel quite confused at first about who and what they are. They feel as if they've become part of a batch of statistics about people who lose out in life, and the only way in which they feel special is that they feel especially unfortunate.

Widows and widowers who have been so closely and happily associated with another person (especially if it was for a very long time) that they have thought of "me-plus-the-other" as a permanent and indivisible unity, rather than thinking of themselves as separate identities, are apt to feel only "half there" once their "better half" is gone. And people who have recently been divorced may feel even more bewildered about themselves.

One frequent reason for divorce is that many people marry before they really get to know themselves (or each other) well enough to know what their deepest interests and desires and values and needs and basic temperamental characteristics are. They conceal and ignore failings during their courtship days because they are so busy trying to impress and please each other, and in their mutual enthusiasm for a few outstanding traits they overlook danger signals about latent ones. Only after they have been living together for a while does he, for instance, find out that the passionate interest she showed in his career was an act —even if a well-meant or unconscious one—and that she is really bored to death by something which interests him more than anything else in the world; or she discovers that certain little quirks and mannerisms and habits of hers which he used to think were "adorable" now, with familiarity and repetition, annoy him terribly.

Just as people today are required to take driver's education courses and tests before they can get a driver's license, maybe people ought to have to take some kind of "self-knowledge" course and test before they can get a marriage license.

Actually, though, even that would not guarantee compatibility, because people keep changing. New events influence us continually throughout our lives. In the modern world we meet more new people and encounter more new experiences in a few years than most of our grandparents and great-grandparents did during a whole lifetime, so we cannot helping changing, developing new interests that a spouse may not share, and making new friends that he or she may not like as much as we do. So even if people were not putting on an act for each other's benefit when they first met, the fervent enthusiasm they then had about each other's ideas, the total agreement they had on every matter they discussed, and the strong attraction they each felt for the other may wane.

People do not necessarily change at the same rate or in the

same direction, so two people who once seemed to have everything in common can grow very far apart—sometimes so far apart that they can no longer stay together and be happy.

During many marriages this sort of change—whether it represents improvement or deterioration or merely variety—occurs slowly, almost imperceptibly, and sometimes people are able to absorb it and accommodate themselves to it without much difficulty. But in those cases where changes carry people off in entirely different directions there is a point of no return, and the marriage is destroyed—even if the couple stays together it is destroyed in the sense that it is no longer a supportive, cooperative, harmonious, fulfilling, joy-producing union.

The survivors of a shipwrecked marriage are then on their own, and it is time for them to take stock of themselves. Each of them, almost certainly, should have done so much sooner, but unfortunately you cannot rewind life like a tape recorder and go back to erase your mistakes. So never mind what you should have done and when you should have done it and what would have happened if you had. Do it *now*, instead of drifting along in confusion or plunging into another equally unsatisfactory relationship with someone else. Start sorting yourself out, so that you can now become the kind of person you really want to be—and the kind of parent who can help children be and become the kind of people you like.

"Know thyself" is such an ancient adage that some people have forgotten it and many pay no serious attention to it, regarding it as just one of many hoary platitudes too obvious to be taken seriously. This is too bad. When people don't take the obvious seriously, the subtleties they do take seriously can be way off-base and get them into trouble. When we don't pay attention to the "obvious" we can become as dotty as an absent-minded professor who wastes a whole morning searching through desks and closets and pockets for his eyeglasses when all the time they are on his head, or as unhelpful as a mother who is such an excellent cook that she thinks it's perfectly obvious how to make a cake or an omelette and therefore never bothers to teach her poor daughters how. Making sure that one attends to the obvious is as important a first step toward intelligent functioning in life as learning to add two and two is before trying to do algebra. We would all love to be so sophisticated and intelligent that we never had to concern ourselves about anything elementary or banal, but we thwart ourselves if we act upon the assumption that we are. In fact, *getting to know oneself is one of the most important things anyone can ever do, as well as one of the most interesting.* And people who never get around to doing it are never able to be as contented or useful or even as attractive as they are inherently capable of being.

You may suppose that everyone actually does know himself, since everyone lives with himself his whole life long, but knowing oneself can be surprisingly difficult. We are very good at fooling ourselves and lying to ourselves, mistaking wishes for realities, thinking up alibis and evading the obvious. And these days genuine self-knowledge is more elusive than ever before—as well as more important—because our world is changing so rapidly and profoundly and has become such a complicated and often alarming place to live in.

People who look for their psychological or moral security in the outside world rather than inside themselves can become disoriented. Both psychiatrists' couches and jails are full of people who are troubled by the mysterious fact that they don't know who they are or what they want and who therefore have pursued goals that have made them unhappy. To keep one's equilibrium amid outer confusion and turmoil one must establish a fixed point somewhere, and the only reliable always-there place anyone can count on is inside oneself.

The search for self-knowledge, in short, is not merely a luxury to be indulged in by people who have an introspective or self-centered or philosophical turn of mind. It is a real necessity, a prerequisite for happy, productive living.

Why is it hard for some people to get to know themselves?

After all, as I said, all of us live with ourselves all our lives, so you would think we would know ourselves. We *are* our selves.

Are we?

Some of us are not! Some of us *lost* ourselves as we grew up, and we became strangers to ourselves, for many reasons—because of the complexity and strength of unknown forces that formed us, because of our often unreliable memories, because of our undeveloped talents, because of our inability to verbalize many of our deepest thoughts and strongest emotions, because of our reluctance to admit and face up to our fears and feelings of inadequacy, and because we may have gotten caught in relationships that were not good for us.

All babies are born with the healthy instinct to know their own needs and to speak up in no uncertain terms whenever they want something. But older people try to train them out of this inborn self-knowledge (and self-centeredness) as quickly as possible. As each child gets older it is forced more and more to repress more and more aspects of its personality so that it can become an acceptable member of society.

This is inevitable, of course. It is even desirable, when it isn't carried too far. All of us must learn to accommodate ourselves to other people's selves. We have to learn to give in at times to other people's wishes instead of always insisting on having our own way. We have to learn to recognize and to accept and to work within limitations. We have to realize that there are other people on this planet who have needs and rights in addition to ourselves.

The trick, however, is not to lose track of ourselves as we discover the rest of the world.

Quite naturally, all human beings establish their sense of being, even their raison d'être, to a large extent as a result of their associates and environment, because each of us lives and grows in a specific social context, not on a statistical chart or in abstract isolation. But we are in for trouble if we let these associations and surroundings swallow us up like quicksand.

I am not, you are not, our children are not merely collages of family, friends, job, nationality, etc. Our relationships, skills, locales, tasks, politics, religion, sex, genes, and cultural milieus all help to describe and conscribe and prescribe what we do in life, but none of these nor all of them put together can fully determine or define who we are. We live in, work in and with, enjoy (or dislike), and are strongly affected by our contacts and surroundings, yet the essence of me and of you is far deeper, more private, more intangible, more impenetrable, more subtle, and much, much more important than any of these things. No matter where you go, or what happens to you, or whom you are with, you are and always have been and always will be your own inimitable self: *you*. A V.I.P. Someone who knows some things and does some things and is some things that no one else in the entire world has ever known or done or been. Unique. Irreplaceable.

What saves us from wandering off into total isolation is the fact that although we never have *everything* in common with anybody else we always have *something* in common with everybody. We can learn to appreciate both our differences and our similarities, and to relish both separateness and togetherness.

The expression "one in a million" implies that something has special value, and this is how we should think of ourselves because we are even *more* valuable than that; each of us is one in 4,000,000,000! Yet we usually don't look at it that way. We notice the huge number of people there are in the world and feel insignificant as a result, instead of special. It's the old question of not being able to see the trees for the forest. Instead of marveling at the inexhaustible variety of people and realizing how each one is born, as Sam Levenson has said, with his own special message for mankind, we lump everyone together, including ourselves, and individuals get swallowed up in the masses. Everybody may *be* important but they don't *feel* important. They leave out the "r" and change the "a" to an "e" and feel impotent instead. Anonymous, submerged.

In many, perhaps all, societies, some people are exploitative and overdemanding, and many others become crushed, overaccommodating, learning to do—even to think—what they think other people want them to, even when this is wrong and quite the opposite of what they really, deep down inside, want to do and think. When Communists manipulate people's souls this way we call it "brainwashing" and deplore it. But all ideologies and systems—and far too many parents—brainwash people to some extent.

Even self-styled rebels are often victims of this sort of standardizing, homogenizing process. They resist it, protest loudly against it, defy it, and think they are therefore being themselves, free agents, but sometimes their protests are so automatic that they resemble blinking and knee reflexes: poke them here or there and they will jump, not because they are actually deciding independently what they should or want to do but because outside pressures are pushing them. They are the individual equivalents of a government foreign policy which, instead of being farsightedly creative, reacts from moment to moment in response to crises arising outside of its control, often doing the wrong things in instant retaliation or else the right things but too little and too late. If we want to be in control of our own destiny we must learn to act on our own, not simply to *re*act to other people and situations.

Many of the most distressing problems we are having in the twentieth century have come about because people want and need to know who they are, but don't.

The women's lib movement is the result of emerging self-consciousness on the part of millions of women who are tired of trying to find their identity only as appendages of husbands and/or children, women who want desperately to be seen and heard and taken seriously by and for themselves. Every Ms. wants to be respected as an individual rather than expected to fit meekly into a preordained role. Unfortunately, women have been so conditioned by the roles in which society has cast them that many of them don't know what to do with themselves once they reject those traditional roles. It is impossible to build a satisfying, creative life on the basis of angry refusal to play a role unless you know what you want to replace that role with, and many "liberated" females, after a great glorious burst of euphoria as they toss off their chains or apron strings or topple the pedestals they have been placed on by a male-dominated society, really haven't the slightest notion of anything meaningful they would like to be now instead of the "little woman" or "earth mother" or "sex goddess" they have hitherto been expected to be.

The emotional volatility, and at times very obnoxious behavior, of troubled and troublesome teen-agers is also due to an "identity crisis." Most adolescents are exploding inside with a jumble of unresolved tensions because they don't yet quite know who they are, so they experiment continually, often daringly, thoughtlessly, foolishly, trying to sort out values and changing their behavior and feelings and theories from one day to the next, veering wildly from one extreme to another, sometimes driving everyone (including themselves) crazy in the process.

Much of the disturbing racial tension that exists today is another sign of the widespread human yearning and need for self-knowledge and self-esteem. So is class tension and belligerent nationalism. Members of groups that are, or feel, persecuted find comfort in group identity because they haven't enough confidence individually, or lack the opportunity individually, to establish a respected identity of their own. Ethnic groups who demand special school courses in Puerto Rican studies or American Indian studies or black studies or name-your-own-favorite-minority studies, and those who demand the right to integrated (or segregated) dormitories, have caused commotion in recent years because of their newly awakened desire to be themselves and to learn more about themselves. The black boys and girls who have stopped trying to straighten their hair and now sport becoming "Afros" are learning to be aware and proud of, and not merely reconciled to, their identity.

Even crimes and wars are often caused by people's desire (no, their need) to be seen and listened to and understood and respected as much as they are by greed or struggles over property or ideologies.

Unless you know who you are, you find yourself frequently doing things which, though they might be pleasing and helpful to someone else, do not help *you* to be as happy or effective as you really could be and would like to be. Adopting other people's judgments unthinkingly, while suppressing and repressing your own, and imitating the way other people think and act may be the most sincere form of flattery to them, but it is not the way for you to become the best person you can be. In fact, it's the way to guarantee that you will become much less interesting and less important than you are potentially.

When we try too hard to live up to other people's expectations or to the models they have presented to us—wishing we were as glamorous or brilliant or successful or something as someone we admire is—we never get around to being ourselves and realizing our deepest aspirations. We try in vain to be something we cannot be, instead of learning how to be what *only* we can be—because we don't even know what that is.

Men, as well as women, need to be liberated.
Women are trained from infancy to meet other people's demands, to please themselves only when they succeed in pleasing someone else, to conform to a prefabricated image of generalized femininity instead of developing their own specific individuality. The result is that many women never learn to value or even recognize themselves except in relation to a particular function or another person. They think of themselves as "So-and-so's daughter" or "So-and-so's wife" or "So-and-so's mother" rather than as "Me."

But, even though this is supposedly a man's world, many a man also feels more like a "what" than a "who," as if he were merely an undistinguished member of a general species. Proudly or apologetically he may identify himself by his tasks ("I'm a salesman" or "I'm a businessman", as if any man were merely someone who sells or buys things), in the same way that so many women think of themselves only as someone who takes care of a house ("I'm just a housewife").

Many men go along for years and years too busy to think much about themselves, doing useful work, being fond of their families (or just taking them for granted), but never building up a strong sense of self. They haven't time to philosophize and feel no need or desire to. But then, if a sudden crisis or change or gap occurs in a man's life, particularly if this is in the intimate area of family life, his frail and neglected self-image may crumble. Something has gone terribly wrong and he feels shattered, even disgraced. But he dare not act or look weak or frightened, though inside he feels like jelly, because tearless, fearless behavior is expected at all times from men.

In short, both men and women are apt to lose themselves in appointed roles. They may not mind fitting into a slot, as long as a job or marriage is going well. They are only partly alive, but they feel fairly satisfied with that part—unless and until the task or relationship which has given their life its meaning and stability ends. Then they are cut adrift. They really lost their way long ago, *in* the job or relationship, but never realized it. Now they do. Painfully.

In such cases, it is much more than a husband or wife or job that has disappeared. The main reason for living is gone. It is essential, if such people are ever going to be joyful and function well again, and if they are going to be able to raise happy children, that they rediscover themselves. Children need a parent, and if there is only one on the scene, and that one is lost, where will the children find one?

The temporary emptiness in your life which is produced by the departure of someone or something you loved is bearable if you are a strong person. However, when you lack a vigorous sense of identity and personal worth, losing any important aspect of your life can make you feel as if you had lost *everything*. You don't merely feel slightly poorer but utterly destitute, and desperate. If you are the ex-wife or ex-husband of a broken marriage or the survivor of a marriage ended by death, you may feel as disoriented as if the very floor had been taken out from under you or as if your whole soul had been ripped right out of you.

What can you do about it if you feel unimportant, worthless, empty, or annihilated?
The most obvious thing, in some ways the most natural and easiest thing, is to crumple, to succumb to despair. Except that there is one hitch if you happen to have children for whom you are responsible. You *can't*. Your children need you. So you *have* to keep going. You have to reorient yourself. You have to find yourself.

You may notice yourself wishing (and then feeling terribly guilty for feeling that way) that you had no children, because they are such a big responsibility and you no longer feel able to cope with responsibility. All you long to do is to give up, collapse, cease struggling.

Life is full of paradoxes, and here is one mysterious and marvelous and life-saving one: *Your greatest burdens are your greatest blessings.* Be glad you have children—very, very glad—because they force you to do what you should do and what you will later be very glad you did, which is *not* give up. You will have to do many things for their sakes which you don't feel like doing, and you will benefit from this fact as much as your children will. By helping them you will be helping yourself. Because of their needs you will keep on going through the motions of living even on those days when you feel like never getting up out of bed again. When you have not yet established an independent identity of your own which is strong enough to make you want to keep on living for your own sake, your children will serve as a bridge over troubled waters.

The littler people are, the bigger help they can be in sustaining you as you cross over from that period in your life when you thought of yourself as half of a pair into that unknown new life when you must learn to think of yourself as yourself: a whole, not a hole.

The one and only safe place to establish your identity is within yourself. You have to learn to find your greatest source of happiness and strength, basically and primarily, there, exploring and cultivating your own inner resources, because other people can always go away and leave you (your children almost certainly will, and should, someday) and external circumstances are always changing. If you have learned nothing else as a result of becoming a single parent, you should at least have learned that!

Yet many people never realize this. They spend their whole lives in a vain, often frantic, search for happiness, looking everywhere else except inside themselves. They think they could become so much better, more useful, more contented, more creative if only they lived in a different place, knew different people, had a more interesting job, had more money, or had . . . name it. They may, in fact, at times need some or all of those things, but in themselves none of them will permanently help anyone unless *inner* strength is also developed. "The kingdom of heaven is within."

Being happy and knowing yourself are inextricably linked. How can you ever be truly, lastingly, deeply, thrillingly happy unless you know what makes you happy and strive for it? And how can you possibly do that unless you know yourself well enough to know what your real needs and abilities are? So it should be obvious (and remember never to overlook the obvious) that you must become aware of, honest with, and understanding of yourself.

Ah yes, you may say, but the trouble is that I do know myself and I do know what would make me happy: a happy marriage would make me happy! And therefore, since I am not married, I can't be happy.

If that is the truth about yourself, what can you do then? You can admit and accept the fact, if it really is a fact, but you must at the same time accept another fact: no one worth marrying is ever going to want to marry you if you are perennially unhappy and confused, permanently lacking in interests and self-confidence, if you remain a forlorn nervous wreck, feeling incomplete and sorry for yourself because you are spouseless.

So get to know yourself well enough to recognize what your best (and worst) traits are and what your strongest interests and abilities are. And then use that knowledge to develop your best qualities into superb ones and to correct your worst failings until they become very tiny ones. Become as happy, interesting, worthwhile, self-sufficient, and attractive as it is possible for you to be under your present circumstances—and you may become an extremely desirable catch for an extremely desirable marital candidate. If you never find a new partner you still won't lose out, because you will have become much pleasanter and more interesting to yourself in any case. Either way, you'll win. Whereas, if you fail to do this, then you and your children will lose out, either way.

Of course, in every generation there are some children who spring up unpredictably, like mutations, into wonderful and successful people even though they were raised by seemingly very inadequate parents. And, yes, some gangsters have had saintly mothers—and some saints have had wicked parents. But these are most certainly exceptions. *To a frighteningly large extent, what our children will be like depends on what we are like.*

We prefer to blame television, our children's peers, their teachers, and society as a whole, rather than ourselves, for traits our children develop which we don't like, but we cannot honestly deny the fact that we are the primary and steadiest influence in their lives during their formative years. Children are great mimics and even though we may not always recognize our own voices when we hear our children whine or shout, and may not realize the source of a child's emotional problems such as insecurity or hostility, outsiders can usually see the family resemblance quite clearly.

If we ourselves are inconsistent, indecisive, panicky in emergencies, habitually worried, unhappy, bored, or cynical, the chances are that our children will reflect and perpetuate these traits. It is a sad fact of life that it seems to be much easier to teach our children to imitate our faults than it is to pass onto them our ideals.

And speaking of ideals, since the world is changing so speedily these days, we cannot expect our children to pick up out of the air, by osmosis, the values we would like them to live by. If they are going to get ideals that we ourselves believe in, they are going to have to encounter them at home.

But still another problem complicates matters: we ourselves are no longer quite as sure as we once were about what our own values are! When the large outside world is being rapidly transformed and our own private world has recently been through an enormous upheaval, we have to make an extra effort to hold on to our values, or to find new ones to replace the old ones if these have slipped out of our hands.

"You are what you eat," say the nutritionists. You are also what you believe—in other words, what you eat mentally. To a great extent our inner outlook affects for better or worse our outer look. We were born with a baby face but we ourselves mold our own mature faces, ironing in frown lines and worry lines and droopy dissipated bags under our eyes, or a pouting or sneering or tight-lipped mouth—or smile lines. Our feelings about life affect our posture (whether it's sagging and stooped or sprightly and erect) and our mannerisms (fidgety, fluttery gestures or calm, graceful ones; wishy-washy handshakes or a firm grip; nervous, shrill giggles, boisterous guffaws, pleasant chuckles; nasal, whiny voices or well-modulated speech; brisk footsteps or a lazy, dragging shuffle, etc.). And because our outward appearance strongly affects how people react to us, our inner outlook's influence on our appearance affects our social lives, our careers, and how our children feel about us—and about life.

This is therefore a time when we must think more seriously than we ever have before, or may ever need to again, about what attitudes and habits we want to develop in ourselves and transmit to our children.

You may be a free spirit who relishes the newfound freedom of the nonmarried state or an affectionate soul who very much hopes that your period of independence will be temporary but, whichever you are, seize the golden opportunity that singleness provides you with and *take the time to get to know yourself.* Become your own best friend, as Mildred Newman and Bernard Berkowitz advise. Find your center of gravity inside your own soul. Make yourself, for the time being anyway, your strongest interest.

This isn't advice to be selfish. As a recent pop song put it, "I've got to be me! How can I be good for you if I'm not good for me?" How can you be good for and to your children if you're not good in the first place? If you want to help your children you must be good to yourself so that you *can* be good to them.

Once you have learned to establish your center of gravity inside yourself a very nice thing is apt to happen. You may become like one of those toys that look like jolly little fat men, with weights inside them that act as balancers so that no matter how hard anyone pushes them over they refuse to lie down. If you can really rely on and enjoy and understand yourself, then none of the hard knocks which life and other people are sure to keep giving you from time to time will be able to keep you down for very long. As a result of your inner balance you will quickly bounce back up again, and hold your head up high.

Another thing: in addition to the many benefits that you yourself will receive from acquiring a deeper and sounder knowledge of yourself, an inevitable and equally important side effect will follow. You will simultaneously gain a greater understanding of your children and hence become a more effective, wiser, happier parent.

I would go so far as to say that no one can be a really good parent unless he or she is an understanding person—and I'm not at all sure that it is possible to be that unless one first understands oneself. The benefits of true knowledge, like true charity, shouldn't stay at home, but they have to begin there.

3
EXPLAINING YOURSELF:
Answering hard questions

It would be so convenient if, while we are going through a transitional period, trying to get to know ourselves, learning to accept ourselves and our new circumstances, preparing to make whatever adjustments will be necessary, people would leave us alone for a little while—not boycotting us, but tactfully averting their gaze just long enough to let us catch our breath. Then we could present ourselves to them later, as new and improved products, with the rough spots and awkwardnesses we are so agonizingly aware of right now smoothed away. We could rehearse our new roles in private instead of having to face an audience unprepared.

That's what you probably feel at times. However, if people actually stayed away from us completely while we were trying to recover from a blow like a death or divorce (and many squeamish problem-avoiders do), we would feel even more isolated and desolated. Anyway, there would always be more rehearsing that could be done to improve a performance. The longer we waited for opening night the more nervous we would probably get. Even as magnificent an actress as Ethel Barrymore never learned to face an audience without stage fright. So perhaps it is just as well that we never have an opportunity to memorize our lines in advance. If we were able to hold off until we were fully ready to look and act our best we might never get around to performing at all.

In any case, whether this would be convenient or not, it doesn't happen. Life jogs along relentlessly. As one person said to me once, "The trouble with life is that it's so daily!" We have to keep on meeting the demands which life keeps on making, as they come at us willy-nilly, not when we wish they would. When the merry-go-round we are on makes us so dizzy that we cry, "Stop the world, I want to get off!" our plea is ignored. The world keeps right on spinning, and before we have caught our breath after one crisis the next one is upon us, yelling at us, as in the child's game of hide-and-seek, "Coming, ready or not!"

In short, the world does not leave us free to adapt ourselves to new situations in peace and quiet. Particularly when we have children constantly clamoring for attention, it remorselessly keeps intruding on us, requiring things of us. And it disturbs us with many questions which we are expected to answer, sometimes before we have any idea what the correct answers are.

Close friends do not wait until we have sorted out our thoughts, established some perspective, and regained emotional balance before they ply us with whys and whats. Everyone concerned about us asks, "How do you feel?" and "Are you going to be all right?" and "Why and how did it happen?" (whatever "it" was), and they want us to tell them, despite the fact that we haven't been able to figure out why and don't want to talk or even think about it. They want to know what we are going to do now (so do we), how we are going to manage (so do we), *are* we going to be able to manage (we fervently hope so but aren't a bit sure) long before we have had a chance to make any plans and while we are still very confused, even panicky. (They also ask, politely, "Is there anything I can do to help?" But that's one question you had better not answer too specifically, because as soon as you say, "Yes! Please come over tomorrow and take care of my children for the afternoon because I have to go to the lawyer/dentist/PTA meeting/grocery store/employment agency/psychiatrist/etc." most of your friends will beat a hasty retreat, saying, "Oh gee, I'd love to, but I just can't—my mother/sister/cousin/husband's boss/daughter/son/niece/aunt/husband has asked me to go to such-and-such-a-place tomorrow afternoon and I already promised, but some *other* time . . ." There are a few glorious exceptions to this general rule, but not many.)

Even near-strangers are apt to mind your business instead of their own. The drama and suspense of an emotional crisis appeals to the voyeur and eavesdropper and kibitzer in everyone. Some people get a kind of macabre thrill out of hearing every gory detail of someone else's problems.

How can you give an answer when you don't know the answer?

Obviously, you cannot explain things you don't understand. So don't go out on a limb and make up explanations just because you think they sound virtuous or clever. Don't pretend to clairvoyance or omniscience. Don't commit yourself to opinions which are the result of momentarily intense emotions and which may come back to haunt you later when you will realize they seemed unduly arrogant or craven or biased.

Sometimes the only, or best, answer you can give to a serious question is simply, "I don't know." You can say, "I'll have to think a lot more about it before I can answer that." Or you can say, "I think what happened (or what I'm going to do) is this—but I could be wrong. I'll have to wait and see after I've had a little more time to think it over. What do you think?" Or you can say, "Well, in part it seems to me that this is how it was (or is, or will be), but I suppose there's more to it than that; I'm still trying to figure things out."

Answers of this type are not evasions, so don't be afraid you'll sound silly saying them. Though incomplete, they are honest. An evasive tactic is to change the subject as quickly as possible, meanwhile either ignoring the question or tossing off a glib reply without thinking about what you are saying, hoping it will shut your questioner up. Devices like that may temporarily fool people, including yourself, but they will not be really satisfying and will not shed any useful light on the matter under question. You owe yourself and your children (and to a lesser degree your friends) the truth, even when you don't know what the truth is or know only a small part of it—so when the only truth you know is that you don't know, then that is the truth you should express.

How can you protect your privacy from overcurious pryers?
Some people are extremely tactless, asking very intimate questions and making offensive personal comments. I remember a beautiful (in every way) girl at college who had only one leg, on which she used to go zipping around campus with the aid of crutches. She developed a stock retort to silence people who stared at her and said, "I see you lost a leg." She'd glance down, look surprised, and say, "Oh, my, how careless of me!" You may be able to think up an equally humorous and withering response to protect yourself from a busybody or sentimentalist who pries into your problems.

But don't be too free with verbal scalpels. Go easy with sarcasm and the tendency to resent people's comments. You may be particularly sensitive right now, and there is only a thin line between being sensitive (which is a nice trait) and being touchy (which is a nasty one).

Don't turn everyone's questions off rudely, automatically, because you think your affairs are nobody else's affair. Give everyone the benefit of the doubt and assume they are asking questions out of sincere interest and concern, not just because people enjoy snooping. If some of them go too far in poking into private territory you can cut them off politely, saying something as matter-of-fact and truthful as "I'm sorry but I'd rather not talk about that right now," but don't snap at them angrily unless you are very sure that your diagnosis of prurience is correct.

If you are overdefensive you may offend someone who really meant you well—and that's unwise, because right now you need all the allies you can get. Also, if you cut people short you may lose valuable chances to gain more insight into your situation. They may be asking questions which you should be asking yourself but which you have been evading. Opportunities to discuss frankly what has happened, to explore the situation, searching for answers to some of the serious questions raised in your own and in other people's minds, may be a very useful counterbalance to your desire to escape unrealistically from facing and acknowledging your difficulties. The shortest distance between a problem and a solution is usually a straight confrontation.

How can you answer your children's endless barrage of questions?

Young children are the champion question-askers of the world. They regard a parent as an infallible and inexhaustible font of wisdom, a source of information about every fact under the sun. And the fact that a question may be too complicated or too upsetting to answer rarely stops them from asking it. Many of their queries are truly unanswerable ("Why is a circle round? Why is water wet?") and I doubt that the parent exists who hasn't at some point in his or her parental career resorted, out of exasperation, to the shut-up reply of "Because I say so" or, even more bluntly, to the one-word answer, "Because!"

It is never wise or kind to cut off a child's questions, even though it is understandable that we do this when patience or time runs short. The child's innate curiosity is one of the most wonderful things about childhood, and it should be considered a parental privilege, not a nuisance, to be able to satisfy and stimulate and channel this God-given gift that enables a child to grow not merely in an accumulation of factual information but in an understanding and appreciation of values.

When a father or mother snappily cuts this curiosity short too often, the child who was originally so unselfconsciously eager to learn everything about everything gradually becomes duller, less curious, less full of awed wonder about the world. The potential poet or scientist or inventor or researcher inside every little child is killed by parents who are too listless or stupid or unimaginative or impatient or plain rude to respect their child's desire to learn. "Go away and leave me alone!" is a parental cop-out, and if we say it too often we deserve to have the sullen, withdrawn, morose children that such treatment helps develop —but, alas, the children didn't deserve to be turned into that kind of person. And yet, unless they have the good luck to find other, more adequate sources of information and inspiration, from teachers and friends and books, or unless they have unusually deep and strong inner resources, the parent's failure to respond constructively to their inquisitiveness will punish the children even more than it punishes the parents ("The sins of the parents are visited upon the children. . . .").

Sometimes, of course, children's questions are not prompted by genuine curiosity as much as by the desire to get a parent's attention. A question may be a ploy, a tactic, a device, and the real answer the child is looking for may have little to do with the subject at hand. Even then the question should be treated with respect, because there is a reason why the child needs attention. A parent must learn to listen carefully and try to answer the unspoken question that is hiding underneath the verbalized one.

This is particularly true of the types of questions children ask when they are emotionally disturbed. They may ask a question which cannot possibly be answered factually at that time—either because there is as yet no clear answer or because the true answer is one they could not understand or accept. The real answer might trouble them even more than does the ignorance or fear which prompted the question (for instance, if the reason Daddy has gone away is because he is a vicious murderer and has been caught and put in jail). At such times you may have to invent suitable and convincing answers that will soften harsh reality. But even then, don't brush off the questions just because they are hard or even impossible to answer. Talk over the subject in *some* way that the child will find helpful.

The shock of death or separation or divorce is traumatic to a young child, almost always. If a parent has disappeared and the child does not seem at all troubled and is not asking where and why Daddy or Mommy has gone, what's going to become of us now, etc., don't think this means you have been blessed with an unusually uninquisitive or considerate child and let the matter go at that. Some children show how troubled they are in delayed or indirect ways, rather than by asking direct questions. They may regress to earlier, babyish behavior or become unusually quarrelsome, whiny, and disobedient. Punishing them will not change them back into happy, well-adjusted children. You must get at the repressed worry or anger that is bothering them.

Such children have deep and urgent questions pressing on their minds, although they may be unable to articulate them. Something very basic which they have always taken completely for granted has suddenly, strangely, been completely altered and they feel as if they have been through an earthquake, only worse. They may be too aghast or bewildered to talk about it. They may be carrying a secret burden, convinced that in some way they are responsible for the disaster. So instead of feeling relieved to be off the hook when your children don't talk about what has happened, draw them out—gently, tactfully, compassionately.

You may not want to. It would be much easier for you not to have to talk about it. But you must. People have a right to information about things that fundamentally affect them. And how you answer (or evade) your children's questions, spoken and unspoken, will be pivotal in determining how the children will react to death or divorce, whether they will be able to take it in stride or whether they will be deeply and permanently scarred, perhaps so closed-in from now on that they are unable to love anybody because it hurts too much.

Little children have complete candor, unless they have become so frightened that they learn to be inhibited and devious. They will look you right in the eye and ask direct questions as hard to reply to as: "What is death?" "Where is Daddy now?" "Am I going to die soon too?" "Are you?" "When?" "If you die too what will happen to *me?*" or, even worse, "Why didn't *you* die instead of him—I wish you had!"

Equally disturbing questions are asked by the children of divorced parents: "Why did you and Mommy fight so much?" "Why were you so mean to Daddy?" (or "Why was Daddy so mean to you?") "Does Mommy hate us?" "Is Daddy a bad man to have gone away?" "Did he go away because I'm a bad boy and he doesn't like me?" "When will he come back?" "If I'm very, very good can I get him to come back?" "I wish you had moved away instead of him—I want my Daddy! Why don't you go away? I hate you!" "How can you take care of us all alone? Are we going to be poor now?" "Are you going to divorce me too?"

An adopted or illegitimate child also has very serious, important, tough questions that need answering: "Why didn't my mother (or father) keep me?" "Didn't he/she/they like me?" "Is it because they are bad? Does that mean I'm bad too?" "What was she (or he) like?" All children long to think that both of their parents are nice people, yet it puzzles and worries them if you convince them that an absentee parent is or was nice because then they can't understand why they have been rejected.

Another common question that children of a single parent often wonder about secretly, or come right out and ask, is: "When are you going to get married again?" This may be an expression of deep worry, because children may be terrified at the thought of having a new (probably bossy and mean) father or a wicked stepmother straight out of Cinderella. Or they may be pathetically eager to have a "normal" two-parent family the way most of their friends do. In either case, the children's fears and hopes may come out in terribly embarrassing questions addressed not to you but to every opposite-sex guest who appears on the scene: the hostile "Are you going to marry my Daddy? Go away! I don't like your face!" or the too-cordial "Isn't my Mommy pretty? Why don't you marry her?" to someone nice you've just met (who thereupon makes the quickest possible escape from your clutches).

You may feel it would require the understanding of a brilliant child psychologist, the tact of an experienced professional diplomat, the wisdom of an unusually profound philosopher, and the rapier wit of Art Buchwald to handle all these questions adequately, but there are certain attitudes and approaches you can take which, though they may not supply you with the exactly right words at the very instant you need them, will help to pull you through most of the most awkward and troubling moments.

Questions about adoption:
The main thing that is vital in the case of adopted or foster children is to assure them (again and again and again and then again, in ways that are convincing, in actions as well as in words) how much and how unfailingly you love them. Even if one or both of their biological parents decided they couldn't keep them, you *chose* to bring them into your family because you *love* them, so they have a very strong reason to feel good about themselves. Don't let them think of the unknown people who spawned them as their only "real" parents, so that you are relegated to a subordinate role. You are their real parent because you love them and take care of them and they can rely on you. Arm them with this source of reassurance early in life. If you wait too long before letting children know they are adopted, the shock when they finally find out can be overwhelming. They may feel you've been dishonest with them and may never trust you (or anyone) again. They may become really disoriented and shattered. I know of one adopted girl who wasn't told about her origin until the night before she was going to get married; she ran away and killed herself.

Also, the longer you put off discussing the subject the more awkward it will be for you, as well as for the child, when you finally do it. The best thing is to refer to it casually, naturally, now and then, from the beginning, rather than to treat it as if it is a worrisome, unpleasant secret. Long before a child realizes it has emerged from some woman's body it is willing to accept fables about being bought in a store or brought by a stork or picked off a rose bush, so the adopted child who hears about the wonderful, exciting day when you went to an adoption agency and saw this beautiful baby and said, "Oh, I want *that* one for my very own!" will be satisfied—in fact, thrilled—to hear about it. "Tell me again, Mommy, about the day you adopted me" was asked purringly over and over again by one very happy little girl I know who thought that was a much more beautiful and exciting story than the Three Bears or Sleeping Beauty or Snow White—after all, *she* was the beautiful heroine in it. (This family also used to make Susan feel superspecial by festively celebrating two birthdays for her every year: the day she came into the world and the day she joined her family.)

"Why did my other mother get rid of me?" need not be answered in detail. You may not know, anyway. "I'm not sure, dear, but she had problems that made her afraid she couldn't take care of a child and she wanted you to be happy so she gave you to me and, oh, I'm so glad she did because I wanted you so much!" That, followed by a warm hug, will comfort and please most young worriers. When they are older you can explain in more detail that things like poverty and illness and emotional difficulties sometimes prevent a girl from keeping her baby with her, even though she may love it and wish she could; and by talking about this honestly and sympathetically you can help your child to become a very understanding, broadminded, realistic person who not only fully accepts you, and himself or herself, but people who are troubled.

Questions about death:

If you have no idea how to answer your children's questions about something as important as death, you had better start exploring the subject in your heart. Some things are much too important to be neglected, no matter how escapist we feel.

I remember a friend of mine who was very squeamish about the subject of death. When her mother died she simply told her children that Grandma had gone away.

"When will she be back?" the children asked, logically enough.

"She's never coming back," she said.

"Why not?" they asked.

No comment.

Naturally, they were stunned, appalled. They wanted to know if Grandma was mad at them. No. Their mother had enough sense to try to persuade them that this wasn't why she had disappeared. But she offered no satisfying substitute explanation, so they had to try to guess what had happened. She just kept murmuring mournfully something about "she can't come back" because "they" had come and taken her away. About a week later she wondered why her little daughter began screaming in terror every time the garbage truck came down the street.

An equally bad (inadequate, scary, untrue) explanation of death, which too many parents offer children, is: "She went to sleep and she's never going to wake up again." This is an excellent thing to say if you are trying to make your children terrified of going to sleep at night.

It is important to remember that, if you fail to answer children's questions in a way they can accept, they will figure out answers by themselves—which will probably be much more distressing than the truth is. They will not remain content with no answer because their minds are too active.

"Death education" is like sex education: the "facts of life" include the fact of death, and quite naturally such basic facts arouse curiosity in children. They *must* be explained some way. If a parent is too ignorant or tense to give sensible, honest answers to questions about these subjects, the children will invent their own inaccurate, bizarre, and sometimes ugly answers to fill the intellectual void their elders have created. The strange and sad thing is that many parents who are intelligent enough to realize that it's better for a child to get accurate information about sex from them than from other children, who don't know what they are talking about and whose misconceptions can produce hang-ups that it may take years to counteract, are often as evasive about discussing death as the prudes they sneer at are about sex.

When anyone close to your children (let alone their father or mother) has died, it is your *obligation* to explain the departure as well as you can. Naturally your explanation of death will differ from that of someone whose beliefs about God and immortality differ from yours, but give the most sensible and comforting answer that you can give. If you believe death is a total stop, you will say one thing. If you believe in an afterlife, you will obviously say something quite different. But whatever you say, make it consistent with what you really believe, keep it simple and clear, and say it as calmly as possible.

If you do believe in an afterlife, try to be convincing about it. This means not going around the house wrapped in perpetual mourning—because children are logical, and if you tell them their father or mother is now going to be happy forever and ever in heaven but, while you are saying this, you are sighing and looking as if *you* will never be happy again, the inconsistency between what you say and how you act will not escape them, and your reassuring words will be far from persuasive. You can explain that you are very sad right now because you miss him or her so much and haven't got used to it yet, but you mustn't let your sadness seem total or incurable or you will seem to be a selfish monster who regrets the fact that someone you love is now happy with God—or else this will show that you obviously don't really believe what you are saying.

A simple and partial explanation is both more honest and more convincing than an attempt to give a complicated and complete one. Answer questions but don't try to anticipate too many further ones—like the father who told his little boy all about ovaries and hormones and genes and chromosomes and wombs and birds and bees in answer to the question "Where did I come from?" when all the boy wanted to know was if he, like his best friend, had come from Chicago.

You can say that heaven is a place of perfect happiness—if

you think so—but stop short of drawing a road map of it complete with pearly gates and streets of gold. Say something about the fact that God who made us all is still ruling the universe and is still looking out for everyone and everything he made, even for those we can no longer see—just as your neighbor who lives down the street is still looking after her children after she has left them at your house and is out of sight. Or say that God is love, and that love is faithful, kind, reliable, eternal, and that the dead are even closer to this wonderful reality than those of us who are still on Earth. But if you try to give a lot of details, since you won't really know what you are talking about, your phoniness and ignorance will almost certainly show through. You can say you don't really know what the next world is like but that someday, when God wishes it, you and your children will join Daddy or Mommy, and then you will all find out, but it's something like Christmas: you have to wait until you're there to know how beautiful it will be.

Children are imaginative as well as logical. Given just a little basic information and a simple explanation they can accept, they will be able to think their way more deeply into a subject, if they feel like doing so, without your step-by-step assistance. They may come up with a concept of eternal bliss that involves eating an endless supply of chocolate chip ice cream rather than listening to an interminable concert by angelic harpists—but their imagery is probably no further from the real truth than traditional formulas. All such images are merely metaphors, human attempts to fathom a reality far beyond our comprehension, feeble efforts to imagine "the unimaginable depths of the riches of the wonders of God which eye hath not seen nor ear heard nor mind conceived of," as Saint Paul put it. So don't try to impose your own complex speculations or imaginings in detail on your children, attempting to explain a lot more than you really know. Just give them a little help and encourage them to work out their own philosophy and theology.

If you are not at all sure there is any afterlife, or if you are personally quite sure there is none, it will of course be harder for you to enable your children to accept peacefully the fact that someone they love very much is dead. It is going to be harder for them, as it is also going to be harder for you, than for children in a religious family (except for those who have been taught the fire-and-brimstone version of religion; if that is your family's faith your children may be in for many nights of nightmares, because atheism and agnosticism are more merciful creeds than that which posits a vicious, vengeful God).

But even if it may be somewhat hard, it is still not impossible for an agnostic or atheist to convey a sense of peaceful acceptance. Children know that flowers are born and bloom for a while and then fade and die. They can accept that fact calmly (after they get used to the idea—I still remember my three-year-old son bursting into tears one spring when the blossoms of a beautiful magnolia tree fell off onto the ground). You can explain that this process of coming and going, beginning and ending, is true of everything and everyone. It is all part of the rhythmic cycle of the universe which is a continuing process: spring is followed by summer, which is followed by autumn and by winter, and then again by spring. . . . Leaves which fall off trees drop onto the ground and disappear, and then provide nourishment for lovely new trees with new leaves, and new flowers . . . and after every day that "dies" in the evening another one is "born" tomorrow.

Children understand about taking turns, except when they are very, very little. You can paraphrase Ecclesiastes and explain that each of us has a time to be born and a time to grow and a time to die, and that this is a beautiful natural process by which the world keeps on renewing itself—if nobody ever died there would be no room in the world for new life, and that would be very sad because life is so good that it is wonderful to be able to enjoy it and to share it with each other.

Just as the world was an interesting and great place long before any of us were here, it will continue to be interesting and great long after we have all gone away, and then it will be someone else's turn to enjoy it and to benefit by whatever good things we have added to the world while we are here, as we ourselves benefit by good things people before us discovered and created . . . so aren't we glad that we are able to be here for a while, and aren't we glad that Daddy (or Mommy) was too, even though we're sorry his (or her) turn is now over?

As one wise and sweet little six-year-old I know said once to comfort his sorrowing mother after his baby brother had died: "Oh Mommy, I'm going to miss him too, just like you are—but wasn't it *nice* of him to visit us for a while? Weren't we *lucky?*"

Questions about divorce:

Death is more tragic than divorce because it is more irrevocable, more ultimate, but in one way it is less awful or at least less difficult. The sadness caused by the death of someone you love, who has had a good life and who has given you much happiness, has a cleanness and inevitability to it that make it possible to accept it more tranquilly than the sadness caused by divorce, which is almost always mixed with rancor and anger, a sense of failure, a history of disappointments, arguments, and mutually inflicted wounds.

It may, therefore, be harder for divorced people than for widows or widowers to speak comfortingly about a departed parent. A large undigested lump of bitterness and resentment may make it almost impossible, for a while at least, to speak of the absent parent without animosity.

If you are temporarily so distraught that you cannot answer any queries about "the departed" without conveying strong negative feelings, starting to choke up or lose your temper, it may be wise to say as little as possible for the time being. But make a strenuous effort to get over this state of mind as soon as possible, to avoid frightening (or disgusting) your children.

You may not feel like being generous in speaking about your ex. You may want your children to know what a no-good heel their father is or what a filthy little tramp their mother is and how terribly much you have suffered because of this. But *be fair*. The so-called "innocent" injured party of the first part in a bitter dispute has often inflicted as much pain on the so-called "guilty" and brutal party of the second part as the party of the second part did to the party of the first part—even if unconsciously. Both parties may have been driven to act the way they did by things they didn't understand, so *be charitable.* And also, *be careful!* Most children are instinctively, valiantly, and passionately loyal, and if you denounce their parent, whom they love, whether you do or not, your condemnations may come zooming back to hit you with the speed of a Frisbee. Absence can make the heart grow fonder and fonder; the absent parent isn't the one who is always saying mean things like "Go to bed" or "No, you can't go outdoors until your cold is over" or "No, you can't watch TV until you've finished your homework" or "No, you can't have the car tonight"—so your children may decide that you are the villainous parent, not the absentee.

They may decide that in any case. If they do, try not to show them how much your feelings are hurt and try to keep on being nice to them—if you are patient and understanding, they may change their minds. Don't try to bribe or wheedle them into liking you; that's like giving into a blackmailer. Just try to ignore their hostility as well as you can, realizing that children's moods are as changeable as Vermont weather ("Don't like our weather?" the Vermonter asks the visitor. "Wait a minute!").

They may miss their absent parent so terribly that they have to take their anger out on someone, and you're there to take it out on. They may really be furious at the deserter, but they can't get at that parent the way they can get at you, and they feel as if they have to get at somebody. It's better that they should blame you for everything, even though it's unfair, than that they should blame themselves, as so many children do after a divorce. If you stay calm they will get over the stage of hating you, whereas if they hate themselves they may have emotional problems for years.

They may decide they like the absent parent more than they like you simply because they are going through a stage. There are certain periods when children normally like their father best and others when they normally like their mother best. This is just a fact of nature—though it's hard on you when the anti-you stage happens to coincide with your divorce.

Or they may decide they like the absent parent more than you because you do *too* good a job of speaking well of the departed spouse and they can't help concluding that if he/she was that wonderful then he/she must have left because you aren't. *Someone* must have been to blame (it takes a lot of living and maturing to realize that in some conflicts no one is to blame). For their sakes, perhaps you should be glad if they are blaming you rather than themselves. But perhaps you should also make sure that you are not unrealistically deifying your ex-mate and downgrading yourself, bending over backward, in your efforts to be fair.

In other words, it's a bit like walking on eggs, or on a tightrope. You must proceed very gently and try to keep your balance. Don't overcomplicate the reasons for the divorce and don't oversimplify them either. Children are often a lot more realistic and understanding and strong than adults give them credit for, if they are told facts.

If your children are blissfully unaware of faults that their other parent had, it may not be wise to try to keep them unaware indefinitely. If you do they may grow up with a very unrealistic notion of people's capabilities or with an imaginary ideal they feel unable to live up to. But if they are aware of a parent's faults, because they remember things or because the parent patently neglects or abuses them, it is far healthier for them to put the blame where it belongs, on the neglectful parent, than to blame themselves for what is going on. A child has every right to resent being neglected or abused, and if you try to pretend that a parent who acts that way is really a great person, your child will either resent you too, or become utterly confused, or think you're nuts.

Don't try to praise or excuse behavior that shouldn't be praised or excused.

Try hard, however, not to convey or build up hatred, even if your ex behaves extremely unpleasantly, lest you become permanently a person who is hateful (hated and hate-full). Try to speak calmly, pleasantly, factually, neither canonizing nor anathematizing the departed parent. If you can think of extenuating circumstances to explain, though not to justify, bad behavior, mention them. Don't dwell on failings. Recall interesting things about good times you used to have together. Describe any real talents and other good qualities that perhaps may balance, at least in part, faults that are obvious. Don't be afraid to recall disagreements, even battles, you may have had (your children probably remember some of them all too well, anyway), but also don't be reluctant to remember the good times. There were some or you would never have married.

Actually, it isn't so much a matter of what you say to your children as of how you say it. The precise words or facts don't matter nearly as much as your tone, the feelings inside you which come across. So if you really feel overadoring or overhostile the best thing you can do is to go to work on your own attitudes. Avoid viciousness in giving criticisms, but criticize what you think should be criticized so that you don't distort your child's values.

It is better to admit, frankly and matter-of-factly, our own and other people's limitations—without exaggeration or hysteria —than it is to put pitchforks in people's hands or halos around their heads when we portray them. Accompany critical comments with (1) observations about mitigating circumstances, (2) sensible explanations, (3) references to compensating traits.

Even the children of a single parent are, in a most fundamental sense, entitled to two parents. They do, in fact, biologically have two. They are the living proof and product of the once-close union of two people, and to a great extent owe their identity to both of these people. It is neither just nor healthy to let them grow up thinking the absent parent was of no consequence. They cannot totally reject, mentally and emotionally, either parent without rejecting part of themselves. If you make or let them do that you will end up the parent of incomplete human beings.

In any conflict there is some wrong and some right on each side. As a priest I know puts it, every dispute between two people has four sides. So try to be a little more humble and a little more generous than you may feel at first. Once a divorce is over it is time to call a truce—both verbally and in your heart.

No matter what painful things may have passed between you and your child's other parent, regard the relationship between you that once produced your child as sacred, because the creation of life *is* sacred. The union of two people produced a new and unique human being, your child, who is now looking to you for encouragement and love, and one question no child should ever have to ask is, "Are you sorry I was born?"

4

ADJUSTING YOURSELF:
The transition from grief to peace

After a tragedy, such as a death in a family or a divorce, you may not at first react with grief. You may not feel much of anything. This doesn't mean you are callous or shallow. It's just that you can't fully comprehend, at first, what has happened.

When a disaster is sudden and unexpected, the first reaction is apt to be sheer disbelief; the sorrow is delayed. You may be in such a state of turmoil for a while that you feel more bewildered than sad. You may be in a state of shock.

If you have been anticipating the disaster for quite a long time, your initial reaction when it finally happens may actually be one of relief—and then, perhaps, a stab of guilt for feeling relieved instead of sorry. Or you may just feel very, very exhausted. Internally bruised. Numb. Limp. Like a zombie. Or, as one new divorcee put it, "like a used paper plate."

Sometimes a marriage has been so unhappy that its end via separation or divorce seems to call for a victory celebration—a "coming out party"—rather than for sorrow. But no matter how necessary, even desirable, a divorce may be, it is like major surgery: expensive and painful. Even if you don't miss the person from whom you are now mercifully separated you may miss the role he or she played in your life or was meant and expected to play much more than you ever thought you would. The result can be puzzling, a strange combination of relief and grief that is all the more poignant because it's hard to understand how you could be grieving for the loss of happiness you didn't have. The fact that you didn't have it adds a dash of bitterness to the already distasteful mixture of relief, grief, and confusion.

If divorce resembles surgery, so does the death of a beloved person. It's like an amputation. Part of you has been forcibly removed. And, as in a physical amputation, it may be quite a long time before you really realize it is missing. You still feel married long after you're not—so the full weight of your sadness doesn't press on you until later.

And then, after the facts have finally sunk in and you have survived, and you think you have made all the necessary adjustments and are congratulating yourself on having gotten through everything so smoothly: *kerplunk! wham! ouch!* It suddenly hits you, hard.

Your next reaction may surprise you. It may not be sorrow but intense anger—at God, at life, at the person who has left you in this difficult situation, at yourself for being in it, at everyone and everything. If the person has died, it seems (indeed, is) irrational to get mad at him, but emotions are not rational, so you rage, "How dare he do this to me! Why didn't he take better care of himself and of me and of the children?" Or "How could she possibly have been so careless, so inconsiderate, so stupid—didn't she realize how much the children and I need her? She should have taken better care of her health (or should have avoided that accident). She was an idiot! And I was an idiot for getting involved with her, and for marrying her, and for getting myself stuck in this situation where I have to take care of these children all by myself instead of being free!" Such thoughts pop into our heads even though they make no sense—and then we are very ashamed of ourselves, and that makes us madder than ever.

Later, after both shock and fury have passed, there may roll over you waves of simple unadulterated grief, sometimes a real flood so heavy and deep that you fear you will literally drown.

And then alarm may get mixed in with the grief. You may really become afraid that you will never be able to feel happy again.

As with a bad case of flu, this sickness—it *is* a sickness—will leave you more quickly if you can stay quiet for a while, surrendering to it, instead of trying to push yourself right away into normal activity. Roll with the waves. Don't try to force yourself to undertake too many distracting activities right now—your thoughts are so oppressive that nothing will distract you. And don't try to make detailed plans—you're not thinking clearly enough at the moment to make *sensible* plans. You are weak, and you need rest.

It may seem odd to advise you to let yourself give way to feelings of sadness, instead of saying "Snap out of it, pull yourself together." But you will find this is welcome advice when you are feeling very, very low. There will almost surely be a period when you don't know how to make yourself feel better and, what's more, don't even want to! You would rather sit around moping than bestir yourself. In a strange, seemingly perverse way, you almost enjoy your anguish.

Why?

Because *at times we actually need our grief*. Forgetting what is making us sad would be even more painful than remembering. To "turn it off" and make ourselves get rid of it would feel like an even more irrevocable good-bye to someone or something we are reluctant to part with than the good-bye which has already been forced upon us. We don't want to "fare well" because that would necessitate another "farewell." Forgetting would be the further, final, separation from the person whose loss we are mourning. As long as we are still linked by memory and sorrow we still feel close, and closeness with that lost person or thing is what we are still desiring so intently. So, for the time being, we prefer misery to pleasure.

This is logical emotionally, even if it sounds illogical to someone who has never gone through this type of experience.

In a transition period be patient with yourself. Respect your grief, recognizing why you cling to it. If you try to cut it short too abruptly or harshly, you will not get it out of your system; it will just disappear underground and may rise up to kick back at you later. Denial of grief will not destroy the grief; it could destroy you, instead, by making you tense, hypocritical, cold, hard. Never be ashamed of genuine emotion.

To deny its power over you by saying sternly to yourself, "Come, come! Pull yourself together! Things aren't that bad. The world hasn't come to an end!" when things *are* bad and a very important part of your world *has* come to an end is dishonest and silly. It's dishonest because it means denying the authenticity of your most spontaneous and deepest feelings and denying the value of that which you have lost—so it's not only a lie but a form of betrayal. It's also silly, because it doesn't work. It actually prolongs, even while it distorts, your grief.

The only way to recover fully from a really deep sorrow is to bear its impact honestly, accepting its reality, realizing that grief is an inevitable and fitting reaction and tribute to the loss of something very precious.

It isn't always possible to be brave any more than it is always possible to be brilliant. And when it isn't we should be understanding of, and patient about, our frailty—as we should be about other people's too.

Try not to make hair-tearing-out emotional scenes straight out of nineteenth-century melodrama in front of your children. These might scare or revolt them. But don't be afraid to let them see you cry. *They* cry when they're hurt, so they will understand and not be shocked. And be honest with them about why you are crying. Some parents try so hard to protect their children from anything unpleasant that the children grow up with an unreal attitude toward life, unprepared to face and handle any disappointments. Another danger of trying to be so brave that your children won't know you are suffering is that the children may interpret your apparent lack of emotion as callousness or indifference toward what has happened. They may think you just don't care, that "it's no big deal" to have some-

ADJUSTING YOURSELF | 61

one die or to get divorced, that loving relationships are unimportant. They may grow up with such a shallow "so what?" attitude toward life that they are as unequipped to respond to life's joys as they are to meet its sorrows. Don't give your children that attitude or the idea that emotions are supposed to be repressed—don't, that is, unless you want them to become unhealthy, dishonest, unloving and unhappy people.

Unless you overdo it continually, your sadness will not unduly alarm them. Children have much shorter attention spans than adults do, so they can feel very unhappy and worried and very sweetly sympathetic one minute and then bounce off a minute later to play happily as if nothing had happened—an ability you will envy and even resent at times. It is their vague, unexpressed fears and hurts that damage them; expressed ones clear the air. So you won't scar their psyches if you and they cry or complain openly nearly as much as if you insist on keeping distress bottled up inside.

Grief to which you sincerely and unaffectedly yield for an understandable cause acts as its own catharsis. It is only when it is clearly exaggerated, disproportionate, out of place, unduly prolonged and therefore debilitating that you need to make strenuous efforts to abolish it.

It is no disgrace to wet your pillow on a lonely night after a hard day or to burst into tears when suddenly overwhelmed by a catastrophe. Under some circumstances it might be a disgrace not to! It would mean you were inhumanly cold. Females usually know by instinct that a "good cry" will make them feel better more quickly than a premature effort to be brave will. It's too bad that so many men consider it "unmanly" to cry—they might be able to shed some ulcers if they would let themselves shed some tears.

Grief isn't a sign of a weak character. It's a sign of the strength of your feelings. In a strange way, it's also proof of your capacity for appreciation and happiness. You wouldn't feel sad at the loss of something worthless, so the pain you feel indicates how much you value what you are missing. Remember that. If there were no such thing as happiness you would not be sad that you lacked it. Sorrow is a shadow cast by joy, and the brighter the sunshine the darker the shadow. So be grateful for what was, even though you can't help regretting that it is no longer.

Be natural enough to admit and to show how you feel. Let yourself feel your feelings in all their fullness. Their depth will reveal the fact that you are alive, a responsive person, a warm person, a *real* person, instead of a machine or a cold fish or a stone. Their intensity will be the measure of how much genuine emotion you are capable of—and take heart, because that means you are capable of great tenderness, and of joy as well as sorrow.

After a while . . . when the first and worst waves of grief are over, kiss your old life good-bye and plunge into your new one. You may not believe it now but you will be equipped to experience new happiness as deep and sharp and strong as the pain you have gone through. You will encounter many new and now unforeseeable experiences, and the pleasure they bring you will actually be heightened, deepened, and sharpened by contrast with the pain you knew before reaching them—as a bright splash of vivid color in a painting looks all the brighter when set off against black. You will appreciate happiness instead of thoughtlessly taking it for granted the way so many people do (until life teaches them not to by taking it away from them).

So don't run away from grief or try to repress it. Just don't cling to it too hard and too long. Let it have its way with you for a while and gradually and gently it will release you from its grip. Then, when you are stronger (or bored by a steady diet of grief), try some simple devices to get yourself moving again. Deliberately take your thoughts off it by turning them onto something else, by (1) opening funny or exciting or beautiful books; (2) going out to theaters or concerts; (3) putting your favorite records on the phonograph; (4) calling up friends you always enjoy talking to; (5) going out for walks to delightful places; (6) cooking some delicious recipes, reliable old favorites or intriguing and challenging new ones; (7) memorizing poetry or going to art galleries, soaking yourself in serene and soothing beauty; (8) finding other pleasant activities to occupy you.

Even after you think you have fully recovered there will be relapses from time to time, almost certainly. When these occur don't get alarmed or angry or discouraged. Expect them now and then, and try to turn them to good use. Instead of evading them, look right at what it is you still miss so much. Don't shove the thought away ruthlessly or just peek at it nervously. Telling yourself not to think of something doesn't work; it's just a negative way of continuing to think of it (if someone tells you "Don't think of the color green," that becomes the one thing you can't help thinking of). So, instead, allow yourself to recall it affectionately, if possible so keenly that you can almost reexperience it and thereby reenjoy it. Relive past happiness: fix up your old photo albums; reread old letters; contact old friends again; tell someone about old times, not with heavy sighs so that they wish you wouldn't, or with countless minor details that are of no intrinsic interest, but with such enthusiasm that someone else can share and savor your experiences with you.

The Oxford Dictionary defines *nostalgia* as "homesickness as a disease; sentimental yearning for some period of the past." The word is a combination of two Greek words: *nostos,* meaning "return home," and *algos,* meaning "pain." People who make the *nostos* larger than the *algos* can give the past a sort of bittersweet immortality that is really much sweeter than bitter (as widows such as Ruby Keeler and Lotte Lenya know and demonstrate so beautifully). So don't just stick your toe timidly in the water and stand there shivering, fearing that the waves will knock you down. Boldly dive in all the way, clear over your head—and you'll come out on the other side of the waves, where you can swim again. Then, after a vigorous swim, come ashore once more, for a little longer this time. But realize you can go back again, in your mind and heart, whenever you really want or need to, and then you won't be afraid to leave.

Any meaningful relationship or experience you have known and cherished can be a source of personal wealth years after it is all over. Your past is one thing nobody can steal from you. And neither death nor divorce can make a former marriage non-existent or unimportant. In that sense every marriage is permanent. It is something significant which has helped to make you the person you are, and it will always be part of you, something to acknowledge and be glad about forever if you look back on it in the right way, with appreciation for whatever it gave you—even if you think all it gave you was a painful lesson.

What if it was too brief, or too imperfect? (Isn't everything?) Instead of focusing on the brevity or imperfection, concentrate on whatever was good about it and recognize what you gained from it. You may bring back to yourself small forgotten moments which you will treasure even more now than you did originally. As Gibran's Prophet said, that which you most love about someone may be even clearer in his absence. When he is with you, that is good. When he is gone, the goodness remains with you.

Staying fixated indefinitely on the past is unhealthy and unproductive. Endless complaining about the fact that something has ended prolongs awareness of what is gone (which, as I said, is the very reason we do it, because we want to prolong the awareness), but after a while, if we don't watch out, the habit of of complaining will sour both past and present.

I have a friend who, whenever she sees me, sighs deeply and says, "Well, here we are! Two of life's rejects!" Her husband left her fifteen years ago and she is as bitter about it today as when it first happened—in fact, more so, because the bitterness has hardened like stale food from having been kept too long. She spurns consolation, always looking back toward what she has lost, stoking the fires of her anger, rather than looking forward to new possibilities life might have in store for her. The result is that life is now offering her fewer and fewer new possibilities. I think she thinks that by setting some kind of Olympic record for prolonged grief she is showing the world how deeply, unusually sensitive she is, but it is a sensitivity focused so wholly on long-ago events that it has rendered her insensitive to everything else—including the current needs of her children.

We spoil what was good in the past, and neglect what is good which has succeeded it, if we let ourselves become embittered. Why dirty something which could be kept bright and shining? Memories are valuable possessions, but we ourselves ruin them if we make them excuses for lasting anguish. Remember the poet who said it is better to have loved and lost than never to have loved at all? To act as if it were worse to have had something good for a while than never to have had it at all is a wretchedly ungrateful attitude! Still, it's a very common attitude among stubborn, persistent mourners.

Sometimes people cling indefinitely to the past even though they didn't actually enjoy it while they had it. Somehow the fact that it is gone sanctifies it, like the memory of a scoundrel whose widow is at first, quite naturally, relieved at his demise, but then, because she considers it sinful to speak or think disrespectfully of the dead, she gradually retouches her picture of him until she ends up idolizing a figment of her imagination—and if she goes far enough along that path she ends up a lonely, pathetic creature out of touch with life, with no friends she likes because no living humans can measure up to the unreal portrait she has created.

If the past was happy there is a temptation to become unduly sentimental about it at the cost of the present, becoming firmly convinced that the world is going to the dogs (because we don't notice today's good points) and has been ever since "the good old days" (because we don't remember yesterday's bad points).

If the past was unhappy there is another temptation: to keep stewing over it, regretting it, beating one's breast about lost opportunities and lost hopes, rehashing injustices suffered, continually chastising oneself or complaining about others for having been foolish or selfish, fretting again and again about what did or didn't happen, wondering (petulantly, not analytically and constructively) where things went wrong, why this or that mistake was made, what could and should have been done differently so that things today would be better than they are. Some people chew over old emotions until they are as tasteless and dry as old gum, torturing themselves with whys and if-onlys.

There are other ways of thinking about the past which are healthy and helpful. We can recall past suffering with the realization that, since the cause of it is no longer here, we now have good reason to be happier than we used to be. We can remember and count past blessings with gratitude and, in the recollection, enjoy them still. Or we can dig into past problems and pains, not with masochistic hysteria but in *depth,* with sufficient determination and objectivity to learn from them and therefore start functioning more effectively from now on.

"Forget about it!" "Let bygones be bygones." "It's water over the dam." "Don't cry over spilt milk." Many people will advise you to rise above past failings and woes, or to tear yourself away from lost pleasures, by just forgetting all about them. Personally, I think that's unnatural. It's awfully hard, it can't always be done, and it needn't be done if you will *use* the past to learn from it and to build upon it.

Gaining genuine understanding of the past illuminates and thus improves both the present and the future—as long as we don't stare at the past so hard and fixedly that we get stuck back there. It is one thing to use the past as a platform or springboard from which to advance to a new place, but quite another thing to try to stay there. We should stand on the past, not sit down in it. It's a departure point, not a permanent home.

So don't dwell exclusively in the past, ignoring the present and its many opportunities, but do invite the past along to join you in the present. Link past-and-present together into an integrated whole, a living continuum which is you.

Don't try to live in the future, either. The same people who tell you to let bygones be bygones say things like: "Look ahead." "Tomorrow's another day." "Start making plans." "Think about the future instead of the past." "Things are bound to be better soon." I don't think these little adages are really terribly much comfort in a time of crisis. It's true that "it is always darkest before the dawn," but when it's still pitch black it's hard to see clearly, even though you will be able to later. And when the immediate past has been extremely unhappy it is temporarily very hard to believe that the future is going to be any different.

Besides, can anyone be sure that the future will be happy? Just as there is no human being to count on in the final analysis but yourself, there is no time to count on which is as certain as the present moment. The world may be blown up in nuclear warfare in a few years. Or we may all die soon from the cold, due to the fuel shortage or a new ice age, or from air pollution, mercury poisoning, DDT in our milk, traffic accidents, murderous muggers or terrorists, or from heart attacks caused by worrying about all these ghastly possibilities. Even if we don't die right away we may find life increasingly miserable in the future because of rising inflation, unemployment, overpopulation, racial tensions, food shortages, ill health, old age. As one gloom-predicting editorial writer analyzing the state of the nation recently put it, "Things are going to get worse before they get worse."

Whenever you are very depressed over anything you can quickly make a mental leap and become depressed over everything. There is no end to the ingenuity of seriously unhappy people when it comes to convincing themselves that unhappiness is the normal and inevitable lot of everyone in "this valley of tears." They believe in "Murphy's Law," which says,

"If things *can* go wrong they *will*." And when you have that frame of mind, trying to dwell on and live in the future doesn't cheer you up one bit more than dwelling on and living in the past.

If you find yourself enmeshed in a maze like this, pretend you're an alcoholic! Don't become one—that will just multiply your problems a millionfold—but follow the procedures which Alcoholics Anonymous have developed for conquering helplessness and hopelessness. Actually, I think we all owe alcoholics a debt of gratitude because their problems caused AA to come into existence (see? good can come out of evil—there's a thought that should help cheer you up!), and AA has developed some extremely effective principles and tactics for dealing with and reducing life's miseries.

First: Don't make grandiose overambitious hard-to-keep resolutions of permanent reform, trying to guarantee yourself a consistently successful future in which you will never again repeat past mistakes. Just work on getting through *one day at a time* successfully. (Christ gave the same sound advice two thousand years ago when he said, "Take no heed of the morrow; sufficient unto the day is the evil thereof." But most people today find it easier to grasp the message when it is put in modern language.)

Second: It helps you solve your own problems if you involve yourself in trying to *help someone else* solve his or her problems. Parents, especially, please note: don't think so hard about your own needs, disappointments, troubles and worries that you increase those of your children. If you can't cheer yourself up, at least try to cheer them up—and you may get cheered up at the same time, by accident!

Third: Memorize, and practice, the AA prayer: Ask God (or whatever source of creative power you think exists which is life-giving) for the *strength* to accept what cannot be changed, the *courage* to change what can and should be changed, and the *wisdom* to know which is which.

"The acceptable time is now," as Saint Paul said.

In moving forward through today—the transition point between past and future—you may need to establish some kind of future goal in order to know in what direction to move, but don't try to reach that goal in one great giant leap. You need to have some idea of where you are heading, just as you need to recognize that the sum total of your past experiences is the background from which you are moving, but you must do that moving now, in the present. We are three-dimensional, not one-dimensional, beings, and the three dimensions of time (past, present, future) are as essential to our lives as the three dimensions of space. The present is never an isolated moment suspended in nothingness. It's the meeting point or passageway between a real past and a real future, so neither past nor future is unimportant—we mustn't ignore them. But they must be kept in their place.

The future may be wonderful or it may not be. The only way to find out, and the best way to make it wonderful, is to live today well. The past, also, may have been wonderful or it may not have been. The only way to profit from it is to live today well.

Every joy life gives us would be ruined if we kept wishing we had had it sooner or could have it longer. The most beautiful flower arrangement in the world is going to wither someday soon and be tossed into a garbage pail. Should that realization keep us from enjoying it while we can see it? There is no such thing in the entire world as a permanent flower garden, a permanent romance, a permanent triumph, a permanent peace (but console yourself with the realization that there's no permanent sorrow, either). Even so, present pleasures can be thoroughly delightful while they last and leave a lovely afterglow when they are gone, to brighten the whole rest of our lives, if we let them.

The past is gone and the future is not yet here. Yesterday was "today" while it existed and tomorrow will be "today" when it exists. So "today" is all the time there ever actually is in which to do anything. If we constantly brood about what is gone or about what has not yet arrived (and which may never come), we waste the only real time we have. "Jam yesterday, jam tomorrow, but never jam today," as Alice complained, is tantamount to never getting around to living at all. And not being alive while you're alive is a greater tragedy than dying when it's time to die.

A Hindu prayer—a salutation to the dawn—puts it this way:

Look to this day, for it is life, the very life of life. In its brief course lie all the verities and realities of your existence: the bliss of growth, the glory of action, the splendor of beauty. For yesterday is but a dream, tomorrow only a vision. But today, well lived, makes every yesterday a dream of happiness and every tomorrow a vision of hope. Look well, therefore, to this day.

5

COMFORTING YOURSELF:
Self-sympathy versus self-pity

A cold is usually not just one ailment. It can be a whole anthology of afflictions: sniffles, runny nose, sneezing, wheezing, coughing, sinus pain, headache, earache, stomachache, diarrhea, constipation, sore throat, chills, fevers, cold sores, fever blisters, fatigue, lethargy. Similarly, grief often brings with it a whole cluster of disturbed emotions all churned up together: anger, worry, fear, nervous tension, restlessness, insomnia, self-doubts, guilt, self-contempt, and self-pity.

All of these are terribly uncomfortable feelings and it would be hard to decide which was worst. And all of them, if they go on too long, can become worse than uncomfortable. They can become seriously destructive.

When grief degenerates into self-pity, look out! Just as a bad cold can develop into pneumonia, which in turn can bring on dangerous complications, a bad case of self-pity can turn into such deep and constant depression that a person is unable to function.

Depression can become so severe that it is truly impossible to rise out of it without outside help. It can assault you emotionally so that you lose all self-control. It can so confuse you mentally that you are incapable of thinking clearly. And it can exhaust you physically until you are literally paralyzed.

So if you find crying jags becoming habitual or notice that you are resorting too often to a bottle (whether it's filled with alcohol or tranquilizers or sleeping pills), get yourself some help quickly, before you turn into an alcoholic or a drug addict or a suicide!

Depression is an ailment which people who are not prone to it cannot understand, and they may view its victim with contempt, so the perennially cheerful and sensible friend you admire, whose example you think ought to inspire you to get undepressed, may be the last person whose advice or help you should seek. You won't be talking each other's language. Professional counseling (situation therapy) may be necessary, to take care of the immediate problems which caused your depression and those which in turn are caused by it. Or more general and prolonged therapy (analysis) may be needed, to uncover and remove its underlying, long-range causes and far-reaching results. (If you think you want therapy but don't know how to go about finding a therapist, turn to chapter 8.)

You may be someone who considers it either nonsense or disgraceful to go to a psychologist or analyst, but it is more disgraceful to continue to expose your children to the hazards of living with a parent who is desperately and chronically unhappy.

I am not saying that all grief turns into self-pity or that all self-pity develops into depression or that all depression requires professional treatment. This is certainly not an inevitable progression, but it is a logical and fairly common one, and it is a danger you should be aware of so that you will guard yourself against it in the early stages, by not letting yourself indulge in self-pity at any length.

Don't take it too seriously if a sudden attack of it knocks you down once in a while (except that the trouble is, it probably wouldn't be able to overpower you in the first place if you weren't already taking everything too seriously—overseriousness about problems is a basic cause *and* a definite symptom *and* a likely result of self-pity). If, however, you notice that it is becoming frequent or unusually acute or prolonged, take definite measures to get it out of your system. If you succeed you will save yourself a lot of money, because psychotherapists and psychiatrists are extremely expensive (though they're worth every bit of the money you give them when you really need them).

It is important to make a distinction between self-pity and grief. As I said before, you may have real reasons for grief at times, because it is the spontaneous, natural, appropriate reaction to a severe loss or disappointment, and when you accept it as such it paradoxically contains a healing power which helps you recover from it. But self-pity interferes with and delays the healing process, encouraging you to wallow in weakness rather than to acquire courage. You keep examining and reopening your wounds, like someone nervously picking at a scab.

Self-pity is grief's egocentric mimic. The suffering which grief entails is caused by and focused on the thing or person one has lost. Self-pity is focused on the loser instead. It is grief turned inward, grief looking at itself in the mirror. It debilitates further an already weakened person, polluting sorrow with selfishness. It causes us to dwell on ourselves and the troubles we are enduring instead of letting us get about the business of figuring out how to extricate ourselves from, or diminish, or abolish, or endure the troubles. It makes us pile prolonged woe, compounded with self-centeredness, on top of brief woe.

When you are a self-pitier you don't sit around thinking about how marvelous the lost and beloved person or thing was. Instead you sit there, hour after hour, thinking about yourself and how unfortunate you are. You moan, "Things like this happen to other people, not to me! Why did it happen to ME?" (Why not? Why should you be exempt from the human condition? Disappointments afflict everyone at times. Are you so self-centered that you really think you are so special you should be immune, and really never noticed how painful pain is until it happened to you? Maybe that's why it's happened to you: you need to learn some humanity!)

It is one thing to be sad, but if you are also sad about being sad and, furthermore, resentful about being sad, you experience a series of negative emotions, adding two or three unnecessary sadnesses to the first unavoidable one. The same is true of worries. They escalate if you let them. At times worry is unavoidable—even useful, because it may prod us into doing something that needs to be done to avert a disaster—but if we also keep worrying about worrying, and then pity ourselves for having to worry, and then perhaps worry about pitying ourselves, we double and triple our worries and sorrows.

How can you help pitying yourself if you are really pitiable?
Plenty of people will say, "Oh, I know I shouldn't but I just can't help it! I don't want to pity myself, but there is so much to pity myself for!" I don't think it is true that we can't help nursing destructive attitudes and that we can't consciously set about replacing them with constructive ones. We can learn (I don't say it's easy, just that it's possible) to control our minds, emotions, and actions to a far greater degree than most of us are willing to admit or attempt.

Perhaps you do have valid reasons to be pitied. But this is one occasion when "I'd rather do it myself" is the opposite of healthy independence. Let *other* people pity you if they volunteer! Pitying you won't weaken them. But pitying yourself uses up emotional energy you need to put to more constructive activities.

Relish the sympathy and admiration friends show you if it is comforting—that is, if it strengthens you and cheers you up. After a divorce you may be in extra need of some kind words, to counteract the harsh, nasty, and hurtful ones recently made about you during the divorce proceedings.

Almost everyone likes compliments, if the complimenter can convince them he really means what he is saying, so remarks about how brave or patient or noble you are being in the midst of a sea of troubles may make you feel better. They may make you admire yourself, which is fine, because self-respect is a toxin-antitoxin which is sure to diminish self-pity. In that case, treasure them. (Some people respond to compliments with caustic cracks, contradicting them and ridiculing themselves, to cover embarrassment if they feel unworthy of praise or to show that they are above flattery. Don't do that. That, in effect, is calling your friend a fool or a liar. Accept tributes gracefully and gratefully.)

But check your reactions, and if you find that well-meaning oversolicitousness is reinforcing your conviction that you are the most unfortunate person on earth, as it sometimes does, watch out. If you start fishing for compliments too hungrily or taking them too seriously, watch out. Keep some grains of salt handy. If you don't, you may end up being less noble than people are telling you you are, and then you may lose not only your friends' admiration but even your friends! Actors who believe all the exaggerated compliments they get from press agents and fans tend to become less and less worthy of compliments until one day they stop getting any. (On the other hand, those things your ex-spouse and his or her lawyer recently said about you were almost certainly also exaggerations, so sprinkle some grains of salt on them too.)

How can you lick self-pity?
First of all, here are a few tactics that, in my opinion, do not work.

Direct attacks at self-pity are often futile. The more you struggle against it the sorrier you get for yourself—because in fighting it you are still concentrating on it. You need to find ways of getting your mind *off* it, not to keep thinking about it.

Do not pester, and thereby perhaps alienate, the nearest available acquaintance, friend, or relative. Don't call people up just to tell them how wretched you are. We all get by with a little help from our friends, but if you are a true friend of your true friends you won't want to get them as depressed as you are, and when you are really in a bleak, black mood that is what you are all too apt to do. First try to get over such moods by yourself, and *then* contact your friends to keep yourself buoyed up.

Rigid self-discipline or heroic patience probably won't cure you either. These may, in fact, actually increase your self-pity by giving you further tension and unhappiness. Most of us are not capable of heroism except in short spurts, and if we attempt it and then fail to achieve it, we find one more reason to be very depressed. Even if we do succeed in being remarkably strong-willed, refusing to give in to any weakness, we may harm ourselves (and our children) by turning into tight-lipped, repressed ascetics who never have any fun, who never are any fun. Dour and forlorn people who live all alone are usually nothing more harmful than eccentric characters, who bother themselves more than they bother other people, but a dour and forlorn parent is a destructive horror.

Another thing, related but a little different, is this: Don't pretend you feel perfectly great when you really feel perfectly rotten. As I said in talking about grief, being dishonest with yourself drives your emotions underground where they can do you even more damage than when they are out in the open.

Don't reject people's offers to help you either, refusing to admit that you need, or could use, help. Don't *demand* help, but don't be too proud to accept it when it's sincerely offered (companionship, baby-sitting services, a loan when it's really urgently needed, advice when you're confused, etc.). It may be more blessed to give than to receive, but learning to receive a gift graciously is one very nice way of giving: you're giving someone else a chance to give. (Why should you be the only generous person?)

What about the "misery loves company" theory? When you are feeling very sorry for yourself many people will attempt to get you over it by saying things like "Oh well, think how much worse off you might be" or "Think how much worse off

So-and-so is." There is a quotation some people toss at you at such times, which many consider inspiring although I consider it a bit ghoulish: "I was unhappy because I had no shoes . . . until I met a man who had no feet."

Are remarks like these consoling? They remind me of the joke about someone who said, "I was told to cheer up because things might be worse—so I cheered up and, sure enough, they got worse!"

It really seems to me pretty selfish to feel enormously comforted by the fact that somebody else is even worse off than I am when I'm miserable. Shouldn't that fact make me, if I have any generosity and compassion, feel sadder than ever, realizing how hard life is if anyone can be *that* sad? We should hate, not love, the fact that misery has company. If we sympathize with ourselves as much as we do, this should teach us also to sympathize with other people, instead of making us glad that they too are sad.

Nonetheless, it is true that, no matter how unfortunate you are, there is someone else in the world who is equally or even more unfortunate. If you doubt that, take a trip to Lourdes or Bangladesh. I guess if that kind of comfort comforts you, you should consider yourself luckier than I am, anyway, at least in that one respect.

The fact that your own problems are less severe than someone else's means at the very least that you have one less reason than you might have for self-pity, and if that realization makes you feel good, good. However, if the resulting cheerfulness boomerangs, making you feel more terrible than ever because you feel ashamed of yourself for being glad you're better off than the starving beggars of Calcutta or the paraplegics in a veterans' hospital, comfort yourself with a different thought: You are not being abnormally selfish, it's just that a stomach ache which is your very own is bound to hurt you more acutely than starvation which is someone else's. Not because you are really evil and cold-hearted, but because it's your stomach that is hurting and therefore you are the one who is feeling it. I think it was

Shakespeare who said that the philosopher has not yet been born who can endure a toothache patiently.

Scolding yourself for not being braver and more selfless than you are almost certainly won't help. If you berate yourself for pitying yourself you will probably just make yourself feel guilty, which may give you still one more reason to pity yourself or which may cause you to substitute self-hatred for self-pity, and that won't make your effort to became emotionally healthy any easier (in that case, rush to chapter 6).

Everyone is inherently self-centered to some extent. We can't help this—though we should try not to let it get too far out of hand. We were made that way. Each of us is at the center of the universe as far as we are concerned, no matter what Copernicus or Galileo discovered about the positions of the sun and the planets. Egocentrism is a psychological fact even though not an astronomical fact.

Also, different people have different pain thresholds, so it isn't helpful to compare your pains and problems with those of other people, trying to see if they are blacker/whiter, heavier/lighter, greater/slighter, longer/briefer. Something which would hurt someone else only mildly might give deep anguish to you or vice versa, not because the one who suffers most is faking, looking for sympathy, or exaggerating, but because that person is actually more tender and vulnerable in some way than someone else is.

A hurt which is merely a temporary nuisance to one person can be truly traumatic for another, because of our differing backgrounds, standards, values, degrees of sensitivity, varying strengths, etc. Some people are simply too numb or dumb to realize how unfortunate they are—so in that respect they are fortunate! And some people are so spiritually, intellectually, and psychologically strong that they actually do not suffer as much or as long as others would in their situations. Some people are far more skillful than others at disguising suffering or shaking it off. One person may never let others know what he is feeling, preferring to withdraw and suffer in silence, so no one realizes the struggles he is going through, while another may crave and need companionship and therefore do his sorrowing right out in full view of everyone. Therefore we cannot possibly tell who is suffering the most.

Not only are we unable to judge how much another person hurts, it's irrelevant. Whether someone feels worse or better than we do, it's *our* suffering that hurts *us,* and what is important is that we should not harp on it or build it up or whine about it.

Once again, it is simple intelligence and kindness to yourself to accept what and who you are, not sneering at yourself or feeling guilty because you wish you were braver, not indulging yourself overdramatically either, and neither envying nor looking down on anyone else. Admit that you hurt and are therefore sorry for yourself, and then proceed from there to try to get over it.

As Dr. Haim Ginnott says, when a youngster spills a glass of milk, instead of going into a long song-and-dance about what a clumsy clod he is—making him feel even more stupid and inadequate than he already feels as a result of the accident, hence more nervous, hence more likely than ever to do it again, hence convincing him that he is incurably stupid and inadequate—it is much more constructive to stay calm and say something practical like, "Oops! Better run and get a towel to wipe that up." This gives the "sinner" a chance to atone—without theatrics— and also to do something that makes him feel competent instead of stupid. Similarly, you will only increase your proneness to self-pity if you keep chastising yourself for it, whereas you could perhaps end it soon by a bit of timely and practical action.

What types of action work?
Part of the solution to any problem is a correct diagnosis. If you are a self-pitier, try to find out why.

Is it because you have suffered so much in the past? Or the opposite, because you were so happy in the past that the present is unbearably dismal in comparison? Or is it because you are afraid of the future? Or because you are worried about money troubles? Or because you are lonely? Or bored? Or feel worthless and useless? Or *too* needed, overwhelmed by responsibilities?

And how serious is it? Could you snap out of it by yourself if you could find something to distract you but you can't think of anything? Or are you afraid you need help to get over it and don't know where to find it?

Every chapter in this book is an attempt to deal with one of the above questions, so keep reading. You will not find any magic formulas that will produce instant cures, but you will find speculations and insights which have helped other people conquer problems as bad as yours.

Diagnosis completed, start attacking the *specific* cause or causes. Trying to worry about everything at once means you'll never stop worrying, so put minor worries to one side and go after those that bother you the most. Start with the worst first. Or, if it seems more likely to result in success, with the easiest-to-solve first. But wherever you start, attack just one or two problems at a time.

Some people are able to lose the blues quite simply and quickly—by indulging themselves. For instance, going forth on shopping sprees. They feel so elated after buying themselves something they like that they forget their woes. This is a splendid idea if you can afford it and the subsequent bills won't bring on an even worse case of the blues than you already have.

Some women scrub floors or clean out closets when they get upset. Having to scrub a floor or clean out a closet adds to my self-pity rather than diminishing it, but some energetic people seem to find such physical activity wonderfully therapeutic. And it's better to beat a rug than to beat oneself.

I have a friend who is a single parent who has installed a punching bag in her bedroom, and when she is suddenly overwhelmed with feelings of frustration or anger or forlornness or nothingness she punches it—hard. If you don't have a punching bag, punch a pillow. Or wash your clothes or your hair and scrub, hard. Or try out a new recipe (even if food would stick in your throat right now, you can serve it to your kids). Try a really complicated one that will force you to concentrate, and remember that it doesn't matter if it turns out badly because there is no one there whom you have to impress, no one who will severely judge you and be disgusted by your failure if it is a failure, so this is a heaven-sent opportunity to practice learning to bake bread or to decorate a cake fancily.

Some men (and women too, now that women are insisting on sharing all traditionally male prerogatives) distract themselves from sorrow by plunging into lots of overtime work at the office, or by going out and getting royally drunk. Both of these distractions may make them forget their personal troubles for a little while, but the fatigue and headaches that are apt to result can be worse than the sorrows they are trying to drown. Also, neither of these devices is a good one for a single parent to employ, for obvious reasons.

Sometimes no special steps are necessary. You can simply ride out an attack of self-pity like a case of flu or seasickness or a hurricane, and it will leave of its own accord in its own time. Sometimes it seems to disappear out of sheer embarrassment or boredom. When you look it squarely in the eye after a while it seems so ridiculous, so inflated, that it loses its power over you. Or you simply get tired of the monotony of sustained emotion: your attention span collapses and you find some other subject genuinely more interesting than your own misery. A new concern takes over.

A sense of humor is an insurance policy against self-pity. It helps enormously if you can see the compensating or cheerful or even funny side of your troubles. There usually is one, though it is pretty well hidden at times. If you can do this you will then probably get more compliments than ever to console you, and you'll actually deserve them—like Jimmy Durante who, when nasty kids made fun of his big nose, instead of resenting it and getting angry, or having his feelings hurt and deciding he was inferior, decided to become a comedian because he was "funny looking" and then, having turned his biggest liability into an asset, became one of the most popular and sweet and successful human beings in the whole world.

I have a friend who suffers from the assorted afflictions that arise at "the approach of middle age," as he calls eighty-two. He says he doesn't yet feel like an old man but like a young one who has something the matter with him—or like a passenger in a balloon which has a slow leak! His memory, legs, and energy are not what they used to be, but far from pitying himself he glories in having lived so long. He cheers himself up about his failing powers by noticing the compensations. For instance, he explains, in old age you no longer have to do things brilliantly to impress people; they are impressed that you can do them at all. And he rejoices that he no longer has to pretend he isn't a coward; he says, "If someone saddles up the meanest horse in the corral and invites me to get on, I can say no."

In short, he doesn't feel so hot, but as his physical health has diminished his wit and charm have increased. Everyone who knows him delights in seeing or hearing from him. And instead of pitying himself for his ailments he says he has made a list of all the diseases there are and has discovered that those he doesn't have outnumber those he has by twenty to one, so he calculates that he is only "five percent ill—a trifling degree."

Good humor can't cure old age but it can certainly brighten it.

But sometimes self-pity lingers on and on and on, and neither yielding to it nor fighting it nor ridiculing it make it shrink or slink away.

At such times, I think, the best remedy is to start deliberately ignoring it, snubbing it. How? By distracting yourself. Many children have been distracted out of tantrums and griefs which they could not have been talked out of or scolded out of nearly so quickly. The smart parent discovers this and applies the knowledge. The smartest parents apply it to themselves as well as to their youngsters.

When we find ourselves persistently thinking self-pitying thoughts it may be time to stop thinking about ourselves altogether for a while—not time to try replacing destructive thoughts with constructive thoughts, which at the moment we feel too weak or discouraged to do, but simply refusing to think about ourselves at all, before we allow our gloomy viewpoint to become a deep-seated habit.

Even very simple distractions may work wonders. Your radio or television set or a chatterbox friend or a child with homework problems may come to your rescue. Or a good mystery story or science fiction novel or a movie. Or the suggestions made earlier about energetic activities. But you may need something with more continuity—a strongly absorbing interest (see chapter 11).

One complication is the fact that we may at times think we want to give up self-pity when we really don't. Just as we sometimes have an emotional need to hold on to grief when we think we would like to be free of it, we have a certain amount of vested interest in cultivating self-pity. Here we are, with a sorrow we must accept or a problem we must learn to face and handle. It's hard work, not pleasant; tiring, not relaxing; so we try to escape from it into self-pity, telling ourselves it's no use working to try to improve our situation because we won't be able to, no matter what we do. If we can convince ourselves of that then we will be able to spare ourselves the trouble of doing the hard work; on the other hand, of course, we will also guarantee ourselves a continuation of the trouble we now have.

By reminding ourselves frequently of how badly life has treated us, of how pathetic we are, we are trying to make ourselves feel a little bit better by giving ourselves the sympathy we feel we are entitled to. We are trying to mother ourselves with the kind of comfort we give small children when they have a hurt or disappointment, saying "There, there, you poor little thing," hoping this will make the hurt go away. That's all right —for a moment or two. But if we go on and on that way, this type of sympathy can make us (and children too, I might add) feel worse instead of better, because we are emphasizing more strongly than necessary how much something hurts, how sad it is. A quick kiss plus a joke, a brief pat combined with a prompt distraction, is far more helpful than endless sympathy.

In a morbid way, self-pity may fascinate us. It may entertain us perversely, somewhat in the manner of an exciting horror film. We are extremely interested in ourselves (we can't help that, as I said before), so sometimes the last thing we genuinely desire is to achieve self forgetfulness. Self-pity makes us feel important, even while it paralyzes us so that we can't do anything important.

When we are in this type of mood and start to read a book, we soon find we can't keep our mind on the words. The plot and characters simply don't interest us as much as our own predicament does. Even though we are finding our own situation deplorable it is still terribly absorbing to us. To take our minds off it we may have to search very hard to find a distraction that is sufficiently distracting. And nobody else can discover what that is, because what would succeed in distracting one person might not have the same power for another.

There was one whole year when I, who am normally an omniverous reader, found I couldn't keep my mind on books. But word games and crossword puzzles and jigsaw puzzles were great. I could do them while still thinking about myself, whereas a really good book would have taken me out of myself, something which I was then too preoccupied with myself to be willing to have happen.

And then suddenly, one day, I decided I had done my last crossword puzzle (not true—I gave myself a vacation and then rediscovered them, along with double-crostics). Somehow I no longer cared what a five-letter synonym for something-or-other was and couldn't imagine why anyone would be silly enough to bother to figure out something so pointless. But when crossword puzzles left me cross, other things came to my rescue: ping pong and bowling and chess and TV and the daily newspaper. And then I rediscovered books! The moral of that story is that you have to *try* things before you can find out what will work. And when one thing doesn't do the trick, try something else. Don't give up. Keep trying.

The basic problem about self-pity is that it is a form of self-centeredness that can grow larger and larger inside you like a cancer if you don't get rid of it altogether. And it is such a gloomy form of self-centeredness—not a bit like the rampant egotism of a high achiever—that when it takes over it discourages you, making you unambitious and unenergetic. It then requires twice the ordinary effort for you to make yourself do something constructive or to notice something beautiul and inspiring, to lift yourself up. Thus, when you most need to engage in a purposeful, interesting project to occupy you, you are least able to think of one or to throw yourself enthusiastically into one.

There is a way to lick this lethal lethargy, not perhaps fully today, but at least to guard against its future recurrence. This is preventive, rather than curative, medicine. The next time you feel cheerful and active, and find yourself too busy to get everything done that you would like to do, jot down a list of things you wish you had time to do. Put aside some special books or a bunch of magazines you want to read, and a few letters you want to answer that are not urgent, and make notes to yourself about possible projects: things around the house that need repairing, photos you want to put into albums, bulbs you want to plant at different seasons, curtains and slip-covers you would like to replace—whatever. Then keep this list handy, to turn to when you feel another dry spell coming on, when you fear that once again you won't be able to think of anything to do. It will come to your rescue.

The principle that is helpful here is one which Saint Ignatius thought up for the guidance of his Jesuits: "In times of consolation, remember desolation; in times of desolation, remember consolation." This rule of remembrance helps protect you from both smugness and despair, keeping you aware of the fact that neither is the whole story.

In other words, now while you're miserable, recall gratefully times when you were not and use that recollection to remind yourself of how circumstances keep changing. This will help you accept the current drought or storm peacefully, realizing it will not—repeat, will not—last forever. That's not brainwashing yourself. It's being realistic. You need not pretend you are feeling any better than you are, but you may actually start feeling a little better when you finally get it through your head that nothing lasts forever.

And then, the next time you feel happy again, don't blithely take the happiness for granted and assume it will last forever, forgetting you ever felt any other way. Instead, remember how low you felt "yesterday" (today) and plan at that time a preventive program to ward off another similar period of emptiness and dryness and pain in the future.

There is an extension of self-pity which a loving parent may fall prey to, which is dangerous for our children and must be guarded against. You must be careful not to let self-pity expand to your larger self, your family, thinking and letting your children think how dreadfully unfortunate they are because they have only one parent living with them.

Both divorce and death in a family are, undeniably, very hard on children. Either of these experiences can tear them apart, at least for a little while, and bewilder and alarm them. But children are less breakable, more resilient, than we sometimes think. Remember that difficulties coped with and survived strengthen people so that in the end they can be better for the experience: "God writes straight with crooked lines." Your children may, as you may, become more understanding, more self-reliant, and generally better people as a result of sorrow.

It is not as much fun to have only one parent as to have two, if the two are happy and loving, that is. But it is far, far better to have one happy and loving parent than to have two unhappy, cross, quarrelsome ones. Many couples who have stayed together "for the sake of the children" have discovered later to their surprise and relief, when they have finally parted, that their children are much better off once the break has been made. The home atmosphere has less tension and rancor in it, and as a result, everybody benefits. So make a positive decision to make your life and your children's lives happier and more productive from now on, instead of deciding you are all permanently doomed.

In the case of the death of a parent who was both loved and loving, of course it is *not* better that he is gone, but even in that case you need not feel that your children's lives are irretrievably blighted. The best tribute you can pay a dead parent is to keep his or her children freshly aware of how good life is even when we don't have everything we want. Instead of feeling sad and thinking all the time about what the "poor dears" are lacking, remind yourself and them of how many good things they have had and still have. One of Robert Kennedy's sons wrote a beautiful essay shortly after his father's sudden death in which he recalled the good times they had had together and said he would rather have had that father for a few years than any other father for a lifetime; rather than unfortunate, he considered himself unusually fortunate.

One point I would like to make as strongly as possible, even though it means repeating myself. Sometimes divorcees, widows and widowers think they would be better off if they had no children because their children are a great burden and responsibility which they don't feel up to. They say, "If only there weren't children involved I could manage this situation." I think they are fooling themselves and slandering their children. Certainly children *are* a great responsibility, but they are also just about the most interesting, and amusing, people in our lives. Watching them grow and playing a significant part in that growth, as Dr. Spock says in his famous book, "gives most parents—despite the hard work—their greatest satisfaction in life. This is creation. This is our visible immortality. Pride in other worldly accomplishments is usually weak in comparison."

Instead, therefore, of regarding parenthood as burdensome, think of it as *creative*. You are being called upon to play this role without the support of a co-star, and although it is a demanding role, you are highly privileged to be allowed to play it. Realize that more and more people are choosing this role. Realize that your children are not rare freaks to be pitied, because many other children also have only one parent and many of them are very happy. Realize too that a lot of people who have no children wish fervently that they did and would be glad to change places with you if they could.

If you live long enough, your children will go away someday and you will then look back, with perhaps exaggerated nostalgia and tenderness, on the days when they were living with you. Someday you may actually think of these years as a peak period in your life. Many of the most irritating things your youngsters do to you and that you do to them, the craziest mistakes you make, the most bewildering and upsetting experiences you have will by then have become family jokes. You won't recall the anguish nearly as vividly as you will remember some now almost unnoticed pleasures. Memory is selective and you will almost certainly have forgotten how scared you once felt or how much you used to pity yourself and your progeny.

Well, instead of waiting until that far-off day to look back on today, why not look at it while it is still here, and savor all the possibilities for pleasure it offers you?

When society was less affluent and blasé than it is now, people used to say (and mean) "Count your blessings" and, continuing that thought with a related one, "May all your blessings be little ones." If you take your ancestors' advice, you will realize that your little ones really are extremely large blessings. You may begin to see how lucky you actually are and start feeling self-envy instead of self-pity.

So be good to yourself and to your children, neither self-pitying nor self-punishing but gently self-indulging. If you are, you may be quite astonished to find how soon you are enjoying yourself so much that it is no longer any effort not to pity yourself or your children, because you are no longer at all pitiful!

6

RESPECTING YOURSELF:
Getting rid of guilt and self-hatred

There is a peculiarly close friendship between self-pity and self-hatred. They often visit us hand in hand. And self-hatred can be as self-destructive as self-pity.

If you are going to be a successful single parent, it will not be enough to get to know and accept yourself, to understand yourself and your circumstances realistically, and to adjust yourself to your situation sensibly and courageously. You will also have to be happily at peace with yourself. This means you'll have to *like* yourself and your life.

Unfortunately, being single may lower you in your own estimation. One of the greatest difficulties about not being married is the fear that this marks you as "queer" (in both the old-fashioned and new-fashioned senses of the word). Many people think "unmarried" is a synonym for "unwanted."

You may not consider this true as an unvarying rule, yet still find this attitude coloring your feelings about yourself. Sometimes, after all, when you were little, your mother used to punish you by making you go away by yourself. So did friends who refused to play with you when you did things they didn't like. Being alone thus can become linked in your subconscious mind with being naughty and therefore ostracized. It can get translated into "nobody likes me," and that in turn can get translated into "I'm not likable."

If you are convinced that everyone except you is mean and wrong and "has it in for you," then you are undoubtedly developing a case of paranoia. This may spare you from the unpleasantness of having to admit that you don't like yourself, but it is every bit as demoralizing and unrealistic to feel that everyone in the world is against you and it's *their* fault, as it is to think they're all against you and it's *your* fault. Neither state of mind is happiness-producing, and both need to be exorcised.

Probably your problem is not that extreme. Most of us are influenced by other people's opinions of us enough to be persuaded (at least partially) that we are sometimes (but by no means always) wrong, and that this is sometimes (but not always) why people leave us alone, so we don't feel totally enraged or anguished when we are alone; but we do frequently experience vague uneasiness mixed with varying degrees of guilt, worry, sadness, self-doubt, and self-disgust when we find ourselves all alone for a long period of time. (Of course, a functioning single parent isn't *all* alone, but the presence of your children may not reassure you about your worth, because children are a captive audience; in most cases they haven't freely chosen to live with you, and even if they have, in a contested custody case for instance, they are so immature that you may suspect the soundness of their judgment and think *you* wouldn't be so foolish as to live with you if you had any choice.)

A broken marriage usually makes its survivors feel even more rejected and dejected and guilty than other unmarried people do. A "gay divorcee" may put up a convincingly bold front and blame her rotten husband for everything that went wrong with her life, or maintain that it's a "civilized" divorce ending a marriage which both partners had simply "outgrown," with no one to blame, but way down underneath the little girl who used to get sent to her room when she was naughty still lives inside her, and at night when it's dark and no one can see her cry herself to sleep, and she lies there recalling some of the insults and complaints her former husband has thrown at her, she may feel very differently.

Feelings of inadequacy and undesirability assail every human being once in a while—even those who never admit it—and they are strongly reinforced by a divorce. You feel that you haven't "made it" with the opposite sex, and even if it was only one representative of that sex that has rejected you, you may feel that your sexual desirability is in serious doubt. Furthermore, even if it was you who did the rejecting, you know that everyone else doesn't know that, so you may worry about what other people (that tyrannical omnipresent "they") think about you and assume that their opinion of you has been lowered. You may try defiantly not to care what "they" think, yet care a great deal inside, trembling before the finger of scorn you imagine "they" are pointing at the "loser," whether they actually are or not and whether or not, in your clearheaded moments, you think you actually deserve scorn.

If you feel at all guilty about your divorce (and most newly divorced people do feel guilty as well as angry and hurt) you may dislike or even despise yourself. You may go so far as to feel you were to blame for every problem you or your spouse or your children have ever had, and that no one with any sense or taste could bear to be in the same room with you, as you swing over in a wild reaction against your original unjust feeling that your vile spouse was to blame for everything that went wrong. One attitude, of course, is as absurdly unbalanced as the other.

In instinctive self-defense, the ego fights off all knowledge that is unbearably painful. Many people can't stand to think about unpleasant things that have happened to them and therefore never learn to cure them or to prevent their recurrence. Many people neither care nor dare to try to get to know themselves because they are so afraid that they will uncover repulsive character defects and discover that they have inflicted serious wrongs on themselves or on others—for which they won't be able to forgive themselves. Some people are sure their divorce proves they are too unattractive or stupid or bad ever to be able to keep another person permanently in love with them. Others are sure it proves they are not loyal or stable or strong or generous enough ever to be able to stay permanently in love with anyone. Both conclusions provide convincing reasons to dislike oneself.

Nearly every divorce does represent a serious disappointment and admission of failure of some kind. If it didn't this would mean that neither party had ever expected and wanted their marriage to last, and this wouldn't mean the marriage had not failed but simply that the failure was built into it and accepted even before it began. And any marriage that terminates in acrimony and enmity is likely to convince both war veterans that they are, at least to some extent, not merely unloving and unloved but unlovable.

Self-reproaches of some kind are therefore almost inevitable. What one must learn to do is to keep these within the bounds of realism, so that awareness of past failings will inspire one to improve in the future, rather than make one feel generally and permanently inadequate.

Even the end of a loving, happy marriage can seriously weaken the ego of the survivor. People glow in reflected glory when someone they love loves them. Mutual love helps them feel and become lovable. But once the person who makes you feel this way dies you lose that source of reassurance and may start to wilt like a flower pulled up by its roots and deprived of water.

In other words, our own sense of our own worth is usually so strongly influenced by what other people think of us that when any marriage ends, for whatever reason, its survivors may lose self-esteem along with a mate. Saint Paul, a very independent guy (whom I find myself quoting a lot), said we shouldn't feel this way. He said something like this: "It doesn't matter what others think of me. It doesn't even matter what I think of myself. It only matters what God thinks of me." This is a way of saying that the *truth* is all that matters. Most of us are not so wedded to truth that we care more about it than about our reputations, but caring about the truth, rather than about our own or other people's unjustly harsh judgments, is the thing that can set us free.

Fortunately, society is kinder these days to "singles" than it used to be. The idea that being unmarried brands a woman publicly as incomplete and undesirable is no longer as widely held as in the good (?) old days when "maiden ladies" were automatically referred to as "spinsters" or "old maids" and divorcees were universally scorned as "fallen women." Today there are chic new terms like "bachelor girl" and "Cosmopolitan girl" designed to make the single life seem glamorous. These apply more to unencumbered young swingers than to women with children, but at least they indicate that some people now realize that some females—like some men—may actually prefer to be unmarried, instead of being so only because they "couldn't get (or hold) a man." Singleness is therefore no longer quite as stinging a stigma as it once was, even though many unemancipated girls still consider not having a husband tantamount to admitting that no man could possibly love them.

Men, too, may feel stigmatized by singleness. "Eligible bachelors" are sought after and admired but if they are past their mid-twenties they are also frequently suspected of being maladjusted, unstable, and immoral Don Juans too irresponsible or selfish to "settle down," or homosexuals, or misanthropes. Achieving a favorable self-image while single can therefore be difficult for a member of either sex.

Women's libbers vehemently reject, of course, the idea that singleness disgraces a woman. Their efforts to get their weak, old-fashioned sisters to acquire more self-respect (and to demand more justice in regard to such matters as job discrimination, credit ratings, and social freedom) are so laudable and important that I hesitate to criticize them, yet I must—because

I think many of them are unwitting victims of, and spreaders of, the self-contempt they decry, rather than inspirers of self-esteem.

Sometimes they talk as if they want to convince both men and women that women are not merely the equal of men in every way but so superior that men are really quite unnecessary —and I vehemently reject that notion! Sometimes methinks the ladies (wrong term: they are not at all ladylike) do protest too much. Sometimes methinks they dislike femininity as much as they dislike masculinity.

Many of them seem to regard pregnancy and childbirth as unfortunate nuisances which interfere with more interesting occupations (whereas I am sorry for men because they can never experience these sublime, self-transcending miracles), and they complain about child care as if it is a demeaning set of tasks to be avoided as much as possible. Motherhoood *is* a tiring, neurosis-producing role when it is so full-time that a mother never has a chance to get any rest, or to socialize with other adults, or to read a good book, or to finish a sentence, or to get out of the house for a change of scene, or to pursue any other interests. But we women might find it a lot easier to persuade men to help us with the myriad tasks involved if we were not so hell-bent on persuading men that such tasks are stultifying and degrading. Mothers really owe it to themselves and to their children and to men to recognize gratefully the great joys that go along with the chores.

Some women appear to want it both ways: they want to be admired as more practical, intelligent, gentle, kind, sweet, loving, wise, unselfish, sensitive, tolerant, patient, understanding, profound, peace-loving, artistic, and spiritual than mere men, yet at the same time they insist that there is no such thing as a specifically feminine trait. They proclaim how glad and proud they are to be women yet deplore and resent the idea that women should have any unique functions, biological, psychological, or cultural. This, I think, indicates an unconscious but strong disguised self-contempt plus self-pity which has become twisted into hostility toward the only available scapegoat: males. (Incidentally, if you are an ardent women's libber with a son, be extra careful not to make him feel guilty for being a male. This is no joke. Militant feminists can give their sons hang-ups every bit as damaging as the hang-ups domineering males can give females.)

Self-hatred is a seriously dangerous attitude. You may think it is merely unfortunate for the individual possessing it, shrug your shoulders, and say, "If people are foolish enough to make themselves miserable by hating themselves, that's their business." But that isn't all there is to it, because human beings have a built-in instinct for self-preservation so strong that they hate hating themselves, since this hurts them, so they turn self-hatred outward and aim it at other people instead of at themselves. A woman who hates herself cannot make an endearing, supportive mother nor is a man who dislikes himself capable of being a wonderfully warm and loving father, because self-hatred (like love) overflows onto others.

The person who holds himself in contempt holds other people in contempt too, as a defense mechanism and because our attitudes toward the outer world are reflections and projections of our attitudes toward our inner world. Thus someone who thinks of himself belittlingly as "only a little guy" but can't bear to admit it (like Archie Bunker) may blame all of his inadequacies and problems on "niggers"—and blacks who are deeply insecure about their own worth in turn hit back by blaming all of their troubles on Whitey. People perpetuate and aggravate, instead of solving, their problems this way, but in the short run this transference provides them with an emotional "out" that gives them deceptive, partial comfort.

It was not an accident or a patronizing concession to our weakness but a profound understanding of human nature that made Christ say we should love our neighbors as ourselves. If he had meant to say that loving ourselves is wrong he would have told us to love others *more than* or *instead of* ourselves. Instead, he recognized that loving oneself is healthy and natural and the foundation for the ability to love others.

There is one thing that single parenthood is sure to do for anyone. It gives a rapid education in what it is like to get along without a partner of the opposite sex. The feminist who has always yearned to have her own way and to do whatever she wants whenever and however she wants, without the interference of a bossy man around the house, now gets her chance to show that she can do anything a man can do—better. Repairing leaks in the roof and electrical wiring and plumbing. Catching and killing mice. Mowing the lawn, fighting the crab grass. Shoveling the snow. Putting up the storm windows. Washing the car. Fixing flat tires and broken windows. Carrying heavy packages. Taking out the garbage. Disciplining the children. Earning a living. Et cetera. She may, to her surprise and annoyance, soon find herself longing for masculine help and advice.

Also the wifeless husband, the male chauvinist who used to wonder contemptuously what on earth women do all day and who wished he could show his lazy and incompetent little wife how some masculine efficiency applied to home management would get the whole house organized and running smoothly in one hour a day, will now get his chance. To wash diapers and other laundry. To wash and dry dishes. Sweep and dust. Plan and cook meals. Comfort sad children, calm down quarrelsome ones, care for sick ones, toilet-train wet ones. Sing and read aloud. Play energetic games. Listen to endless riddles and jokes. Supervise homework. Shop, chop, mop and hop all day long, never getting done, never getting a day off. He may, with surprise and new respect, find himself yearning for a female helper.

Both of them, in short, may find out that, as Oscar Wilde once said, the only thing worse than not getting what you want is getting it.

There is a huge, almost unbelievably huge, amount of strenuous, monotonous, tiring, boring work involved in running a household that has children in it, and there is simply no way to get out of it. Washing machines and vacuum cleaners and frozen foods and electric cooking appliances help a great deal—and God bless their inventors—but they don't end it. Both male and female single parents will find that being a single parent is no snap. It is much more strenuous than being part of a cooperative parental team. And if they get so far behind in their backlog of endless chores that the house is a mess and the children are constantly yelling and disobeying, single parents may begin to feel so inadequate to cope that they are convinced more than ever that they are failures in life.

When guilt and self-hatred get a strong hold on you there may not be much your children or friends can do to comfort you. You probably won't believe anything complimentary anyone says to you. You will think people who praise you are just being polite or kind, or that they simply don't know you well enough to realize how dreadful the "real" you is—if they did they would surely abandon you just the way your spouse did. And if a friend comes over and tries to help you out by scrubbing your floors or washing your dishes (as a good friend of mine once did for a birthday present), you will probably interpret this as nasty criticism of your sloppy housekeeping instead of being grateful for it as an act of kindness.

If no one you know can help you at times when you are convinced you are awful, who can? You can!

How?

The first step is to stop exaggerating your woes and defects.

The second step is to realize that everyone else has woes and defects too; every other parent—single or married—at times feels as inadequate as you do, but it's a well-kept secret.

The third step is to be like Saint Paul and stop worrying so much about what you think other people think of you.

The fourth step is to realize that not everything which needs to be done needs to, or can be, done in one day; make time your collaborator and let *it* do some of the work.

The fifth step is to look at your faults candidly but separately and choose a *few* to correct, instead of lumping them all together and trying to attack the entire batch in one fell swoop.

The sixth step is to remind yourself of your good points. There *are* some, even in the worst of us, so you are not entirely worthless. Build on them.

Even people who have too exalted, rather than too low, an opinion of themselves occasionally succumb to self-hatred, because an inflated self-image is like a balloon: it can get punctured by a pin prick. Sooner or later a situation occurs which shows up the egotist's inadequacies and then Newton's law of motion goes into operation: there is an equal and opposite reaction toward inflated self-hatred.

Some people are neither overbearingly conceited nor cravenly self-critical. They don't overrate either their faults or their virtues. They don't go so far as to hate themselves but they are perpetually discontented with themselves just the same. What's wrong? They don't know and they are too lazy or uncurious to find out. "Who cares?" is their reply to most difficult questions. They put up with their discomfort like someone who is trying to ignore a swarm of mosquitoes that are buzzing around him on a hot summer night because he can't be bothered to go and get some insect spray and besides he hates its smell. Since they never examine themselves thoroughly enough to get to understand themselves, they are never able to lose that uncomfortable feeling of inadequacy, but they would rather overlook it and live with it than go to the trouble of analyzing and curing what is responsible for it. Their slogan is "Why look for trouble?" and the result is that they are forever in trouble they haven't looked for.

In short, different people have different reasons for not wanting to get to know themselves and for not learning to accept themselves and for not being able to adjust themselves and, therefore, for not honestly liking themselves.

One of the most pervasive and persuasive reasons is that many people are afraid that if they really think about it they will realize it is incumbent upon them to develop *new* attitudes, behavior, habits. They don't want to have to do this. Besides, they might not succeed, and then they'd feel worse than ever. So it seems easier just to bumble along, trying not to think about it.

Seems. Not is. In the long run, evasiveness makes problems harder. One cannot treat an undiagnosed disease. One *can* be seriously hurt by an unseen, unknown danger. *Awareness is always preferable to ignorance.*

It is true that as we get to know ourselves better we usually become aware of hitherto unsuspected imperfections in addition to those we already knew we had. But even that is no reason to hate oneself. Not being perfect is nothing to feel guilty about; it is human nature not to be perfect, even though it is also human nature to wish we were or to think we are. (There's an old Quaker saying I like: "Everyone's crazy but thee and me, and even thee's a little odd.")

A "perfect person" is almost a contradiction in terms. Every human being is finite, after all, and the word *finite* means "limited." So if you think you are, or can be, or ought to be, or someday will be, perfect, you don't know either yourself or human nature as well as you think you do. You are almost certainly suffering from delusions of grandeur and you are in for many bitter disappointments. I am sorry for you and for your children, because a perfectionist is hard on himself and can also be an extremely hard person to live with. Both you and your children are going to be constantly distressed at their imperfections. You will probably make unrealistic, unachievable demands on them, as you do on yourself.

Or you may kill them with kindness—like one mother I know. If you are always noble, kind, self-sacrificing, infinitely patient and understanding you may take out a monopoly on virtue and end up with children who are such unruly, selfish, undisciplined monsters that no one else will be able to bear having them around, even if you remain so heroic that you can. They won't even be able to bear themselves!

I have a good friend whom I really like and whom I used to

consider "the perfect mother." But when it dawned on me one day that I was extremely fond of her but heartily disliked her children, it suddenly occurred to me that she couldn't be a perfect mother after all, because she was raising antisocial hellions. I finally realized what it was that she was doing wrong. She was being so perfect that her children didn't have to be even minimally good.

When she had a headache she endured it bravely and permitted as much noise and activity around her as when she felt fine, so her children never learned to be thoughtful of someone else. When her children were bored or sad, she was there in a minute, ingeniously providing an instant cure, so they never got any practice in resourcefulness. When they were rude to someone she made up for it so quickly and sweetly that one would have been ashamed to notice their behavior and almost didn't—until it became habitual and she didn't happen to be around.

Patience and understanding are great virtues in a parent but they can be carried too far. Acting natural with your children will educate them for real life in this imperfect world much more effectively than being perfect would. It will help your children to know that there are limits and to learn to be adaptable, patient, considerate, and realistic. Nature knows what it's doing, letting children be raised by imperfect parents.

What if you are not an exaggerator in any way but honestly know that you have some very serious faults? Ask yourself some really tough questions. Were you to blame, at least in part, for your marital break-up? Do you have real reasons to feel deeply ashamed of many things you did or failed to do in connection with your spouse, who is now gone and to whom you will therefore never have a chance to make amends? Awareness of this type of failing is terribly painful, and terribly real. What to do if this is the case?

You will become frantic if you try to cure all your faults at once. It cannot be done. No sooner will you have conquered impatience than you will be faced with smugness. No sooner will you attack smugness than you will find despair rearing its ugly head. You will go after that and find presumption in its place. You will fight laziness and become a compulsive busybody. Fighting evil in general is fighting a Hydra-headed monster.

It is much more sensible to realize that you are *never* going to be perfect in all respects and to work on a few things that you find most inconvenient or most harmful or most embarrassing about yourself (or your youngsters) and let the rest go for the time being. A war fought on several fronts at once is less likely to be won than a one-front war where all of your enemies are in sight, instead of sniping at your rear while you're warding off others. So go after one or two weaknesses at a time, with determination but also with calm.

Nothing is gained by endless clobbering of yourself. Even if you have genuine reasons to be frightfully ashamed of past behavior you can learn to think about it in a way that will not further depress you and cause you to continue to be inadequate. You can examine, regret, and analyze both past and present failings—without wallowing in them. You can admit to yourself that you have had experiences you would much prefer never to have had, disappointments that made you extremely sad, caused in part by defects for which you are truly sorry—without becoming basically maudlin or gloomy. You can admit where you have failed, through your own fault, your own most grievous fault—without regarding yourself as thereby locked into a state of permanent failure in every respect.

After all, we often congratulate ourselves on successes without becoming cocky. You can know that you looked well and had a very good time at a particular party without therefore concluding that you are the most beautiful, popular, best-dressed, and wittiest person who ever lived. You may know you did a particular job extremely well, yet that knowledge doesn't fool you into thinking you can do every job equally superbly. But somehow with failures we tend to generalize from the particular, and if we have done something wrong or foolish or unfortunate, we conclude that we are inherently and perpetually wicked or stupid or unlucky—though this is ridiculous and unwarranted.

Telling yourself you are being illogical, when you are exaggerating a problem or failing, will not automatically cure you. When you are being illogical it is often because overwhelming emotions are interfering with clear thought processes, and your emotions at such moments have far more power over you than any intellectual appeal to logic. But even if you are convinced, and even if you are right, that you have been—so far—an utter failure, you can still turn yourself around, now, if you will use your failure by examining it to learn why it occurred, and then move beyond it.

There is a very helpful book called *Advice from a Failure* (by Jo Coudert, a Dell Publishing Company paperback) which deals with, and can help its readers deal with, long-standing emotional difficulties. It effectively demonstrates the fact that one can learn from and profit by mistakes.

Bad examples can be as educational as good ones—in fact, in some cases even more educational, if looked at in the right way. When we see a good example we ought to be inspired to emulate it, and when we see a bad example we ought to be equally inspired, to avoid it. Success teaches us what to do. Failure teaches us what not to do.

This is true when we dislike the way other people act and also true when we dislike the way we ourselves have acted. If we scrutinize poor behavior frankly, fearlessly, and intelligently, instead of evading and covering it up with phony excuses, we will be strengthened in the process.

Some of our worst traits are so deeply imbedded that it is enormously hard to shake them off, but when we become fully aware of them and of the harm they are doing to us and to others it is much easier to get rid of them than if we don't even know we have them. This, of course, is the basic contribution to psychological health that has been made by psychotherapy (which is discussed in the next chapter on how to change habits) but it has application in daily life even for people who wouldn't think of going to the expense and trouble of seeing an analyst.

There is another modern psychological theory called *psychocybernetics* which can also be helpful, although it operates on a very different principle. It maintains that if we continually keep thinking about how terrible we have been, we simply reinforce our failings by convincing ourselves that we are hopelessly awful, and we then become incapable of becoming better. Instead of examining one's conscience scrupulously, reminding oneself of and deploring and apologizing for one's sins and failures, this system suggests that we forget about them and remind ourselves instead of our virtues and triumphs, to reinforce our positive, rather than our negative, feelings and traits. If we can remember how we felt and what we did when we did something good, we may begin to feel that way again and repeat the successful behavior.

Personally, I think it is important to recognize *both* our defects and our assets, our failures and our successes. When we have done wrong I think we should admit it, be sorry, try to figure out why we did it and why we don't want to have it happen again, and how to prevent it. But I think it is equally important when we have done something well to realize it and be glad, allowing ourselves to take satisfaction in it and figuring out how we did it and how we can do it again.

Too many people, however, think that knowing one has good points is "pride" and knowing one has bad points is "humility." Since pride is a sin and humility a virtue, they actually think self-hatred is preferable to self-respect. But true humility is not a lopsided dwelling on one's failings; it is a realistic recognition of one's limitations and a willingness to acknowledge one's debts in regard to *everything* we have received, all our gifts, including our good qualities.

We inherited certain traits and tendencies, some good and some bad, from our parents and their parents and *their* parents. What we do with these is up to us, but we had no power to pick and choose our genes. We have also been subjected to many other influences during our lives, some of which have benefited us greatly and some of which have handicapped us. Again, what we do about these is up to us but no human being is powerful enough to select the century or the country or the family which will mold him. We do not create ourselves, in other words. Realizing and acknowledging this is what humility is, not cringing and wringing one's hands, cowering, or glowering at oneself.

If we are looking for a model of humility (and other virtues) to emulate, the Virgin Mary is a more attractive example than Uriah Heep. Uriah was 'umble but had no self-respect at all. Mary was humble and had a great deal of it. When told she would be the mother of a savior she didn't denegrate herself and say, "Oh my goodness no! I couldn't possibly! I'm not nearly worthy enough. Ask someone else." Instead she exclaimed delightedly, "He who is mighty has done wonderful things in me—all generations will call me blessed!" She knew her claim to fame was due to God's greatness rather than to her own independent achievement, so she was grateful instead of conceited about it, but she also knew she was doing something great, and she rejoiced accordingly. We, in our own much less exalted way, should adopt the same attitude, knowing when something we do is good and rejoicing in it, instead of perpetually worrying about, dwelling on, and blaming ourselves for our faults.

One woman I know once told me, "Everyone is entitled to three faults." I don't know why she picked precisely three, but I have found her attitude useful in getting myself to be more tolerant of other people's defects and of my own. Despair assails you if you expect perfection in yourself or in others. It is unattainable by humans. Every one of us is fallible. But knowing this does not mean that people—you and your children included—are not worthy of respect. In fact, this realization actually gives us an additional reason to respect ourselves and other people, because we manage to achieve things despite having failings, and it is a greater achievement to succeed in spite of handicaps than it would be to succeed without any.

Don't demand the impossible of yourself or of anyone else. The possible is possible. The impossible isn't. Allow yourself and your youngsters at least three faults apiece and respect each other in spite of them, even because of them.

7

CHANGING YOURSELF:
Breaking old habits and establishing new ones

By whatever process you arrived at the state of single parenthood, your arrival almost certainly means you have experienced a big transformation in your style of living, and there will be many other changes, both large and small, in the wake of this major change.

If you only feel comfortable ("groovy") when in a familiar groove, this prospect will frighten you. You may think you're not up to it.

Well, it's no doubt harsh to say so, but how you feel about it is irrelevant. You are going to go through changes whether you like the idea or not.

If you cling too tenaciously to possessions and habits and attitudes associated with a life style that no longer exists, you will get trapped in inconsistencies and anachronisms. So instead of wasting time and energy trying to avoid the unavoidable, spend your time and energy constructively and creatively. Otherwise you'll be like a baby trying to push back a tooth that is cutting through gums—this won't make the pain go away and it can't stop what is happening from happening.

It has been said before but is important enough to repeat: *All life involves growth and all growth involves change.* In fact, growth *is* change. And if you want to make the process of change easier on yourself, you won't just accept it reluctantly or stoically but actually learn to like it.

You may not yet be able to see where change is leading you, or *how* or *if* it will benefit you, but you can learn not to mind living in suspense—like a child who tingles with anticipation waiting for Christmas presents, though he doesn't know if he will get what he wants, or like an eager reader wondering how an exciting mystery story is going to work out. Embarking on the unknown is a thrilling adventure, if one cultivates curiosity and flexibility.

They say you can't teach an old dog new tricks. Maybe that's true of dogs. But why live a dog's life? I know humans of all ages who have learned lots of new tricks. And one of the cleverest tricks you can learn is to turn your attitude toward life around, so that although you cannot have everything you like, you at least like everything you can have.

Teaching ourselves (and letting life teach us) new tricks from time to time helps us do two important things: meet new situations easily when they arise, and stay interesting. People do not stay interesting unless they keep growing and changing. Becoming a "grown-up" does not mean becoming permanently set, like jello in a mold. Even though adults no longer grow bigger physically they should keep growing bigger mentally and spiritually, through added experiences, increased knowledge, and heightened understanding. (I should amend the first part of that last sentence which implies that adults stop growing physically, because although we do stop growing taller we usually, alas, keep growing wider!)

It really is important not to shrink back in fear when growth is being required of us, because if we do we will not merely fail to improve, we will regress. Shrinking doesn't mean staying still; it is literally the opposite of growing and means growing backward. Things and people that don't change *do* change—for the worse. A plant grows and blooms, or it rots. A white fence, in order to stay a white fence, must be repainted regularly or it will turn into a dirty gray fence. Similarly, humans need to be continually refreshed and renewed or they stagnate and deteriorate. Most of us, however, wouldn't have enough initiative to bother to grow and learn new things unless we had to. We are inclined to be overcautious, lazy, and unimaginative, except when changes are forced on us. Yet once we have gone through a never-before experience we almost invariably find ourselves richer, stronger, and happier, and are glad we were forced. This is why it is not sentimental rationalization but simple accuracy to call many disasters "blessings in disguise." Everything doesn't always happen for the best, but one can always make the best of anything. If you can't see this, get yourself a new pair of glasses . . . rose-colored.

What can you do if you realize the desirability of change but nonetheless feel incapable of it?

Perhaps you have made sincere resolutions, again and again, to try to enjoy and take advantage of whatever new opportunities your new solitude (or, to call it by a more attractive name, your new freedom) opens up . . . but it doesn't seem to offer any. You never meet anyone new. You never do anything new, because you're too busy on your familiar treadmill. You never go any place new, because you can't afford it (or can't get a baby-sitter). Everything you do, everything you see, everyone you know, everywhere you go, reminds you over and over again of how things used to be or of how you wish they were but are not, and it's not because your attitude has locked you in but because your circumstances have.

If this is so, you may have to force the issue and take deliberate action to alter your circumstances, even doing something as drastic as moving to an entirely new locale and entering a brand-new social circle.

Does it seem a bit much to be told to make one more big change on top of an already enormous one that has occurred in your life? Yes. At first thought, it seems not only unnecessary but rash. You don't want to change more than you have to. Your children need security. You need stability. Everyone needs continuity. You and your children may be extremely fond of the home and habits you are used to, and of your old friends and neighbors and possessions. That sense of identity which is so important for everyone's well-being is strengthened, after all, by familiar customs and associations, so why turn your back on them?

"I've already lost so much. Must I lose still more?"

Sometimes, yes.

"Why?"

In order to gain more. In order to get a new perspective. In order to become free to discover new things you will enjoy as much as or more than the things you have lost. Familiar routines and places and friends are extremely comforting, but sometimes they may be too comforting, causing you to be content in what amounts to a pleasant prison when you could and should be traveling freely.

A caterpillar would probably prefer to stay curled up comfortably inside a safe, cozy, familiar cocoon, but when it is time for him to be transformed into a butterfly that cocoon must be broken. Don't be sorry for him. The cocoon's tenant may be very discombobulated in the transition, but once he has known the fun and freedom of flying I am sure that nothing on earth could ever make him wish he were back in that small, dark, confining place.

Changes may be necessary in your daily routines. In the late afternoon, if you used to get out the cocktail shaker and have a relaxing drink with your glad-to-see-you mate, and if this moment was one of the high spots of your day, you may now find late afternoon a hard time to get through. A cocktail mixed by and for yourself is not as enjoyable as one that represents conviviality and companionship, and the once delightful martini may now seem as flat as ginger ale that has lost its fizz. You may find yourself drinking too many martinis, in a vain effort to recapture the jollity they used to provide, and as a result spend too many evenings in a blurred stupor instead of a warm glow. If so, this is probably your cue to alter your mealtime, moving supper up to an earlier hour, using this part of the day for animated conversation with your youngsters instead of preceding dinner with a pause that no longer refreshes.

Of course, if you are like many parents, that particular time of day may be the opposite of a treasured memory. It may recall chaos and mayhem, when the children were always fighting as a result of end-of-the-day tiredness and screaming for their supper, while you frantically tried to get them to calm down and take their baths or do their homework, and wished that dinner would cook itself so you could rest your tired feet and your aching back and that your equally tired mate would show more interest in you and help you more. For many families, late afternoon is the most hectic time of day, when a mother needs three extra hands, the disposition of a saint and the resourcefulness of a magician.

In that case, you may find single parenthood a great deal easier and pleasanter between the hours of five and seven o'clock than married parenthood is. The Children's Hour may never become as elegant and tranquil as Longfellow's glowing description of it, but at least you can give your children undivided attention and take care of their needs without having to worry about a spouse's needs at the same time.

However, there may be some other time of the day or week which is harrowing now in contrast to the way you used to spend it. For many people the weekends are awfully hard. Time drags by so slowly. They miss the Saturday night movies or social functions, or Sunday afternoon walks and chats that were once a regular habit. The whole pace and flavor of a weekend is altered when one member of a family has gone away. If Sunday dinner now seems like an enormous amount of work to go through for just yourself and your children (who don't appreciate your cooking efforts anyway), perhaps on Sundays you and the children should go out on the town in search of delightful new restaurants or a movie, or develop a brand-new habit such as regularly inviting friends over for Sunday brunch.

For many ex-marrieds, bedtime is the hardest time of all. They miss the ex and the sex (although many women hesitate to admit the latter fact outright, partly because "the frustrated female" is as apt to be the subject of cruel and dirty jokes as the object of sympathy in our sometimes crude culture), and as a result they find it terribly hard to get to sleep. Foolishly they resort to too many sleeping pills, or stay up much too late, endangering their good health and their good looks, watching the late-late show even when it bores them, or going in for endless nocturnal floor-pacing and sheep-counting.

This problem is harder to cure than the other two, because you can't give up going to bed every night, whereas you can skip a cocktail or change your mealtime. Would taking on a roommate or a lover help? You may think the first suggestion untempting and impractical and the second tempting but immoral. And perhaps nobody you know except you could stand living in the same house with you and your noisy brats. Besides, you may not know anyone you or your children would want to live with. Even if your morals, and your charms, make it possible for you to acquire a lover, you undoubtedly couldn't be with each other every night; you might like the idea, but what would your neighbors, let alone your children, think of you?

Though the possibility of obtaining a permanent roommate may be out, it might be well worth considering a temporary one or two. Is there some old school friend or a cousin you're fond of, with whom you have made vague plans over the years for a reunion? This might be a good time to extend an invitation for a weekend, a week, or a month. There are times when the changes of routine caused by a house guest are a nuisance, but this is a time when they'd be welcome.

Changes in your physical surroundings may be a good idea. You might change the bedroom decor in such a way that it will remind you less vividly of your previous sleeping arrangements. How about buying a piece of furniture your previous spouse wouldn't like: a very flouncy, flowery, feminine bedspread, for example, or a huge, hideous but gorgeously comfortable armchair? Or curtains in a color he/she loathed? Or something modern if all he/she approved of was antiques, or vice versa? Changes like these would help you feel more like *you* in your own room and remind you less of the person you used to share the space with.

You might also get a clock-radio that plays soothing music to fall asleep by. You might stock a bedside table with a good collection of interesting (or dull) books that are sleep-inducing. You might try vigorous calisthenics or peaceful Yoga exercises or transcendental meditation just before bedtime, to get yourself more thoroughly relaxed. Or change your schedule by eliminating a cool brisk shower in the morning in favor of a long, hot, sudsy bath at night. (Not so soothing and steamy that you fall asleep while soaking in the tub though.)

In any case, whether it is pleasant little things or important big things that you miss the most, if you do find that your physical surroundings as well as some of your too-well-formed habits are too constantly reminding you of what you are missing and thereby making you feel deprived, get rid of those surroundings and habits or at least modify them sufficiently so they are no longer your persecutors. If your living room has a chair or table you can never look at without remembering how he or she used to sit there, or if your bed invariably reminds you of the missing form that used to warm it up for you, perhaps you should, seriously, get rid of that furniture no matter how much you still like it, replacing it with something new and dramatically different.

These may seem to be small things, but our moods are strongly influenced by small things.

And, speaking of small things, start going through your closets and desk and bureau drawers too, tossing out accumulations of old things, particularly clothes you may still like but which have gotten a bit out of shape from hanging too long on their hangers, and which are no longer as fresh or stylish or becoming as they originally were. It can give your morale a big boost to throw them out and get yourself some nice new ones, to help you change your mood and your image a bit. Go in for more cheerful colors, newer fashions; they'll help you feel younger, springier, more daring, and more attractive. And a new hair style sometimes works wonders. Getting complimented or whistled at by the opposite sex is a superb cheerer-upper.

Don't feel there's no point in getting new things and sprucing yourself up because there's no one there to see you. *You* are there and your children are. And when children have only one full-time parent it is all the more important for them to feel that it is an attractive parent.

What is true of weeding out your closet is also true of other things you've accumulated, ancient souvenirs and bric-a-brac. Of course, some people don't need to be told this. They are not afraid to change themselves and/or their possessions. They refresh themselves and their homes regularly. But those of us who are clingers and collectors need to shake ourselves up once in a while.

This doesn't mean going to an absurd extreme and trying to rid yourself of things just because they are old or have associations which are currently painful. If you throw out too much you may regret it later. "Junk" has been defined as something you never need until the day after you have thrown it out. So don't throw everything away; just *put* it away for a while. The Japanese, whose homes are so exquisite, have a clever habit which keeps their small rooms uncluttered and ever-interesting. They display only one or two art objects in a room, put only one vase on a table, with a book or two, keeping the rest of their possessions out of sight in a chest of drawers, but they regularly vary the arrangements. As soon as they are used to one, they put those things away and replace them with one or two other things until they are used to the new arrangement—so they never get bored with the way their home looks, nor is it ever overcrowded, yet they still cherish old possessions, thus benefiting by both continuity and change.

It may be that you would benefit by even more fundamental

changes. To build a new life, perhaps you should move out of your current home and ensconce yourself in an entirely different type of place where nobody knows you—in a brand-new neighborhood, or even a new city—if your opportunities to meet new people and do new things are too restricted where you are. You may need to meet some people who will not associate you with your former life but will accept and know you only as *you*. You can still, of course, keep in touch with old friends if you want to, but it is important to meet new people too.

Redecorating your home or moving to a new one that needs to be fixed up can give you a consuming new interest, a very effective distraction from other thoughts. You will be so busy figuring out new furniture arrangements and exploring your new environs that you won't have as much time to brood.

So far I've been talking primarily about changing one's exterior environment. *But what about the need for some interior changes in habits and attitudes?*

If you are a confirmed creature of habit you may have to be quite firm with yourself at first in teaching yourself to cut loose; mechanical about learning to become spontaneous; strict about learning how to be free. Think carefully about what you would really like to do most if you could and knew how, and then figure out step-by-step how you could achieve this goal. Don't yield to your first mad impulse, unless the impulse lasts for a week or so. But set yourself a D-day. Before that day arrives think over the implications of the change, to double-check on its desirability, and start taking some tentative steps in its direction. But then, once D-day arrives, plunge—and don't look back.

Groups like Weight Watchers, Smoke Watchers, and Alcoholics Anonymous have studied many people and learned how to help them change long-standing habits. They know that some people have to go cold turkey, while others do better weaning themselves gently, taking one small determined step at a time. They have also learned that most people do better when they take other people into their confidence and get psychological support from people who are cheering them on. So tell your youngsters and your friends about some of the new plans that are rolling around in your head. If they are enthusiastic and supportive, and expect you to succeed, your effort to live up to their expectations and to win their approval will add to your motivation and make the changes easier.

If you are contemplating very major changes, such as a move to another city, you probably shouldn't talk these over with young children too far in advance, because you may worry them needlessly; children are often more conservative about change than Barry Goldwater is. But sound out a few people whose judgment you respect. Play with various alternatives mentally, before you commit yourself irrevocably. And then, once you have made up your mind, let your children know about it and bring them into the planning, and then *act*—decisively, enthusiastically.

The main thing to look for, in planning basic changes, is your real desires, not the most "practical" or "sensible" or "easiest" changes but the most joyous and exciting and potentially fruitful ones, those which offer you the greatest opportunities for new breathing space, those which will open up to you hitherto unexplored possibilities for adventure and fulfillment. You will probably make a few silly mistakes, but they won't be fatal if you keep yourself flexible. You will grow through new experiences and become more and more *you*.

There are many changes you can decide on and carry out all by yourself, or with the help of your children and your friends, once you have really made up your mind that you want to. But *there are also certain kinds of personality changes you might like to make which it may be tremendously difficult, if not impossible, for you to accomplish by yourself.* Some people are so paralyzed by fears or by ingrained habits that they cannot change even when part of them really wants to. They cling to destructive patterns of behavior even against their will, though neither they nor anyone else can understand why. Some people are so tense and rigid, or so flabby and lacking in self-confidence or the ability to make sound judgments, or so perpetually tired (without any apparent reason), or so accident-prone, or so prey to psychosomatic illnesses, that they can hardly go anywhere or do anything. They want to change, should change, must change—but don't know how.

In cases like this it is important to seek help—competent, trained help. It may not be as immediately and obviously urgent as in the case of a pathological depression, but it is essential if they are ever going to get free of what is crippling them.

If a few consultations with someone are sufficient, fine. If not, if it seems that you really need therapy or analysis, have the humility and common sense to get it.

You need not fear that if you go to a psychotherapist he will hypnotize you (unless you want him to) or brainwash you, destroying your personality in order to put one he prefers in its place, making you become a marionette while he pulls the strings. On the contrary, he will help you discover your own personality. He will help you contact and activate the real you that has been in hiding, helplessly pinned down inside a shell encrusted with irrational habits and anxieties. He will liberate, not destroy, you.

A therapist will listen patiently and sympathetically to your repetitious remarks and gradually see patterns of thinking and acting that you don't realize you have. Gently but persistently you will be forced to become aware of them, to recognize and acknowledge hitherto repressed longings and loathings, secret terrors and forgotten dreams. These new insights will increase your ability to make constructive changes and to begin acting the way you really want to—not necessarily the way your mother, father, husband, or wife wanted you to act, not even the way the psychologist wants, but the way *you* want.

Not that all psychotherapy or psychoanalysis is that successful. There are no guaranteed "cures." You may know someone who has been going to an analyst several times a week for years and years, who is still neurotic, or someone who "gave it a try" once and soon gave it up because "it wasn't doing any good." But if you are not happy with yourself it is at least worth trying to learn to be, and the results can be real and important even when they are not clearly visible. No one can judge from the outside how much better about himself a person may learn to feel inside, or conversely how much worse he might feel if he had never had any therapy.

This is illustrated by a joke about a man who went to an analyst to get cured of a stutter. Years later, an old friend met him and exclaimed, "Those sessions didn't do you any good—you're still stuttering!" The stutterer replied, "Oh, b-b-b-but they d-d-d-did! I've l-l-l-learned to l-l-l-live with it!" That joke is really no joke, because it's true that sometimes people can't change as much as they want to, yet therapy is still not a waste of time or money for them because it enables them to learn to bear and cope with defects that used to crush them.

Delving and probing into the inner mystery of yourself is a fascinating experience. As one satisfied customer said, "It's like being present at your own birth!" It *is* a birth or rebirth process, rather than a final solution to life's problems. There cannot be such a thing as a perfect and final psychological "cure" because nobody's personality is ever a finished product until his whole life is finished. But it is no small thing, in the meantime, to be put in touch with your emotions and to feel new energy and confidence surging into you as a result of new awareness and understanding.

If you do decide to go to a therapist make sure you go to a competent professional (how to find one? see the next chapter) and then *trust* him and the therapy process. Be patient, even when it gets very difficult and uncomfortable. It is long, slow, and painful work. There are no shortcuts where growth and understanding are involved. But if you are patient and persevering you *will* feel the benefit of it. Therapy provides no instant miracles and no guarantees against future problems but it does bring about important interior changes which unlock blocked-up potentials. A good "shrink" doesn't shrink you; he does quite the opposite, helping you to expand and grow, to become freer, realer, you-er.

Growing is always to some degree scary and painful. Birth is. Teething is. Studying is. Adolescence is. Conquering defects is. Facing the unknown is. And you may have thought that once you passed your teens you were through forever with that kind of pain because you thought you were all grown up. But no one ever is, entirely, until he's dead.

Realizing that sobering fact may seem like one more reason to feel permanently worried and depressed, if you think of yourself as a perpetually unfinished product, forever partially unfulfilled and incurably prone to imperfections and weaknesses. But it can be a very stimulating and encouraging thought instead, if you focus your sights not on your imperfections but on the unlimited vistas in front of you, the further opportunities and improvements which your imcompleteness implies, the inexhaustible openness that lies forever before you, always inviting you to learn and to see and to hear and to taste and to touch and to feel and to enjoy more and more and more and more and more . . .

Life may at times exhaust you, but you will *never* be able to exhaust *it!* There are now, and always will be, new things to look at, new people to meet, new experiences to have, new places to go, new things to learn and to do—more than you can ever possibly see or meet or possess or explore or learn or experience.

Think of emptiness as something to fill. Think of incompleteness as an opportunity to grow. Think of suffering as educational, which it invariably is if we allow it to be. All pains can be turned into growing pains if we grow through them and learn from them to be more resourceful and resilient, more real, than we have ever been before.

When we accept peacefully the discomforts and uncertainties that the life process makes inevitable at times, when we learn to cooperate with this process instead of resisting it, the pains it causes are reduced. It is like natural childbirth: knowing what is happening to you and relaxing, instead of stiffening in fear, can reduce the agony of severe labor pains, turning them into quite bearable contradictions and speeding the process of delivery. So instead of dwelling on pain sorrowfully and anxiously, pass on through it to get on with the exciting business of growing, of giving birth to a new you, of becoming more and more real.

Also think about this: There is one extremely pleasant by-product of growing up, even though the process is never fully completed. You keep liking yourself, as well as life, more and more and more as you keep getting smarter and smarter and smarter. You may not be inspiring or brilliant company today, but you can start today to become a more attractive and interesting person by the simple device of starting to notice attractive and interesting things you have hitherto been neglecting. Instead of concentrating so much of your attention on how painful the process of growing is, think about how exciting your new discoveries and interests and improved talents can be and are going to be if you work at acquiring them.

Don't make changes just because you think they are expected of you. Only make those you think will be improvements. Make those you really want to make, those that will help you. Don't try to impress anyone else. Don't be affected. Be real.

There is a lovely children's story called *The Velveteen Rabbit* which has a scene in it where two stuffed toys are discussing life. The subject of their conversation is reality:

"What is real?" asked the Rabbit one day when they were lying side by side. "Does it mean having things happen inside you and a stuck-out handle?"

"That's not how you are made," said the Horse. "It's a thing that happens to you. When a child loves you for a long time, not just to play with, but *really* loves you, then you become real."

"Does it hurt?" asked the Rabbit.

"Sometimes," said the skin horse, for he was always truthful. "But when you are real you don't mind being hurt."

"Does it happen all at once?"

"You become. It takes a long time. That's why it doesn't happen to people who break easily or have sharp edges and have to be carefully kept. Generally, by the time you are real, most of your hair is loved off and your eyes drop out. You get loose at the joints and very shabby, but those things don't matter, because once you are real you can't be ugly, except to people who don't understand."

Living is a combination of being and becoming. As long as we are breathing we will always be engaged in the mysterious process of becoming something beyond what we have been in the past or are at any given moment. Each of us is continually learning to become someone who never existed before, and learning to do things which have never been done before in quite the same way under exactly the same circumstances. Even though the results of our activities may be far less earth-shaking than the achievements of Columbus, Thomas Edison, or Michelangelo, every one of us, in our own sphere, is an explorer, an inventor, and a creative artist.

When we have reached a peaceful plateau where we wish we could rest for a long time, or even forever, life still requires us to move on. No one is allowed to stay in one place or attitude for very long, because life is an endlessly flowing river pulling everything in it toward an open sea. And it is equally true that when we find ourselves in a sad state or place and feel doomed to endure it forever, we are mistaken: we will be moved on. Life will give us new experiences and new changes, unfailingly, continually. All we need to do, to smoothe and ease the process, is to keep ourselves aware and open and receptive.

Each of us has talents we never develop or use to the maximum. Each of us has opportunities we fail to notice or grasp, either because of laziness or timidity or lack of curiosity or because we are too busy doing something else. This means that each of us could, if we wished, know more and do more and be more. Each of us has the capability of becoming increasingly happy and increasingly successful, no matter how happy or unhappy, successful or unsuccessful, we have been in the past, because we are never permanently what we are now.

Naturally, the constancy of inconstancy makes life difficult, suspenseful, sometimes uncomfortable, frightening, and exhausting, and it involves real possibilities for dangerous accidents and for failure. But it is also an unending, exhilarating adventure with real possibilities for further and further progress and for victories. Our *attitude* toward life is what makes the difference. We cannot always control our external circumstances but we can always, if we want to and learn how to, be in charge of our attitudes toward those circumstances. We can choose to be reluctant or eager. We can choose to be impatient or patient. We can choose to be resentful or forgiving. We can choose to be timid or adventurous. We can choose to be sterile or creative. We can choose to be phony or real, hostile or loving, negative or positive.

Once we realize this, the whole panorama of reality opens out before us and we see how large and magnificent the arena is in which we can exercise our freedom of choice.

The fact that the only permanent thing in this world is impermanence means we can never altogether escape problems but it also means we need never despair of new achievements.

8

RELYING ON YOURSELF:
Learning to be self-confident and independent

Being help-less does not mean you have to be helpless! It means you have to learn how to help yourself.

Being intelligent doesn't mean being born pre-stuffed with knowledge. It means being capable of acquiring knowledge and of using it correctly.

Being self-sufficient doesn't mean always being by yourself and doing everything all by yourself. It means being capable of going it alone when necessary but also finding out where to acquire help when you need it and then following through on it independently, applying it constructively and creatively to your own situation.

Being self-reliant doesn't mean never relying on anyone else for anything. It means doing willingly whatever you can do by yourself, without bothering other people unnecessarily, and also being farsighted enough to prepare for both foreseen and unforeseen situations.

Being self-confident doesn't mean having no confidence in anyone except yourself, nor does it mean being conceited. It means having the courage to do things you must do and faith in your ability to do them well.

Intelligence, self-sufficiency, self-reliance, and self-confidence are qualities that belong to the type of person on whom other people can depend. So when you are a single parent, these are the qualities you must develop in yourself so that your children can safely depend on you.

Upon first becoming a single parent these adjectives probably don't describe you. Self-confidence is built up by experiencing success, just as success, reciprocally, is acquired in part as a result of having self-confidence. When you haven't yet had any experience as a single parent you can't tell what your capabilities are, so you are apt to feel uncertain of yourself at best, and at worst utterly terrified at the thought that henceforth the welfare of the child or children whom you love more than anyone else in the entire world rests in your hands and yours alone. That's an awesome enough responsibility to frighten even a very stalwart person—and while you are still reeling from the shock of a death or divorce, feeling sad and full of self-doubts, you are hardly the most stalwart person alive.

To feel worried, even panicky, is understandable—for a few days, even weeks. But if you stay panicky after that you had better take yourself firmly in hand before you and your children get seriously hurt. Turn off the faucet of tears and use your free time (those long, sometimes deafeningly quiet, evenings after the children have gone to bed) to do a lot of hard, practical thinking. Make up your mind to take definite steps to develop abilities you have neglected and are now going to need, because —I repeat—from now on you must be self-sufficient, self-reliant, self-sustaining, and self-confident.

Do all these adjectives that start with the word "self" make your life sound pretty grim, as if you have been sentenced to solitary confinement and condemned to live in isolation ever after? That's not it. Learning to be contentedly independent isn't the same as learning to become isolated or selfish; it means learning to become *resourceful*. And this means that, at the same time that you increase your ability to function on your own, you will also increase your chances to become a vibrant, dynamic, sought-after, helpful, beloved person, far more attractive and popular than any clinging vine could possibly be.

A truly self-confident and independent person is not unloving or unlovable. Such a person, in fact, inspires love in others and, in turn, is able to give love to others freely, generously, eagerly, out of an overflowing abundance of inner strength. This is a far lovelier, warmer, more fulfilling love than the kind which is disguised neurotic need, helplessness masquerading as love. That type of love is often an unconscious emotional bribe, a search for security motivated by "the gimmes." It is demeaning and demanding, greedy rather than giving.

So don't be fearful that by concentrating for a while on self-improvement you are going to become self-centered and selfish. You may learn to become truly "selfless" for the first time.

If you are inclined to be overdependent, this means you don't have a strong enough sense of self. Your problem is related to the earlier discussions in connection with self-knowledge and self-acceptance. You may not dislike yourself, and maybe you're not prone to depression, but you don't think enough of yourself *as* and *by* yourself. You see yourself so constantly in relation to other people that when you have to be on your own you seem to evaporate, to disappear. You simply don't feel complete as an unmarried person. But if you don't learn to—beware! You will switch over from having been first an overdependent child and then an overdependent spouse into becoming an overdependent (hence also, probably, overdemanding) parent, seeking all your emotional gratification and reason for living in your children. And that could do both them and you great harm. That is the surest way for you to destroy the possibility of a lifelong healthy and happy relationship with your children.

When we turn to our children to make up for a loss or lack in our own lives or in our own personalities, seeking to find and fulfill ourselves primarily through them, we draw them too close to ourselves and they suffocate from "smother love." We turn "Sonny" into a "Mama's boy" or a reluctant carbon copy of Daddy, a perpetual "Junior," and we make our daughter stay an eternal baby or a cute little doll; or else we force our children to pull away from us, to rebel and run for their lives (which they will do if they have any spunk). *In seeking to cling too hard to children a parent either maims them or loses them—or both.*

People who, whether by temperament or training, do not function well on their own, who are not self-starters, who need frequent morale-boosting encouragement from other people in order to keep going, cannot expect to transform themselves into live-wire go-getting high achievers overnight. But their case is not hopeless.

They will, in the beginning and perhaps always, have to consult friends and advisors more than a naturally independent person would want to do. They will have to discover where to find new sources of support when they have no spouse to rely on, diversifying and spreading out among a number of different people interests which used to be focused on and combined in one person. They will have to find ways of enlisting the cooperation of neighbors, remembering also to help their helpers as much as possible so that help isn't always one-way traffic and they don't become a nuisance. They will have to develop a strong sense of responsibility and cooperativeness in their children, working out schedules for the sharing and exchanging of chores, and bringing the children into their confidence about many matters in a sort of participatory democracy, with policies and plans worked out in family conferences.

If they do this skillfully, they will have turned their weakness into an asset, and will end up with more friends (and more help) than ever.

Some people have the opposite problem: they are too arrogantly independent. They seem to be self-sufficient by nature. They function, on the whole, better by themselves than as part of a team or than when surrounded by willing assistants, who just get in their way. They don't like or know how to delegate work or authority. They are opinionated and don't know how to compromise, usually feeling they can do everything more quickly and efficiently by themselves. They dislike divided responsibility and have a great deal of initiative.

Obviously, this type of person is going to find the job of being a single parent far easier than an overdependent person will, at least in the beginning. But they too will run into roadblocks that they probably do not expect. Do-it-yourselfers need to learn to share authority and tasks and to check opinions more than they are naturally inclined to do. Nobody knows everything, and if you are inclined to think of yourself as omnipotent and omniscient, watch out or you may become a parental tyrant.

Super-independent people, when they become single parents, usually start off with a burst of enthusiasm followed by a letdown. They are bubbling over with so much self-confidence about how superbly they are going to manage, now that nobody is going to be able to interfere with them, that they spurn all offers of assistance or advice. And then they crumble suddenly if some major crisis arrives, finding that being help-less actually does make them feel helpless after all. The blow to their ego is horrendous, unexpected and disillusioning.

Until now, perhaps, they were able to hide the weaknesses and failings which they share with the rest of the human race behind those of someone else, but now their alibi has disappeared and they stand exposed, psychologically naked, embarrassed, ashamed, and scared. A woman who has always said smugly, admiring and pitying herself simultaneously, "I could have been a brilliant actress (or artist or business woman or politician or whatever) if I hadn't given up my career for my husband," may now finally get the chance and be a flop. Or a man who has complained, "My wife never understood or appreciated me; she was always carrying on about my being extravagant (or stingy)," may find himself in chronic financial troubles now that he is running a household on his own and discover that she wasn't exaggerating or making it up to annoy him but was right all the time.

It is foolish to say, "I refuse to bother anyone about my problems; they're mine and it's up to me to solve them all on my own; people have to stand on their own two feet." It's foolish and it's untrue, because we were not created by ourselves nor have we been kept in existence all by ourselves. We are the result of loving collaboration. We were brought to adulthood with the help of many other people: parents, teachers, doctors, siblings, friends, even strangers who helped us when we didn't expect it or know it: correcting things, running things, inventing things, improving things we need and use. All of us are interdependent.

People say "God helps those who help themselves," but the Bible, which many of us consider the most authoritative source of information about God's attitude toward the kinds of attitudes we should have, says "Ask and it shall be given to you." Nowhere does it say that if you don't ask it will be.

It is natural to have to depend on other people at times. If we were truly all alone in the world, totally independent, would we feel happy and gloriously free? Of course not. We'd feel thoroughly miserable. We were made to be the type of creatures we are, who need each other. Giving-and-receiving is our life's blood. We need to do *both* just as much as we need to breathe in and out.

The illusion that anyone can and should always be completely self-sufficient is not really an illusion. It's a delusion. (Illusions are innocent and harmless; delusions are stupid and dangerous.) It is a denial of the humanness of humans. Admitting it when you need help from someone doesn't turn you into a weakling instead of a hero; it makes it possible for you to get the reinforcement you require so that you *can* be a hero! Knowing when, where, and how to find such help is an important aspect of true self-reliance, rather than a contradiction of it.

Whenever one generalizes about any subject one finds oneself having to make cautious qualifications and subtle distinctions, remembering to say "also" and "but" and "however" and "on the other hand." This is one of those times. It is important to realize that a single parent, more than most people, must operate independently *but* it is *also* important to realize the necessity of turning to other people for help at times, and it is vital, *on the other hand,* not to abdicate one's responsibilities to the extent of turning them over to others and becoming a parasite.

Therefore analyze yourself and your situation—thoughtfully, honestly, practically, clearly, specifically—in order to decide what things you *can* do by yourself and what you *cannot* do alone. If you realize that you or your children are in need of a certain kind of help you are not equipped to provide on your own, don't berate yourself for inadequacy; just go and get the help you need which will make you more adequate.

False pride is something no single parent can afford. It is more expensive than the most expensive diamond necklace in the world. The willingness to admit realistically that you have a problem you don't know how to handle, and then to take whatever steps are needed to enable you to learn how to handle it, without procrastinating until it is too late to do any good, requires humility, especially when you don't enjoy taking those steps (like having to go on welfare if you are in a really serious financial jam, something many single parents have had to swallow their pride and do, or having to admit to a social worker how ineffective you are in coping with your hysterically disturbed child), but it is an essential part of becoming self-reliant in the long run, even though in the short run it looks like the opposite. The effort to go it alone when you shouldn't or can't will end up making you more, not less, dependent on the kindness of other people, because they will have to rush to your aid when you have collapsed from a neglected, unsolved problem.

Admitting and surveying and tackling problems is quite different from building them up unnecessarily through worry or overdramatizing them. Many (perhaps most) of our problems we are perfectly capable of handling on our own. In fact, one of the happiest discoveries most single parents eventually make (except for those mentioned above who start off much too cockily) is that they are far more capable of exercising independent initiative and resourcefulness and good judgment than they thought they were before they needed to be.

It would be ridiculous to rely on a crutch if you are able to walk without one. It would be equally ridiculous to refuse to use a crutch when you need one; if you did you would lengthen the period when you couldn't walk well. So ask for help when you need it and don't when you don't. Keep a sensible balance, neither regarding yourself as utterly incompetent and helpless nor as all-knowing. You are somewhere in between, with your own individual combination of virtues and faults, partial knowledge and partial ignorance, and once you know yourself well enough to know what your main strengths and weaknesses are, you can use the former and compensate for the latter.

Where can you find reliable help when you need it?

These days, as life gets more and more complex, there are more and more specialized sources of assistance. In every city and in most small towns there are people trained to give different types of aid: psychoanalysts, psychologists, psychotherapists (some of whom specialize in family therapy), guidance counselors, pastoral counselors, career consultants, financial consultants, tax advisors, lawyers, doctors, visiting nurses, physiotherapists, speech therapists, remedial reading teachers, social workers, consumer representatives, welfare agencies—spiritual firemen all. Some charge for their services; some are available for the asking. If you don't know how to find one, or if you find several and don't know which is best, ask friends or your doctor or a hospital or the Board of Health or a schoolteacher or a minister, priest, or rabbi.

There are also many self-help groups that have been formed by people who have special problems or whose children have: parents of retarded children or of youngsters with cerebral palsy; alcoholics and drug addicts; parents who need to go to work and leave their children, who form co-op day-care centers to help each other out. In an increasing number of communities there are chapters of "Parents Without Partners," an organization which publishes a monthly magazine. The chapters hold regular (usually weekly) meetings and social functions, where both male and female single parents get the chance to socialize and talk over problems with each other. Write to their international headquarters (80 Fifth Avenue, New York City 10011) to find out if such a chapter exists near you, or if you could form one.

Some people hold back from joining this organization out of embarrassment, for fear it is really just a camouflaged dating service; others join it in the hope that it is! It may serve that function, and that really isn't anything to be embarrassed about; it's a valuable function in small communities where most social life is arranged primarily for married pairs. But that is not its main purpose. It was organized by partnerless parents who felt the need to meet with other partnerless parents in order to compare problems, to exchange advice, to help and to be helped in finding solutions.

Watch out for so-called self-help groups which can be more upsetting than the problems they claim to solve: some "encounter groups" and "consciousness-expanding groups" are run by enthusiasts unqualified and unable to handle the situations that arise. They open up a Pandora's box of inflamed emotions and then don't know how to put out the flames.

When you are seeking help for a serious problem, whether it is physical or psychological, you want to entrust that problem to a trained, registered, licensed, reputable professional, not to a quack. Check credentials in addition to getting recommendations.

When should you seek outside help and when should you work things out on your own?

You may agree with everything I have been saying about the need to help yourself when you can and to turn to others for help when you need to, but still not be sure how to tell when you need help and when you don't. You don't want to delay in seeking help if it would really help, but you're not sure if it would.

Prevention is better than cure. In matters of physical health if your tooth or ear or throat or stomach or head is hurting fiercely, you don't need to be told to run, not walk, to the nearest doctor. But there are some diseases which do not reveal symptoms until they are far advanced. It is a good rule to have annual, even semi-annual, physical checkups. They provide better health and life insurance than any insurance company can. If the examination reveals that you are in fine condition, you haven't wasted your money. The certain knowledge that you are healthy is well worth paying for; it makes you feel healthier than ever. If an examination does reveal something which needs attention, this means you have caught it before it is serious and dangerous. So go to a doctor when you do feel well, as well as when you don't. Specialists who should be seen regularly, in addition to the dentist, are eye doctors (growing children, in particular, should have periodic eye examinations to forestall difficulties with reading in school) and gynecologists (a mother should have Pap tests and breast examinations regularly).

Incidentally, you may be interested to know that if you are divorced you have already taken steps to improve your health! A doctor in California recently studied approximately 4,500 families and compared the health levels of (1) happily married people, (2) unhappily married people, and (3) divorced people. The healthiest were the happily married. The sickest were the unhappily married. The divorced were found to be consistently "healthier, happier, and less isolated" than the unhappily married. The study concluded that there are two main ways in which people respond to an unhappy marriage: the stronger and more intelligent get divorced, the weaker ones lapse into chronic poor health.

In the case of emotional problems, if you are so confused that you are not sure you need help, and if you find the subject persistently worrying you, this may be a sign that you would benefit from it. Even if you are not deeply upset, psychologists advise that whenever patterns of behavior have undergone severe, disruptive changes (as they certainly have after a divorce or the death of a spouse) a consultation with a therapist can be very helpful even if not strictly necessary. Again, prevention is better than cure, and although it may be possible to manage without the help of therapy it can perhaps be a lot easier with therapy.

If many people you know are urging you to seek professional help, your difficulties may be serious enough to warrant it even though you yourself don't realize it. Accept, at least tentatively, the judgment of other people when you are confused. It will do you no harm to seek help, temporarily, when in doubt. You are always free to discuss things with an expert and then weigh his advice and decide not to take it if you don't want to—but listen to it carefully before rejecting it.

A sure sign that you need help is if you have extremely serious problems for which you can think of no solution and for which there seems no rational explanation. For instance, it would be quite appropriate to feel terrified if you were in a jungle with an angry tiger racing toward you. But it is irrational to feel scared to death all the time if you have a comfortable home and enough money to pay for food and rent and you and your children are in good health. If you frequently get fierce blinding headaches or rashes or agonizing attacks of cramps and indigestion, even when the doctor has checked you out and tells you there is absolutely nothing wrong with you, then there *is* something wrong with you—but it's not physical.

If you feel inadequate, in a dither, dissatisfied, always tired, yet unable to sleep, if you have great difficulty in getting along with people, not some of the time but almost all the time, if you are unable to stop thinking about your worries, if you are deeply suspicious of everyone (even of friends), if you lose your temper at your children so violently that you frighten yourself as well as them—these are all definite signs that you need help.

Another sign is if your children are constantly misbehaving in bizarre ways, to a degree that you find nearly unbearable, and nothing you do seems capable of stopping it. Brattiness is a loud cry for help. Both you *and* they may need help. This is the kind of situation where family therapy may be advisable, and invaluable.

In many cases your family or friends can give you whatever help you need to get over a rough period. But in other cases it would be an imposition and strain on friendship to expect them to give the kind of close and sustained attention you require. That is one of the reasons it is morally wrong, not merely foolish, to refuse to avail yourself of professional help when it could solve a problem that otherwise will continue to plague you and your family.

Many people are afraid to go to a therapist because of the stigma attached. They think they are diagnosing themselves as crazy or committing themselves to a very long and expensive treatment. Not so. People nowadays often get psychological counseling to work out a specific temporary problem which can be handled in a few weeks.

Even when people are so deeply troubled that they have to go to a mental hospital, this is no longer a life sentence or death sentence as it once was. According to the National Institute of Mental Health, one out of every ten Americans suffers from some form of mental or emotional illness ranging from mild to severe, and there are more patients in hospitals receiving treatments for mental illness than for heart disease or pneumonia or cancer. Most of them are there only for a brief period. There was a time when, if someone had a nervous breakdown, that person was branded and eyed with suspicion forever afterward. Not anymore, fortunately. (You may not be considered eligible to be Vice President later, but would you really want to be, anyway?)

Consulting a therapist isn't a weird hobby indulged in by rich and self-centered people who enjoy paying someone to listen while they rant on and on and on about themselves. Its purpose, and its result when it is successful, is to help people learn enough about themselves so that they can become more capable, happier people, by discovering what it is that has been holding them back from successful achievement.

The reason most people cannot do this alone is because they lack objectivity about themselves and also because many of their self-defeating motivations and fears are deeply buried in the unconscious, so trying to fight against them is like fighting against an unseen enemy in the dark. But when you talk things over at length with someone trained to be understanding and observant, hitherto unnoticed clues and cues come to light. This enables you to learn how to lick problems and fears instead of continuing to be licked by them. People who cooperate intelligently and perseveringly with a therapist do not become overdependent on him or her (except perhaps in an early stage of the treatment). On the contrary, they become capable of being truly independent people when they have never been able to be in the past.

I am certainly not advocating that every time you have a worry or emotional difficulty you must rush to the nearest friendly neighborhood psychiatrist. *Some anxieties are comparatively easy to eliminate, and self-reliance in certain matters can be achieved by taking a few very simple, practical steps.* For example, something as simple as a handy list of phone numbers can put your mind at ease and forestall and solve problems.

One of the first things to do when you are starting out as a single parent is to eliminate fears by preparing ahead for emergencies. You cannot foresee and forestall them all, but some are quite predictable. For example, if you have young children you can be fairly sure they are going to get, one of these days or years, an earache or toothache or heavy cold (even pneumonia), chicken pox, mumps, measles, strep throat—probably in the middle of the night, because of "LMI," a law of life that a brilliant scientist I know discovered. This is "The Law of Maximum Inconvenience." It explains why you hardly ever get a flat tire when you are right near a service station, but only when you are all alone on a dark country road, and why your child never gets sick when the family doctor is next door but only when no doctor is available. LMI also explains the annoying statistical fact that most babies are born between 3:00 and 6:00 a.m. instead of at a sensible hour—that way they can start right off, from their very first moment, making you realize that life is not arranged for your convenience. So, to outfox LMI:

Be sure you know how to get hold of a doctor in the middle of the night. If your pediatrician doesn't make house calls, get the phone number of another doctor who does, and keep it right by your telephone.

Keep other numbers there too. Write them down and paste or thumbtack them to the wall, now. Don't wait until you actually need them. You should know in advance how to get hold of an ambulance, a taxi, a policeman, the fire department, at a moment's notice.

Here are some important phone numbers to write down:

The poison control center, if there is one where you live (if not, the emergency room of a hospital) in case your toddler, while roaming around the kitchen one day, drinks some cleaning fluid or liquid shoe polish or gobbles up a whole bottleful of aspirin; it's astonishing what distasteful concoctions little children who won't eat what you serve them are willing to consume when they are in an exploratory mood. (Of course, an additional and even better way to eliminate anxiety about something like this is to keep certain items—all poisonous, sharp, and breakable objects—completely out of reach of small children.)

A plumber, in case your pipes burst or your toilet overflows after one of your children has decided to flush a toy down the drain.

An electrician, in case your refrigerator or washing machine goes on the blink, or all the fuses blow, or you have an electric fire. (Also make sure you know where the fuse box is and that there are always ready-to-use fuses right next to it. And that you know how to unplug electric appliances if they start smoking or spitting or making nasty, growling noises. And keep candles and matches in a convenient place in case there's a power failure.)

A hardware store or locksmith that makes keys, and makes house calls in emergencies, to enable you to get into your house the evening when you or the children have locked yourselves out (you must keep this number in your purse as well as by your phone, because it won't do you much good there in the house if you can't get into the house to get it).

A TV repairman, for the day when the television set breaks down right in the middle of Sesame Street and your children start howling.

A general repairman or handyman, for all the other things that break down. It is so easy to get royally gypped by repairmen if you rely on the nearest available one when there is an actual need. Need does not seem to bring out the chivalrous qualities in man as much as the desire to gouge, so it's wise to build up a friendly relationship with repairmen who want your regular business and therefore will not take advantage of you. And by the way, part of their regular business should be to repair *promptly* shaky ladders, broken stairs, windows, lamps, and other items around the house which could cause accidents. According to the National Safety Council the average home is the most dangerous place anyone can be; more accidents occur there (almost all preventable) than in airplanes and automobiles, and more young children die from accidents than from diseases. Next year—unless it is a very untypical year—four thousand children under the age of four are going to be killed by accidents at home, and one out of every three children will be seriously enough injured to need medical attention.

A service station, for the day when your car won't start and you have an important appointment. It is even more essential (and difficult) to find an honest, reliable auto mechanic—especially one who will spring forth gallantly to help you in an emergency instead of explaining that you'll have to wait three days for service—than it is to find an honest repairman. So sound out every car owner you know for recommendations.

The gas company, if your house is heated by gas, for that night when the furnace suddenly goes out and it's five below zero outside, and also for the day when there is a leak in the gas pipes and your family is about to get asphixiated. (Another incidental note: make sure you know how to fix your stove's and furnace's pilot lights, and keep long matches on hand so you won't burn your arm off when you have to reach in to find those inaccessible objects—LMI again explains why the manufacturers make them so inaccessible.)

A dentist, to take care of that excruciating toothache you or one of your youngsters are going to get one day.

Your child's school, and teacher.

The vet, if you have pets (a vomiting dog or a cat with convulsions is so distressing to children that if your pets get sick you will want to be able to have them attended to almost more promptly than you would a sick child).

An all-night drugstore.

The nearest hospital, in case you have to rush your child there after an accident someday; if you phone the emergency room ahead of time to tell them you're coming, you'll get faster service when you arrive, and they will also tell you what to do for the patient before you get there.

Several reliable baby-sitters.

Your nearest neighbors and best friends and closest relatives.

All of these numbers should be kept by the phone at all times, and many of them also in your purse for when you are away from home. There are times when help is urgently needed within a matter of minutes. Write the numbers down even if you have them memorized, because your children or a sitter may need them someday if something happens to you instead of to them.

This kind of advance preparation does not imply that you are brooding unduly about all the dreadful possibilities life may have in store for you. Once you have assembled such information, so that you know where you can obtain help the instant you require it if you ever do, you can safely and serenely forget about such dire possibilities.

To be even more thoroughly prepared to handle possible future emergencies—again, not because you are neurotically worried about them but to eliminate having to worry about them—it is a very good idea to take a Red Cross course in first aid. Then, if your child (or anyone else near you) is ever in a serious accident, you will know exactly what to do before the doctor gets there. Such knowledge doesn't merely save you anxiety; it might save a life. You should know how to handle a shock victim, how to apply traction, a tourniquet, a bandage, and a splint, and how to administer mouth-to-mouth resuscitation in cases of near drowning. Accidents do happen, at beaches and wherever there are active tree-climbing, racing, bicycling, ball-playing or fist-fighting youngsters around, as well as on highways.

There is another readily accessible source of help that should not be overlooked: books. Consider your local bookstore and/or public library as excellent sources of expert advice on a great many subjects—legal, financial, medical, psychological, etc.

There are so many books on child care that I cannot begin to recommend or even name them all, so I shall mention only a few of my own favorites. This doesn't mean I am giving the others negative endorsements. It doesn't imply that there are no other equally good books which, for various reasons, you might prefer. Browse through bookshelves freely and make your own selections. These are simply mine.

I mentioned Dr. Benjamin Spock in chapter 5. This may date me, but I consider his book *Baby and Child Care* just about as important to the mother of a very young child as diapers are. Its sales have fallen off in recent years (even so, more copies of it have been sold than of any other book except the Bible). After Dr. Spock's antiwar activities became well known, it seems that many parents feared that if they learned how to make formulas and take temperatures, how to recognize the differences between one type of rash and another, how to deal successfully with such things as temper tantrums, bed wetting, sibling rivalry, nightmares, learning and feeding problems from an ardent fighter for peace their children would grow up to be draft dodgers. I still consider this book the most practical, most sensible, most detailed, yet most concise, most readable, most complete of all the books on child care that I have seen. With my three children I read it about a dozen times per child, always discovering in it new things I needed to know. It gave me information and confidence, and I am very sorry for Dr. Spock's own mother because she had to raise a son without the help of his book. I don't think I could have.

Several other books published in recent years I have also found very helpful. Among the best, I think, are Dr. Haim Ginott's *Between Parent and Child* and *Between Parent and Teenager*. Dr. Ginott is sometimes a little too gimmicky, overglib and oversimplified in his suggestions about tactical formulas, but his basic points are vital. Wittily and clearly he explains why and how we should show respect to all children, even when they are being naughty and difficult, and how we can show disapproval of unpleasant behavior without criticizing and destroying the self-respect of the misbehaver. He explains the importance of empathizing lovingly with a child's feelings, even with destructive or angry or depressed or silly feelings, instead of attacking them head-on or trying to talk the child out of them; the latter approach, which is the one most parents use, reinforces the misbehavior instead of getting the child to change it (and I know his approach works because I have tried it and seen amazing before-and-after contrasts). Also he reminds us of how important it is to keep a sense of humor and perspective when confronted by the various types of exasperating behavior that are typical of different stages. Incidentally, all of his advice is as useful when applied to oneself or one's adult associates as it is when applied to one's youngsters.

Dr. Lee Salk's books *How to Raise a Human Being* and *What Every Child Would Like His Parents to Know* are also wonderfully wise. His understanding of the child's mind and emotional needs makes him an invaluable aide to any parent, single or otherwise, and to every child.

There are also extremely useful books on special subjects related to independent parenthood. These can be verbal first-aid kits, even lifesavers sometimes, when particular problems arise.

For example, there are good books on:

Legal problems that may come up re estates, lawsuits, custody, wills, etc.

Financial problems: investment advice, tips to keep taxes at a legal minimum, etc.

Sex education, designed for different ages and stages

The infant, the toddler, the middle years child, the adolescent

Special problems involved in raising boys, girls, twins, only children, or large families

The underachiever, or the child with a very high or very low IQ

What to do if a child has difficulties at school, either general learning problems or problems specifically related to reading or speech or behavior

Physically handicapped children: the deaf, blind, crippled

Emotionally disturbed children

Brain-damaged children (this frightening term mustn't put you off; it covers many more types of children than you

might expect, those who have speech or hearing or visual or behavior problems, those who are retarded, or hyperactive, or autistic, or epileptic, or cerebral palsied)
Physical education, health, and exercise
Child nutrition, and eating problems
And . . .

There are still a few people who sneer at the idea of "raising children by a book." But what makes them think that because parents consult a book they must do everything it suggests? If a book makes recommendations or stresses values you disagree with, you are obviously free to disregard it. But it doesn't hurt you or your children to acquaint yourself with the thinking of people who have studied problems which you and your children encounter—whereas it could hurt you and them not to. You can make up your own mind on a more intelligent basis after you have heard the arguments for or against a particular point of view. Even when you reject an idea, reading about it will make you clearer in both mind and conscience about doing what you yourself believe in doing than you could possibly be if you were not aware of other attitudes.

No author is the last word on any subject (not even me!) but in almost any book there will be some valuable nuggets of gold. Use a mental sifter to separate them from what you consider sand. You already believe in doing this, I guess, or you wouldn't have bothered to read this far in this book, so perhaps these comments are superfluous.

Some child-care books deal with special subjects that are of particular concern to single parents:

> How to guide children through the emotional trauma caused by divorce or death in a family (there are also books written *for,* rather than about, the children of divorced parents, full of reassuring common sense, some aimed at very young children, some for older children—ask a librarian for titles)

How to deal with a child's grief so that it will leave as few lasting emotional scars as possible

How to help a child accept changes relatively peacefully

Where to go for counselling in regard to emotional or financial or legal difficulties.

It is advisable for a single parent to read what different experts have to say on subjects like these, but I think it is equally important to read general advice applicable to *all* children. Even if married parents think they can raise children without consulting books (which I think is doing it the hard way, the hazardous trial-and-error way), no *single* parent should try, because there is no full-time partner to assist and advise and argue with you. You need to hear someone else's views to balance your own prejudices, both conscious and unconscious, and to supplement your own limitations.

In this sense a good child-care book is a good husband-or-wife substitute. A very incomplete one, no doubt, but a helpful one.

Pamphlets are another excellent source of needed information. If you are not a quick reader, or think you haven't enough time to read books on all these subjects, or if you tend to get confused when you read too much, or even if you simply would like to have everything on one subject presented concisely and separately, you might prefer short, pithy pamphlets which are pinpointed to particular problems, instead of full-length books.

If you write and ask for it, the Superintendent of Documents at the U.S. Government Printing Office (in Washington, D.C.) will send you a bibliography of many tremendously useful publications issued by the Government's Department of Health, Education and Welfare on subjects related to family life and child care.

There are also private sources of pamphlets on such subjects as the one-parent family, the mother who works outside the house, helping children understand death, divorce, and other family crises, adopted children, emotional problems, moral problems, financial problems—almost any subject you could think of that affects your family's life. The three top sources are The Child Study Association of America (9 East 89 Street, New York City), Public Affairs Pamphlets (381 Park Avenue South, New York City 10016) and Science Research Associates (259 East Erie Street, Chicago 60611).

The public health departments of some insurance companies (notably Equitable and Metropolitan Life) also publish pamphlets on some of these subjects as well as on first aid, children's contagious diseases, etc.

Write these organizations for their lists of titles. Some of the pamphlets are free, most of them cost a quarter, none cost more than a dollar, so they are outstanding investments.

And don't overlook magazines. They are a regular, continuing source of the most up-to-date information about subjects like health care, nutrition, and child development. Go to the periodical room of a public library and browse, and subscribe to one or two. *Parents Magazine* has been a reliable assistant to parents for several generations; it wins my own personal nomination for the most vital source of aid after Dr. Spock. Other useful specialized magazines are *Family Health* (for information about general health care) and *Prevention* (for detailed information about nutrition) and *Psychology Today.* Also, women's magazines frequently contain very helpful factual articles sprinkled among the fiction, gossip, and recipes.

Remember that the desire to achieve true independence does not require your being a "know-it-all." It requires you to take the trouble to equip yourself with useful information and skills so that you can take care of yourself and others. Supplement your limitations by turning gratefully to people who are ready, willing, and able to help you.

If you feel beholden to people who have helped you and are anxious to "pull your own weight," there is a wonderful way you can thank them and exercise independent initiative at the same time: *Pass it along!*

We can't always pay people back fully and directly for the help they have given us. They move away, or die, or we are out of touch with them, or there is simply nothing they need that we can give them. But we can still show, and act upon, our gratitude, by finding other people who could use some assistance. We can do something as comforting and helpful to someone else as the thing that was done for us. We can start a lovely chain reaction that will make our lives, and those of everyone who comes in contact with us, happier.

9

ASSERTING YOURSELF:
Learning to be decisive

Independence is not an end in itself. It is something to be used for something else. It is freedom to do things.

To do what? That's the question. You must decide how you want to use your new freedom. If you are inclined to be an eternal vacillator, once you are on your own you will never accomplish much. Now that you are your own boss you must learn to be a good one.

If and when you were married you probably shared in the process of decision making about all matters that affected important aspects of your family life. You probably sometimes resented having to give in to another viewpoint—and you probably sometimes liked doing so, because if a decision turned out to be wrong you could always blame it on your partner—unless: (a) you were a henpecking wife or a browbeating husband whose decisions were never questioned; (b) you always saw eye-to-eye with your spouse on every matter so that you never disagreed on a single decision (is there any couple in the world about whom that could truthfully be said?); or (c) you have an exceptionally sweet and generous nature—or no mind of your own—so you really enjoyed having someone else make all decisions for you.

The ability to submit unprotestingly to other people's decisions does not come easily to most of us. And these days obedience has a lower rating in the hierarchy of virtues than it used to have. Women's lib is a comparatively new social movement but even before it began sweeping across our planet a few years ago like a global forest fire there were little sparks of wifely rebellion flaring in the embers of nineteenth century feminism. All over the world women in our century have been omitting from their marriage vows, in increasing numbers, the traditional promise to obey, and even more women have been refusing, in practice, to obey. Children have become noticeably more rebellious too.

Most people today value intelligence and initiative more highly than obedience. We think the stress on submissiveness which used to be made by almost all moralists and legislators and educators and rulers was often destructive. It encouraged those in power (e.g. husbands, parents, teachers, army officers, politicians, religious superiors) to be tyrants, and others (e.g. wives and children, servants, and subordinates) to become slavish and unthinking. In the twentieth century our "ideal family" tries to distinguish between marital and martial virtues, preferring to operate as a democratic, cooperative team than to have a relationship in which a domineering male lords it over an acquiescent, spineless "little woman" and cowering, intimidated children.

Yet even in a democratic and harmonious marriage, where the decision-making process is shared, there are many times when each partner must bend his or her will, renouncing personal preferences in order to give into the other. Not only wives, but husbands too, must be accommodating if a marriage is to be peaceful and happy. Nice men as well as considerate women frequently agree to things to please their families when they would much rather do or have something else. Among the basic reasons why so many marriages are far from blissful and end in divorce is the fact that so many people fail to act this way, or do it but hate it, or do it but their spouses don't acknowledge or appreciate it.

Everyone has personal desires, interests, moods, and needs, which frequently conflict with someone else's desires, interests, moods, and needs, even when that someone else is a person one loves very much. When this happens, one either has to hold out for one's own viewpoint (which may precipitate a quarrel) or give in (which requires making a sacrifice, something we don't enjoy—if we enjoyed it, it wouldn't be a sacrifice).

Well, here's some good news! Being a single parent isn't all thorns; it has its rosy aspects. Now that you are the sole adult in your household, such restrictions, compromises, frustrations, and annoyances will be far less frequent. To a much greater extent than if you were married you can now—in fact, must now—make up your own mind and do what *you* want to do, when and how and where you want to do it.

From now on there will be a great many matters you will have to decide on your own. To a large extent your welfare and that of your children is going to depend on your ability to exercise sound judgment in making decisions.

What if you are, by nature or habit, timid and indecisive? Perhaps you are a Casper Milquetoast or a fluttery, helpless "little thing" who has always, until now, been looked after by a Big Strong Masterful Man, and you therefore feel the need for constant protection and guidance.

Well, we've been speaking of changes that your new circumstances have brought into your life, including the need to learn to become self-reliant, and here is another change that must be made. A mother on her own will have to alter her concept of herself if she has always considered decisiveness and assertiveness "masculine" traits and thought it was much more "feminine" to be passive, receptive, and docile. She will have to get hold of some of that "women's intuition" which male chauvinists think resides inside her "pretty little head" in the place where brains are in a man's head.

Often, let's admit, we females have a strong vested interest in cultivating weak "feminine" traits instead of striving to be strong, because this frees us from the danger of making mistakes due to incorrect decisions. Being responsible for decisions involves having to stick your neck out, to commit yourself, to take risks, and to accept the consequences of those risks. Some of our passive "adaptability" and "sweetness" has not really been due to our being feminine and/or considerate but simply because we have been lazy and/or cowardly and men have been kind enough to let us get away with it.

So a woman who has hitherto been proud of her humilty and her adaptability will now have to exercise that ancient "women's prerogative" of changing her mind. She will have to become adaptable in a new way: adapting to the need to acquire more firmness and a greater sense of responsibility. Any woman who operates as a single parent must become a lot more aggressive than a wife can be, and more decisive, energetic, and assertive than she may feel inside.

Perhaps she is energetic, brave, and bright yet even so is unprepared to take over the role as undisputed Head of the Family. She has never been trained to be a boss. The first time she has to make a really important decision without a partner's advice she may go into a tailspin. And the first (or the nine hundredth) time she makes a firm decision that affects her children and they defy it, she may not have the slightest idea of how to enforce it, now that she can't rely on the old threat to "tell Daddy when he comes home." The tiniest decision may throw her into a tizzy at first. She may say, "I can't decide this all by myself!" But she can't say can't. That is one decision she must not make. *An unmarried parent has no one to pass the buck to.*

Most men who are single parents have had prior training in making decisions, so their adjustment to this particular facet of partnerless parenthood may be comparatively easy—yet they too will probably have problems with it at first. They will now have to start making decisions about so many trivial yet inescapable matters that most husbands blithely ignore. A husband can rely on his live-in cleaning woman, cook, waitress, laundress, seamstress, messenger, chauffeur, personal shopping service, interior decorator, traffic cop, PTA-meeting-attender, nose-wiper, diaper-changer, quarrel-settler, tantrum-ender—in short, his wife—who attends to all minor but endless daily decisions for him. An ex-husband may feel somewhat demeaned at having to bother his head over such pesky and petty decisions as what to order for dinner tonight and what socks the children should wear today. He may consider this sort of thing "women's work" far beneath his dignity. But he too will have to stop passing the buck. And he too will eventually live through this transformation—and discover, with relief, that his "masculinity" hasn't been destroyed by this new, broadened role.

In short, whether you are a male or a female, as long as you are a functioning single parent you have to undertake all the tasks involved, playing both the "male" and "female" roles in your family, taking responsibility for all decisions both major and minor. You have no choice in the matter. You can't get out of making decisions because even postponing or refusing to make a decision is—de facto—a type of decision.

Even if you are an extremely permissive parent who believes in leaving a large number of decisions up to your children, you cannot escape from your role as final authority—because it is you who have made the decision to be permissive, whether or not your children would actually prefer to be given more detailed and firmer guidance (like the child in the old New Yorker cartoon who asked his kindergarten teacher plaintively, "Do I *have* to do whatever I want to again today?")

Fortunately, once we get used to it, most of us thoroughly enjoy being our own bosses. You'll probably feel very scared the first time you have to make a truly independent decision affecting your family's welfare, but afterwards you may feel startlingly exhilarated. The second such decision will come more easily. And eventually decision making will be positively delightful. Even too delightful. Then you may have to watch out for a new and opposite problem: *you'll have to cultivate flexibility along with firmness.*

It is so easy for single people to become ornery and willful, insisting on having their own way all the time even in very trivial matters, to the point of eccentricity. This is an unattractive trait of many people who live entirely alone and is the source of the cranky "old maid" image (and men can be cranky old maids too). Don't go this far.

Actually, you probably won't be able to, quite, because our children protect us to some extent from our all-too-human desire to be selfish. After all, they too have needs, moods, and desires of their own, and if we are fond of our children or simply normally conscientious we accommodate ourselves frequently to these, doing many things that don't thrill us, just to please or help our youngsters. In our decision making, even though we may be top boss, our children's needs must always be taken into account along with our own desires; so in this respect single parenthood isn't totally different from marriage, and it is psychologically and morally a safer state of life than living all alone is. We are still part of an intimate community and still required to be social and sociable, considerate and patient, accepting certain limitations on our personal freedom for the sake of other people. There is one less person we must try to please than if we were married, so we have a bit more scope than a wife or husband has, but our freedom is not unlimited. (No one's ever is, totally, since we all live in a world that has other people in it besides us.)

But that's all right too. Selfishness is not admired as a moral quality any more than obedience is, even in this modern era of rampant individualism. And fortunately most of us aren't even tempted to be *totally* selfish, so that's no problem. We just like to be a bit self-indulgent now and then—and that's fine. That's healthy. Things we decide to do for ourselves that please and satisfy us improve our dispositions and this results in our making other people around us happy too. When we are nice to ourselves this makes us feel like being nice to our children too, so everyone benefits—assuming that the niceness we show ourselves is genuinely nice, not the kind or degree of self-pampering that causes us to neglect the rights and needs of others.

Decision making can be hard when you are a single parent with no other adult nearby to advise you or back you up—but *decision-sticking-to can be even harder than decision making.*

Too many parents (and not only single ones) are guilty of wishy-washy wavering, scolding their children one day for behavior they permitted the day before and vice versa, so that their poor children can't tell what kind of behavior is "right" and what kind is "wrong." Also many parents lack the courage of their convictions, so that—for instance—instead of saying, "Come and help me with the dishes" in a tone of voice that makes it perfectly clear that this is a normal and legitimate request and that the child is expected to obey it without any fuss, they put the request in the form of a question ("Won't you please come and help me?" or, even more foolish, "Wouldn't you like to stop what you're doing and help me?"), which makes the child feel he has the right to refuse. When you make an order apologetically or indecisively it is harder for a child to obey it. And then, almost before you know it, a heated argument may arise. You'll feel you have rude and ungrateful and uncooperative children and your children will feel that you are being "mean" and unreasonable, goofing off on your parental responsibilities and making them carry the ball.

By and large, children act as we expect them to act. If we take it for granted that they will accept our authority, they too will usually take it for granted. But the more worried or timid about it we are, the more they will sense our uncertainty and maliciously (or opportunistically, anyway) take advantage of our hesitation, or else become genuinely confused about how to act.

How do you enforce a disputed decision?

"To spank or not to spank" is a question that parents have been debating ever since Plutarch eloquently condemned spanking as an inhumane method of discipline. Most parents do spank upon occasion (even if they don't really believe in it; simply because something their child does makes them so mad that they can't think of any other way to react), but many don't. For example, American Indians, despite the reputation of some tribes for fierceness and physical cruelty, never did; there is an Indian saying that "if you beat a child you beat stubbornness into him."

If you do spank, be careful. Especially when you are very angry you may not know your own strength. Never slap a child's face (you could hurt his eyes or knock out his teeth). Thomas Edison got his ears boxed once in his childhood and was deaf for the rest of his life as a result. A tap on the rear is the safest form of spanking.

Spanking has only one advantage over other methods of discipline. It is quick and direct and provides an outlet for parental anger so that as soon as it is over the parent doesn't feel impelled to go on and on forever about the now-punished offense, and the child feels he has expiated his crime and therefore doesn't go on and on forever feeling burdened by guilt. It is more effective and less deadly than a punishment which is delayed or prolonged so that the child forgets why he is being punished, and it is less destructive to family harmony than continual nagging is. It is also certainly preferable to fear-inducing punishments like shutting a child up in a closet or dark room, which should never be done. But its promptness and brevity are about all one can say on its behalf.

If you had never been spanked yourself and therefore assumed that it was a normal thing, it would seem a barbarous and repulsive notion that people intentionally inflict physical pain on children they love. Even if you are not a pacifist, one of the basic ethical principles of fair fighting is to "pick on someone your own size." A parent who spanks is purely and simply taking advantage of size and strength: "I'm bigger than you are so what I say goes." He is applying physical force to try to solve a nonphysical problem and the main thing this teaches is the pernicious doctrine that "might makes right."

A rational punishment more specifically adapted to fit the crime is more educational. For example:

"If you waste your allowance money on foolishness and

therefore have nothing left later in the week for something you really want, I will not bail you out." Or, "If you dawdle too long I won't take you to the park, party, movies, etc." (You have to harden your heart temporarily to stick to decisions like these but you are being kind in the long run because children will learn a lot faster if you do this than if you are always rescuing them from the consequences of their own decisions.)

"If you use those words, or speak to me in that rude voice, I simply will not answer you. When you decide to be nice again I will." (To help yourself stick to this decision turn on a radio or open a book and try not to hear your child's efforts to goad you into showing him you didn't mean it.)

"If you refuse to share your toys with your friends I will not let you have a guest come here tomorrow," or "I won't let you go to Billy's house tomorrow." (One offense deserves only one punishment; don't extend this type of deprivation so long that you delay your child's learning what you want him to learn.)

"If you carelessly break something I won't replace it." (Be sure you distinguish between deliberate destructiveness and accidents. Don't punish the latter; on the contrary, show sympathy.)

"If you hit each other (or shout like that) you'll have to play separately." (Don't get trapped into endless wrangling over who started what. In a war, aggressors feel just as self-righteous as defenders do. There is always a cause that caused the cause of the cause and arguing about it forever just keeps the battle going forever. The only way to stop a fight or a war is to stop it.)

My examples all involve small children, which is cheating a bit because it is obviously easier to stay in control over the behavior of small children than of someone who is bigger than you are. You cannot pick up rude and resisting teen-agers to remove them bodily from your room if you have said "Leave the room until you feel like being pleasant" and they have bluntly refused to go. Your job is enormously harder if you haven't succeeded in inculcating habits of obedience, courtesy, consideration, cooperativeness, etc., in the early years. The older children get, the more verbal they become, the more sophisticated and stubborn in argumentation and the more keenly aware of your soft spots so that they know just where to puncture your armor. The only tactics you can apply to teen-agers (at least as far as I know) are patience, consistency, rationality, clearness in expressing your wishes and convictions, and appeals to the goodwill that is in everybody if you can only reach it.

There are several things a parent must try not to do:

1. Don't express anger that isn't relevant to solving the problem at hand. So often, when our children defy us, we suddenly remember every other thing they have ever done that also annoyed us and we bring them all up, thus almost ignoring the one thing we are at present trying to correct.

2. Don't displace anger, venting it on the wrong person. If one of your children is being so difficult that you can't stand it, you may snap at another child who is an innocent bystander. It's very unfair to take your frustration out on someone just because you can get away with it. And it doesn't teach either the guilty or the innocent child anything except cynicism.

3. Don't show elephant-sized anger at a mosquito-sized offense. Some parents turn into raging lunatics at tiny provocations—which may seem enormous to them at the moment because their anger has been building up over a lot of other small problems which they haven't tackled promptly and directly. Disproportionate anger makes the people you are angry at think *you* are wrong, not them.

4. Don't attack childish behavior with an equally childish burst of temper or crying jag. You want your children to respect you and pay attention to what you say, but how can they if you lose all dignity and go berserk?

You have to learn to control yourself if you expect to be able to control your children. This doesn't mean never feeling anger or never letting them see it. You *should* let them know when they have made you angry, so they will learn what type of behavior people will put up with and what type they dislike. But express your anger in a civilized and appropriate way.

Tiny children need to have you react immediately when they do something wrong, because they have such quick "forgetteries," but with older children it often helps to wait a while before discussing what they have done that has upset or infuriated you. If you feel so heated that it is hard to make yourself calm down and postpone discussion, get a sitter to come to your rescue and go out for a long, vigorous walk or to a movie (maybe a violent horror film would suit your mood) or take out your feelings in a bowling alley or in vigorous housework. Physical activity or a change of scene can help to relieve psychological tensions.

After you have given yourself a chance to calm down and think things over, then discuss the problem. Don't decide that now that things are serene again you won't bring the subject up anymore because that will cause a new fight. The time to solve the things that cause fights is when you are *not* in a fighting mood. You may find that the offense which so upset you doesn't seem as serious as you thought it was in the heat of the moment; if so, fine—say so, and apologize for your previous lack of understanding.

People in authority are often afraid to admit they have been wrong for fear they will lose prestige. But they gain credibility, gratitude, and admiration when they are truthful and humble and realistic enough to admit their own faults instead of always chastising others. And people are more willing to cooperate with someone they believe and admire and are grateful to than with someone who rules only because he is in a position of power. (I wish politicians and prelates would realize this, as well as parents.)

When you are able to discuss a subject calmly and rationally you may find it amazingly easy to get your children to see your point of view. ("Oh, Mother, if only you hadn't said what you said in that nasty tone of voice I might have listened to what you were saying!")

No method of punishment is ideal. Punishment itself is not an ideal. The ideal, where discipline is concerned, is to guide your children in such a way that punishment is never or very rarely necessary. Too many people think of discipline as something you apply *after* an offense. But good discipline is an atmosphere which a skillful parent creates which *prevents* offenses that would need to be punished.

Parents must have the courage and intelligence to hold to their opinions and decisions (unless the reason they were made has ceased to exist)—not arbitrarily, stubbornly, or dogmatically, but nonetheless firmly—when they have really thought them through and are convinced they are right. It is very destructive, both for a child and for an entire family's peace, when parents let a child talk them out of what the parents consider important and reasonable, or when the child is allowed to ignore parental opinions and rules. This is true whether a regulation was made for your own needs or for the child's. You must have the guts to stick to a viewpoint you really believe in—even when it makes your child mad at you and even when he thinks you are being unfair.

It is a Fact of Life that at times our children will be mad at us. If you don't particularly esteem yourself (and, as I've said before, this is a problem that plagues many unmarried people), you may be terribly anxious to have your children love you and feel that you can't stand having them mad at you, even briefly. Giving in to this feeling can be fatal. If you change your views out of fear of your child's anger you will be giving in to emotional blackmail, which will get more and more expensive as times goes by (and it's not good to teach your child to be a blackmailer, any more than it's good to let yourself be someone who is blackmailable). No one can go through life never disagreeing with another person. You are an adult and you do know more than your children do about certain things, so you can't expect them always to understand or agree with your decisions. However, if you are reasonable and act confident, your children will be able to accept your decisions even when they don't understand or like them. And if you don't make a big production of it, they won't be apt to either.

The desire to bribe our children into loving us every single minute, by giving in to them on all occasions, is as futile as the desire to buy anyone's love. Love isn't for sale. Cravenness earns scorn, not love. Affection, friendship, and respect may come to us as pleasant by-products if we genuinely deserve them but it is not only unnecessary to sue for them, it won't work. A child whose parents are strict but consistent and loving is much more apt to respect them than one who knows his parents can be twisted around his little finger. So if you want to win your children's real respect, don't be afraid to act like a parent.

There is a lot of talk these days about the need children have for parents who are pals. This is very true, within limits. It is great fun to do entertaining things with your children, fun to have them enjoy your company and for them to know that you enjoy theirs. It's fun to live in an affectionate atmosphere. But these things cannot be achieved by abdicating from the parental role.

Does all this talk of firmness—which some might translate as "bossiness"—mean that you shouldn't be a companion and playmate to your children, one of their very favorite people? Of course not! It makes it all the more necessary for you to make sure you have fun with them and do things together, to make sure that you appreciate your children's charms and talents (and let them know it), and to show them your affection in ways they can really feel. Remember that awful era when mothers thought it was wrong to compliment a child because if you did the child would become conceited, so they were lavish with scoldings but miserly with praise? When admiring a child they would say to another adult, "Isn't she p-r-e-t-t-y?" or "What a s-m-a-r-t child!" Fortunately we have learned something since those days; we know that praise encourages children to be good more than scolding does and that self-confidence is a better foundation for virtue than fear is. When your children enjoy being with you and know that you both love and like them, they will accept more readily the rules you lay down, your boundary lines, and then, within those boundaries, you can encourage complete liberty.

Spirited children of course sometimes resent having to give in to a parent, but they can also resent *not* having to give in. They may think a parent is incompetent or uninterested in them if the parent always lets them have their own way. I remember one time when my small son looked at me in disgust after he had been very rude to me, and instead of punishing him, I let it go. He said, "You're my mother, for pete's sake! You shouldn't let me do that. You should *make* me be considerate of you! Don't you have any self-respect?" Out of the mouths of babes . . .

If you have been a fairly decisive person all your life and are used to running a well-organized and unhectic home, your children have probably already learned, or soon will learn, to abide by your rules, considering most of them by-and-large fair, or at least normal and thus bearable. On the whole they will feel peaceful, knowing there's nothing they can do about it because that's just how things are—in the same way that we don't object to laws of nature which may cause us inconvenience at times because we know they can't be changed. Your certainty gives them a degree of emotional security and stability which makes them feel good underneath their occasional grumblings.

Quite the opposite happens when we are unsure of ourselves —like when a parent asks wistfully, pleadingly, "Wouldn't you like to go to bed now, dear?" instead of establishing a bedtime. What healthy, self-respecting child in the history of the world ever wanted to go to bed as long as there was anything else to do? Such a parent may think he is being kind, by giving his child a choice, but it is actually a lot less kind to allow your child to stay up to the point of exhaustion and irritability than to decide what bedtime should be, on the basis of your knowledge of his health and age and need for regular rest.

Learning to be able to endure a few frustrations patiently is an important part of growing up. You have had to learn this, and how hard or easy it has been for you has depended to a great degree on how successfully you learned it when you were very young. So, in child-size portions, your children too must learn to face and tolerate occasional disappointments. If not, they will never mature emotionally and will have difficulties at school and, later, at jobs and in personal relationships. So don't feel guilty when you have to deprive them of something they want, if you know that you have a valid reason.

Inconsistency and indecisiveness are actually more unjust and upsetting than most individual rules that a child might consider unjust. So be very careful about making exceptions, once you have made a decision, and never back down under threat of a tantrum. Be flexible when you think you should be, but not when your child is trying to force you to be: that isn't flexibility, it's weakness.

Having to accept rules made by a loving but firm parent is not nearly as upsetting to children as having to live in constant uncertainty about when they have to take an instruction seriously and when they can ignore it. In the latter case children feel bewildered and also honor-bound to challenge the parent's will frequently. They can soon become alarmingly adept at indulging in longer and longer and louder and louder battles, ruder and ruder insults, more and more frightening displays of temper, trying to get their way, testing the limits of their parent's endurance. If they find that you weaken and give in to their demands after five minutes of screaming on their part then, the next time, when you intend to put your foot down and not give in, they will manage to keep up the screaming for six minutes, and if that doesn't work, for seven. They have very strong young lungs and vocal cords and the chances are that these can outlast your older, tireder ears. The only means of avoiding this mutually harrowing escalating contest of wills is to make sure your children realize very early in life that when you say something you really do mean it—unlike the parent who keeps saying, "I've told you for the last time for the last time!"

So make sure you always say what you mean and mean what you say—even if this means you must sometimes be "mean." It may seem theoretically mean, for instance, not to treat all children exactly alike, because if you don't you are "playing favorites." Again using the example of bedtime, a child who isn't allowed to stay up as late as another one may resent it and scream, "You're not being fair!" But children differ, and so do their needs. Some children are healthier, stronger, more self-reliant, less timid, less absent minded, more mature than others, and therefore something which would be safe for one child to do might be unsafe for another. "Why did you let him cross the street by himself when he was only three but you won't let me?" a child may ask. You may not be able to make him understand why. If *you* know you're not being unfair, that will have to satisfy you.

What *is* unfair is avoiding your parental responsibilities. I realized this one time when I said, as I then frequently did, "What would you like for supper tonight?" to my little girl, and she started to cry. I suddenly realized that I was turning over the burden of decision making about menu planning, part of my job, to an immature, inexperienced little person who knew far less than I do about nutrition and cooking. I thought I was being considerate but I was really being lazy.

The role of guide and decision-maker is yours, not your child's. Chickens don't teach hens. Baby birds don't teach their parents how to fly. Baby seals don't teach their mothers how to swim. Of course you shouldn't be a dictator. Of course you should listen to your children's requests and protests with patience and understanding and respect. And when they make valid points, of course you should consider altering particular rules and making appropriate modifications and variations. Bedtime obviously gets gradually extended as children get older. Allowance money increases in view of increased legitimate expenses and as children demonstrate that they can handle money sensibly. Privileges of many other kinds increase too. To take children's wishes and changing needs into consideration when making decisions is only common sense and justice. But don't change rules in such a way that your children feel you have lost control. No matter how much they may protest, children feel safer and therefore happier when they can count on the fact that their parent is in control.

Every child needs parental authority for many, many reasons —some of which he fully realizes, some of which he only vaguely senses, some of which he doesn't comprehend at all. It is unreasonable to expect your children always to think you are being reasonable, but it is up to you, as their parent, to have enough courage, intelligence, foresight, and perspective to be the kind of parent you believe in being, whether your children agree with all of your decisions or not.

You have the right and also the duty to set certain standards of behavior and taste in your own home and to see that your children live by them. When they grow up, if they don't share your values and preferences, they can live by their own rules (and they will, you can be sure) but while they are immature and inexperienced and living with you, you are the person who is meant to be in charge. So be sure you *are* in charge.

There is one sensible precaution to take, however, when disputes arise. Because you have no full-time colleague to consult, you are deprived of the normal system of checks-and-balances which is a protection against the abuse of authority. You may not realize sometimes when you are being unfair, so you should take extra precautions not to be. It may be, at times, a good idea to check your opinions with those of another adult who knows your child—a teacher, pediatrician, or friend—or of the parents of a child you like, whom you think is being brought up in a way you approve of, whose behavior you consider attractive.

It is probably unfair, for instance, to insist on a bedtime that is hours earlier than that of every other child in your child's class, unless your child's health is frail. Or to forbid TV programs that every other child is allowed to watch, so that your child is embarrassed at never being able to join in classmates' conversations about them. Or to forbid lipstick on the grounds that it is too grown-up, if practically every other girl your daughter's age has already started wearing it. You want to raise normal children, not conspicuous freaks who feel "out of it" all the time. So if you find yourself locked in perpetual conflict over certain issues, do some discreet inquiring and consulting.

Children will often moan, "But everybody else's parents let them do that!" Find out, when they say this to you, if it is true or if they are trying to con you. If it is true, you still have the right to hold out for a minority viewpoint if you think the issue is important ("I don't care if every other mother on earth allows her daughter to stay out with a boy until three in the morning on a school night—*this* mother won't!") but on matters where safety or good taste or morals are not seriously involved, a bit of flexibility is preferable to old-fashioned, stubborn rigidity.

You should allow children some leeway in making some of their own decisions wherever safety is not involved and an action is not seriously inconvenient or harmful. It would be tyrannical and the opposite of educational if you tried to decide everything for them. Allow them as much freedom as you think they can handle wisely. But when you think a line should be drawn, draw it—clearly, fearlessly, unapologetically, calmly.

Set reasonable limits on your children's behavior as far as schedules are concerned and regarding eating habits, the amount of permitted noise, good manners, bedtime, the extent to which you expect help around the house, the amount of time you like them to stay outdoors, or indoors, and so forth. All of these are small but important personal decisions which a parent has a right to make. And if you make such decisions in accordance with your own standards and temperament and stick to them consistently, you will have a far more peaceful household and more contented children than if you try to be so "understanding" that you permit more noise than you can bear, later hours than you think are right, etc.

When you try to put up with more than you can bear, you get more and more irritated until suddenly you explode, blowing up over something your children do that is not really wrong simply because your supply of patience has run out. We all seem to have a certain endurance quotient and boiling point and, if we don't set a few definite rules that take this into account, suppressed annoyance snaps out of us at times when it is inappropriate, to the bewilderment and distress of our poor families and even of ourselves. Our delayed reaction may be so fierce that it is worse than the behavior we have been trying to put up with. So establish guidelines that you can live with and save your anger for serious misbehavior.

Don't decide to be a martyr. Just decide to be YOU. Not a doormat, not a dishrag, not a patsy, not a whipping post, not an angel, not a saint. Nor a bully, Hitler, martinet, or devil, either. Just yourself. A loving and understanding, but sensible and decisive, you.

10

ENJOYING YOURSELF:
Eliminating loneliness

Although the adjective *merry* frequently precedes the noun *widow* and *gay* precedes *divorcee* in songs and stories, in real life *lonely* would often be the more appropriate adjective for both nouns.

Even in a bad marriage, wives and husbands take for granted and depend on (often more than they realize) a certain amount of comfortably reliable day-in, day-out companionship. A spouse may be grumpy, overdemanding, dull, neglectful of your wishes, but at least he or she is *there* a lot of the time. However, when you are spouseless there are, inevitably, gaping voids in your schedule when you are all by yourself. At times it's hard to decide which is more upsetting: the hectic, incessant, ear-splitting, headache-inducing *noise* young children make all day long, when you can't get away from them for even a minute because there is nobody there but you to look after them, or the equally inescapable, oppressive, relentless roar of *silence* you hear after you've kissed them good-night, tucked them in bed and then find yourself uninterruptedly and totally alone.

Nothing to do.

Nobody to do it with.

You may feel isolated, purposeless, pointless. In short, miserable. And to add to your misery, you feel guilty about feeling miserable, because you tell yourself that if you were more popular your friends would be beating down your door every night and if you were more loving your darling children would be enough to keep you happy. You must be a monster to be so dissatisfied, an ingrate, a born complainer. So, once again, you succumb to the depressing thought that you are not only wretched but deserve to be.

And this mood may afflict you from time to time not only in the first few months when you are adjusting to the state of single parenthood, but for years; in fact, it can get progressively more frequent and more intense, if you don't take definite steps to prevent and cure it.

The trouble is that no matter how lovable your children are or how devoted to them you are, they are *not* enough. You are a whole person, not merely a parent. You're an adult, not a child. So children cannot fill your entire life or answer all of your emotional and intellectual and social needs. Through their dependence on you they make many demands which keep you from feeling useless and which fill much (but not all) of your time, and through their companionship and affection they reduce your loneliness, but they cannot eliminate it entirely—nor should they be expected to. They can even, innocently and paradoxically, add to it, because when they do something cute there is no one there to chuckle over it with you and when they do something that fills you with parental pride there is no one else around to share in equal measure your delight.

How can you protect yourself from this occupational hazard of single parenthood? You can do two things. First, take sensible steps to see to it that you aren't alone on more evenings than you want to be. Second, build up your intellectual resources and physical energy so that you can fill those evenings when you have to be alone with such interesting things that you actually relish having time by yourself. I'll discuss the first remedy first, and the next one in the next chapter.

You don't have as many free hours as many other people do, if

ENJOYING YOURSELF | 171

you are a hard-working single parent (and that is a redundancy if there ever was one), but during the free time you do have, *you may find yourself rattling around in a social vacuum.* You may not get asked to dinner parties by conventional hostesses who prefer to invite matched pairs rather than "extras." You may not be invited out as often as you used to be by singles either, because those who have children are frequently too busy or too tired and those who don't have children are bored by your conversational preoccupation with such subjects as teething and bed wetting and your baby's weight and how cute your children are or how hard it is to get them to eat their vegetables or how mean your child's schoolteacher is and how hard it is to find a pediatrician who will make house calls. Even if you are invited somewhere, often you can't get there because you can't find (or afford) a baby-sitter. As for meeting new people and finding good dates, the playground and the supermarket are not exactly equivalent to a swinging singles' resort as a happy hunting ground.

So an evening (or several) or a week (or several) may occur in which loneliness sweeps over you as bitingly as a chill north wind and as excruciatingly as a heart attack (it *is* a heart attack, of sorts, as a matter of fact). You feel a persistent, aching yearning, which seems unassuageable, for companionship and love that isn't there, for someone . . . anyone . . . something . . . anything that could fill with comforting warmth the icy hollow inside your soul—and the empty space inside your arms. (And if you think that description is melodramatic, it just means you've never been truly lonely—so be very, very, very grateful to God!)

It may require every bit of whatever psychological and physical stamina you possess to fill up both the internal and external vacuums with things which will make them less empty and less large. You may feel you would be glad to be married to the world's biggest pill or dreariest bore, just to have someone there to look at and to talk to.

Of course, if you think seriously about that for a minute you will realize it isn't true and that if you were married to a pill or a bore you would be every bit as miserable as you are now, if not more so. But it's part of the grass-is-always-greener-on-the other-side-of-the-fence delusion to feel, right now, as if you are more unhappy than you could ever be in any other circumstances. (One possible cure for this mood is to think back to the time in your life when you were the most miserable and compare it with the present moment; you will probably be glad to be in your current situation rather than back there.)

This is a dangerous, as well as uncomfortable, mood to get into. It's the kind of mood that makes some people commit foolish, even fatal, indiscretions. Your children still need you, even if you're wretched because nobody else does, so don't go out and pick up a stranger at a bar (and thereby perhaps get robbed or raped). Don't get roaring drunk (and thereby get disgraced or at least deeply embarrassed and hung-over). Don't take too many sleeping pills or jump out a window (and thereby get dead).

You must not let yourself give in to the violent emotions that a time like this can nudge you toward despair and tempt you to lose all common sense. But you feel as if you must do something, anything, to fill the time until this mood leaves you. Sure. Do something. But do something safe.

One thing you can do is to take the social initiative. If you would really like to have a more active social life but invitations are slow in coming and/or you can't leave the house, don't sit there moping. Ask people over to *your* house. Become a host or hostess instead of wishing you were a guest.

But what if you don't have enough money to be able to entertain lavishly? Well, there are ingenious and delightful ways to entertain without spending much money if you can rid yourself of phony pride and cultivate some imagination.

You can give a big jolly spaghetti or pizza or fondue party, or a tea party or coffee klatch, or an old-fashioned taffy-pull or marshmallow roast, for very little money. You can invite people over for dessert and coffee, or simply to spend an evening, instead of thinking you must serve them a full multi-course banquet. You can serve punch or beer instead of expensive Scotch. You can even frankly ask people to bring their own booze and they won't mind if you give them a particularly festive excuse, providing the locale for a happy Special Occasion. Almost anything can be a Special Occasion. You can throw birthday parties for your children, for friends, for dogs, cats, celebrities, for George Washington and Abraham Lincoln and Martin Luther King, even for Thomas Jefferson or Alexander Graham Bell if you feel like it. Look in an encyclopedia or *Who's Who* and pick a favorite hero or heroine to honor, with decor and food and phonograph records to fit the occasion—French pastry if it's Maurice Chevalier, pretzels and beer if it's Beethoven, caviar and vodka if it's Tchaikovsky, prochuto and red wine if it's the Pope (or Sophia Loren), smorgasbord if it's Garbo, curried rice and tea if it's Gandhi, fish and chips if it's Noel Coward or Queen Elizabeth, hot dogs if it's Eleanor Roosevelt . . .

Or celebrate a holiday: Christmas, Easter, the Fourth of July, St. Valentine's Day, Halloween, or the national holiday of some interesting country your children are studying in school. Invite their classmates, along with the classmates' parents—and feature unusual recipes and appropriate games and decorations.

Or celebrate some more personal occasion: a bon voyage or welcome home, a housewarming, a friend's good fortune (engagement, anniversary, promotion, recovery from illness, etc.) or a child's graduation—and you needn't wait until a child graduates from high school or college; the graduate of first or second grade will be just as, or even more, thrilled to be honored. Or throw a party to celebrate the loss of a tooth or the end of wearing braces or the end of exam week. Or throw a seasonal party —to celebrate the first day of spring, summer, winter, or fall. You can celebrate anything!

Good conversation, games if you're the game-playing type, music if you have a phonograph or guitar or piano, a TV special that you know would be enjoyed by a group of your friends, a relaxed gathering of convivial people with shared interests—these are what make an evening fun, far more than the expensive and fancy food and elaborate frills, elegant silverware and crystal, special flower arrangements, etc., that some hostesses think are obligatory. Many magazine articles on how to be a successful hostess terrorize readers into feeling they wouldn't dare entertain unless they hired musicians or decorated their home suitably for a White House state dinner. This is nonsense.

Some of the best parties I have ever been to were in homes that had no special visual adornments. You don't have to go out and rent extra chairs from a local funeral parlor or political club (although, by the way, it is good to know that if you don't have enough chairs and/or glasses and/or dishes, there are nowadays in most cities places where you can rent these—look in the Yellow Pages). I vividly remember one wonderful party given by a friend who had just moved into a new apartment. She gave it before she had bought any furniture and we all wandered around freely or sat on the floor. The informality and novelty put us in a marvelous mood. We had a picnic on the floor and felt like happy kids.

If you feel that special decorations provide a gala atmosphere which helps put people in a happy mood, your children can come in very handy. Most children are born artists and enjoy nothing more than helping to decorate a room for a special occasion. They can make funny and original invitations, they can design pretty or cute table decorations and place cards, they can deck the walls with topical posters: "portraits" of the guests, appropriate symbolic designs, or large and colorful abstract paintings or collages. If you can't afford to buy expensive flower arrangements or just don't feel like it, your children might be able to make big artificial flowers out of crepe paper (or leftover gift wrap), ribbons, and wire.

Giving a large cocktail party can be extremely expensive—and tiring. Not only is it expensive because of the high cost of large quantities of alcohol (and it is amazing how much even your most abstemious friends can stash away at a cocktail party —you must be sure to have on hand at least twice as much alcohol as your most generous estimate of what you think you will need), but there is also the high risk of drinks spilled on upholstery, food ground into the rug, and cigarette burns on tables. This really isn't such a wise thing to try to swing, unless money is no object.

Besides, at this type of party the host or hostess doesn't really have much chance to have fun. They're too busy rushing around introducing people and making sure that everyone has enough drinks, and providing first aid for those who have had too many, and then when the afternoon is over they're left all alone with a great big Anticlimax, a living room full of stale smoke, cigarette butts and ashes, spills to wipe up and mountains of glasses to wash. It is far more sensible, I think, especially when you have no one else around the house to help you mix drinks, to give smaller parties more frequently, rather than an occasional big bash. You have more chance to talk with and enjoy people when they come in smaller batches, and it doesn't require nearly as much money or energy.

My idea of a successful party is usually not more than six or eight people (unless someone else is giving it), because once you go over that number the people tend to divide up into little groups and you often find yourself stuck off in one corner, unable to hear what the other groups are laughing at so happily. This is frustrating and a waste of good guests.

It's fun to mix friends, sometimes, in unusual combinations, instead of always trying to bring together like with like— though obviously you risk trouble if you invite an Arab and a Jew or a fervent rightist and a militant left-winger to the same gathering. You must use your head as well as imagination and not try to combine people whose basic interests, convictions, or personalities are sure to clash. But you probably know some people who don't know each other and who, at least for an evening or two, would find each other interesting or amusing. If you select your guests well, that in itself will guarantee a pleasant evening for both your friends and yourself, without your having to go to any extraordinary expense or fuss.

One thing which single parents must learn to do is to plan social activities ahead of time. These will not always happen spontaneously (which doesn't mean you shouldn't be flexible enough to take advantage of it when spur-of-the-moment opportunities do occur), or at least you cannot count on them often enough to keep you unfailingly happy and busy. If you don't plan ahead you are sure to find yourself, now and then, for a number of weekends in a row, with no companionship other than juvenile.

It is also wise to foresee when special attacks of extra lonesomeness are apt to arrive and to arrange specific things to do at such times. Former wedding anniversaries, holidays, and birthdays can be bad scenes if you are all alone and feeling neglected.

Sometimes what holds people back from socializing when they would like to is not lack of opportunity or money as much as excessive shyness. Many single mothers, having no man around to act as host at home or as escort outside, feel they haven't enough to offer people all on their own so that people would really enjoy seeing them for a whole evening. And many men who have always relied on women (mothers, sisters, wives) to see to all the details of hostessing feel utterly incapable of entertaining without such help. This is a sad commentary on how they feel about themseles, but it's a common problem.

The very times when we most yearn for companionship may be the times when we feel least capable of obtaining or enjoying it. This is why we must *force* ourselves to socialize, in order to become more capable. What you never do, you will never learn to do.

When we feel terribly lonely and long to have someone come over to spend an evening with us, we may hold back from inviting them for two reasons: we fear that they will say no and our feelings will be hurt, and we equally fear they they will say yes and then they will come and be bored. Our loneliness keeps building up along with our shyness until, from lack of social practice, we become less and less able to be friendly and therefore less and less worthy of friends. Social failure thus becomes not a dreaded future possibility but a present certainty.

Act as if no one could possibly like you and soon no one will. Act so glum that everyone near you feels sad in your presence, and everyone with any sense will avoid you as if you had a dreadful contagious disease (which you do have). Act nasty to people and they will act nasty to you. Act nervous and people will feel edgy when with you. Act bored and you're sure to be boring.

But guess what? This natural law of reciprocity and prophecy-fulfillment can work the other way too. Act cheerful and people will feel cheerful when they are with you and therefore will enjoy being with you and therefore will seek you out. Act confident and people will respect and trust you. Act friendly and most people, in turn, will feel friendly toward you.

Some won't. No one can please all of the people all of the time. Whenever you offer someone friendship you are taking the risk that the offer will be rejected. Some people can't bear someone they think is too cheerful or friendly. I know a man who fired his receptionist because she greeted him too pleasantly in the morning; when he got to the office he was still half-asleep and didn't feel cheerful or chatty enough to respond to a bright "Good morning." But most people will respond to you in the same way that you act toward them. And *all* people will respond in kind if the way you act is morose or hostile.

In short, anyone who dismisses himself as boring, unpleasant company eventually turns out to be right. There isn't much that friends can say to reassure you when you are busy putting yourself way down, except that you shouldn't and that you should *act* as if you didn't. Unfortunately, though, well-meant advice about how you should act may not be well taken. When you are a firm self-putter-downer you are apt to interpret all comments about how you should act as confirmation of your worst fears, and this will make you withdraw more than ever. You'll mumble to yourself, "See? I'm not merely unattractive and boring and a marital has-been; I'm not even sensible enough to know how to have a normal social life!"

But maybe you can lick this problem by applying a little hypocrisy. It has been said that man is the only creature there is that improves himself through hypocrisy. Do you know the story of "The Happy Hypocrite" who was always glowering because he was so unpopular and who was unpopular because he was always glowering? He went to a costume party one night, wearing a mask that had a big jolly friendly smile painted on it, and the people he encountered responded to him as if he were really giving them a big jolly friendly smile. They were so pleasant to him and he had such a good time that by the end of the evening, when he removed his mask, there actually was a big jolly friendly smile on his face for the first time in his life.

The moral is: *Act toward other people the way you would like them to act toward you. That's the Golden Rule of sociability.*

If you use shyness as an excuse to hide from people you will become increasingly shy. The longer you hide the harder it will be for you ever to emerge as a poised and pleasant guest or hostess. In order to avoid a brief pain you will therefore be forcing yourself to endure a lasting one.

Accept invitations when you receive them, sometimes even when you don't feel like going out. You might meet someone boring and you might meet someone interesting; it's worth the gamble. Don't give up after a few disappointing occasions. Gold miners and archaeologists have to hunt through tons of sand and dirt to find a few priceless treasures. Pearl divers have to collect tons of oysters before finding one with a pearl in it. An awful lot of tadpoles have to be born to produce a frog, but mother frogs keep trying!

Even a bore can serve useful functions. The agony of shyness is usually caused by uncertainty about how to behave, or the fear that you are a poor conversationalist, or unattractive, so if you are shy practice your social graces on people who don't particularly interest you, preparing yourself for better things. These people may later introduce you to someone else who really is interesting. And besides, most people are not bores if you really take the trouble to find out what makes them tick, so don't be an overcritical snob. Someone somewhere once said that only one person in a thousand is boring if you really get to know him, and even that person is interesting because of the fact that he's one in a thousand.

Read a news magazine just before you go out, and you'll be sure to have *something* to say when and if the conversation sags. And instead of thinking about yourself and worrying about whether or not people will like you, start thinking about them and drawing them out. If you learn the art of being a really good listener you won't have to bother to learn the art of being a good talker. People will think you are charming and perceptive and unusually intelligent and witty if you laugh at their jokes and let them talk about what is on their minds.

I am not trying to be glib and laugh off the difficulties that a very shy or very sad person has. Particularly in the earliest stages of single parenthood, many people feel too depressed and embarrassed to be able to entertain. But you may be able to ease yourself out of this state, by gentle and gradual but definite efforts. *There is a sensible social compromise you are probably capable of making even when you don't feel up to having adult friends around: entertain your children's friends.*

Even more than you, when your family is learning to adjust to the fact that there is only one parent in the family circle, your children need to be constructively occupied and distracted from self-pity. They need close contact with happy people whose happiness they can catch like a benevolent case of measles. So be friendly to their friends.

The presence of children will probably not make you feel as ill-at-ease as that of people of your own age. You won't feel as threatened by their opinion of you as you feel with contemporaries. You won't be so worried about "Were they really his (or her) friends or mine?" or "Are they accepting my invitation only because they feel sorry for me?"

Offer an overnight visit to a sociable little girl from your daughter's school class. Give them popcorn to pop, toys to play with, television to watch, records to listen to, and let them stay up an extra hour so they can enjoy the thrill of feeling really privileged and deliciously wicked. You can give them a good time easily that way, regardless of your social shyness on the adult level. It's fun to hear happy giggles and see activity in your now-too-empty house. Even the "noisy noise that annoys" at other times can be a welcome antidote to loneliness after too many too quiet evenings.

If your children are sons instead of daughters it may be a bit harder to entertain their friends, because boy guests can carry noise and pandemonium to ghastly extremes. They have a way of rasping the nerves with roughhousing and fisticuffs and they find confined space more confining than little girls usually do. Keep them well occupied and well fed if you want them to be peaceful.

Most of the young boys I have known respond to invitations to stay overnight less eagerly than most little girls do. Girls always seem to love the adventure of packing a suitcase and wearing their best pajamas and having a chance to whisper titillating secrets to each other far into the night. Boys are more blasé about this type of socializing. However, you can still invite your sons' pals to a movie, a baseball game, or a bowling alley, and to lunch or supper, and if you plan wisely you can give them and yourself a very good time.

It's prudent to have lots of games on hand, ranging from old reliables like chess, checkers, cards, Scrabble, anagrams, cribbage, Monopoly, and other standard games to the latest novelty advertised on TV—if you are lucky enough to have boys who will sit still long enough to play them. It's splendid if you possess electric trains and construction sets and other equipment that can keep them occupied in an absorbing and quiet project for more than two minutes at a time. If your boys are so athletically inclined that the only thing which amuses them is punching things or people or throwing or kicking balls around or running, you had better limit invitations to brief periods during good weather and arrange to keep the youngsters outdoors as much as possible, bringing them inside only at meal and snack times.

Make sure there is lots to eat and to imbibe. Fortunately, most children are easy to feed, as long as you're not their mother and therefore are not worrying about giving them a balanced nutritious diet. You rarely have to go to elaborate lengths trying to be original. In fact, if you do you are apt to be very disappointed by their reaction, because almost always they would prefer something simple and unoriginal, like hot dogs, potato chips, hamburgers, or peanut butter sandwiches, to fancy concoctions. Ice cream in the freezer is, of course, a must, and so are cookies, Cokes, ginger ale and fruit drinks—and that's about it. You can be an Ideal Host or Hostess as far as the young are concerned if your home is well stocked with these simple provisions.

Entertaining boys may be more expensive than entertaining girls because it may be necessary to give them movie money or to take them somewhere where they will be kept too busy to beat each other up and damage your furniture or nerves (I'm sorry if all this sounds "sexist" but these are honest opinions based on years of experience). However, unless you are in terribly straitened circumstances you can afford such outings now and then. If you have a puritanical conscience, justify the "extravagance" by realizing how much your children benefit emotionally from companionship and shared activities and the social practice they gain by being hosts.

A single parent is sometimes tempted to live too exclusively for, with, and through the children, and when this happens the parent-child relationship becomes too ingrown. It is stifling to the children as well as stunting to the parent. People who live in a one-parent home (usually so embarrassingly described as a "broken home") have an even greater need for satisfying emotional relationships outside the family than people in a two-parent home. Its members should live pleasantly *with* each other, but not entirely *for* each other, and certainly not to the exclusion of outsiders.

The term "single parent" is really a misnomer, since no parent is ever truly single. A parent is a pivotal, influential part of an important social unit, the most basic unit of society: a family. And a family can never be all it could and should be unless it is an active part of a larger social unit: a pleasant community.

If you are friendly and sociable your home will be a happy place and your children will bloom in it.

Your children didn't ask you to bring them into the world; you invited them here. So it is your responsibility to look out for them and to help insure their safety and happiness. But you alone cannot, and must not try to, give them everything they need. In addition to needing you they need other people to relate to, both older people and people their own age, and some of the time they also need privacy and freedom. Don't hover over them and their guests anxiously, trying to make sure they have a good time; they'll have a better time if you don't worry about it and give *yourself* a good time. When they are little, of course, you have to keep a discreet eye on them for safety's sake, but even then, stay in the background independently occupied to give them a chance to be independently occupied too. Everyone needs a combination of companions and solitude, of attention and independence.

Speaking of independence, when you arrange it so that your children have a happy social life of their own, they won't resent it when you have one of your own too. They will be too busy to feel jealous or neglected. They will only notice your social life, as a rule, if you don't have any, if you spend most of your time sulking in solitude, becoming droopy, dried up, sour, and unfriendly. It's like housework: no one notices it when you dust and make the beds and do the dishes; they only notice it when you don't.

This, incidentally, is another hazard of single parenthood. Even though, in its first stages, you yearn in vain for an active social life to alleviate your loneliness, after a while you can get so used to solitude you become addicted to it. Entertaining your children's friends is therefore a good way to keep yourself in the habit of entertaining—but it should *not* be considered a permanent substitute for adult socializing. You need the company of people your own age some of the time, unless you want to end up an eccentric hermit—and a functioning parent cannot afford to have that ambition, at least not for many years.

So look out for your own social needs as well as those of your youngsters—not instead of their needs, not ahead of theirs, not in spite of theirs, but along with theirs.

Speaking of your needs brings me to an important question. What about sex?

In pre-women's-lib days most females were presumed to be "nice girls" and "ladies" and therefore were extremely delicate about discussing sex, reluctant to do so even with close friends, sometimes even with husbands. Nowadays, however, almost anything goes, verbally and nonverbally, ever since "J" undressed in public and wrote a phenomenal best seller about the Sensuous Woman. She started the now worldwide fad of kissing (et cetera) and telling, and made a lot of money thereby—one of the more notable examples of turning a hobby into a career.

Rumor has it that all widows and divorcees, except those who are flagrantly repulsive or in their late nineties, spend most of their days and nights, especially nights, dodging passes from lecherous men who assume they are sexually frustrated and therefore almost as eager to hop into the nearest bed as the men are anxious to have them do so. I suspect that jealous wives and husbands are more apt to believe this humorous rumor than divorcees and widows are. It has not been (alas?) my experience that long queues of panting males appear on the doorstep as soon as a divorce decree is final. I admit that it's rather embarrassing to admit that (though I can comfort myself with the memory of a handsome moving man who, the day I moved from the house I had lived in while married to a smaller apartment, suddenly realized he was moving the furniture of a divorcee and really began to *move*. He looked like an unintellectual Marlon Brando and I marveled at my virtue as I resisted him, keeping bureaus and chairs and lamps between us. He was importunate for about a week and phoned me several times a day and I was just about to consider succumbing when he gave up—maybe he found another divorcee to move!)

Nowadays, with the new morality, it's hard to decide which is considered more disgraceful: the admission that one is reveling in multiple illicit love affairs or the admission that one isn't. But the harsh, unromantic fact is that most single parents sleep alone at night in single beds.

On the where-there's-smoke-there's-fire theory, I presume that many widows and divorcees do console themselves for the absence of a legal mate by accepting amorous attentions from other men whenever they have a chance, even when these others are only looking for part-time playmates rather than for lasting attachments. The life of ex-marrieds has been described as a constant swing between unhappy love affairs and sexual drought. On the other hand, there are many people who find casual sexual relationships unwelcome and who are also in no hurry to get involved in new deep emotional entanglements, because they loved their former mates either too much or too little to want another one right away.

But whether they crave or dislike sexual encounters, single parents are, as a rule, far less apt to be dined, wined, and bedded than ex-spouses who are childless. Most men on the prowl would rather go after a girl who is totally unattached. As for widowers and divorced men, many girls pretend to be enchanted with their children in order to win admiration and gratitude, but even so the children are a nuisance and impediment when parents are wooing or being wooed. Children have a way of getting in the way.

Your children can be an advantage to you if you are interested in protecting your virtue and/or your reputation for virtue and/or discerning the true intentions of a wooer. People who like your children are, obviously, the best candidates for friendship, romance, or matrimony you could have, so your children perform a useful function in helping you separate the sheep from the goats among your friends. But children are a big disadvantage if you are eager to be known as a femme fatale or a lady killer. You have to find sitters or else entertain people at home with the children underfoot and within earshot—which can interfere rather seriously with intimate conversation and other kinds of personal communication. Children are not insurmountable obstacles to romance, but they are a complicating factor, and the exact opposite of a dowry.

A man has to love a woman a lot more to propose to her if she comes supplied with a ready-made collection of offspring than if she is unencumbered. A Moslem or Pacific Islander might welcome this unmistakable proof that she is fertile, but a modern American man is more apt to think apprehensively of how expensive it would be to support both her and her progeny. Of course, if he does, even so, propose, that's all the more wonderful: it's proof that he loves you enough to override obstacles that would defeat a lesser man, and it's sort of like being the princess in a fairy tale where the valiant hero is willing to conquer dragons in order to win your hand.

Anyway, barring above-average luck or allure, a single parent's romantic prospects leave something to be desired. It is by no means certain that your children's missing parent will be replaced by a stepparent in the near future. Ex-marrieds have a fairly high remarriage rate but it is nowhere near 100 percent and has decreased markedly in recent years, dropping in half since 1960. You might as well make up your mind to realize this and to stop yearning, if you are yearning.

If you are a yearning female you had better take care not to look or act like one, in any case, because nothing turns men off faster than that desperate I-need-a-man look in the eye. Most men instinctively protect themselves from predatory females. On the other hand, unless a girl's eyes have some kind of glint or twinkle or wink in them, how is any man going to know that she is eager, able, and willing? She has to give out some indication of interest before a man will venture to try to sweep her off her feet. As they used to say, she must chase him so he can catch her. So if you want to be caught, give out friendly "vibes" but not anxious ones.

Your children are apt to have serious conflicts in their minds —and even more so in their hearts and subconsciouses—about any intense interest you show in members of the opposite sex or that they show in you. On one level they may be delighted. On another, priggishly disapproving—considering you much too elderly to go in for that kind of stuff. On another, apprehensive. Who is there who hasn't heard stories in which a wicked stepparent was the villain? "If Mommy loves a new man enough to marry him, how do I know she will still love me?" "If Daddy marries that new lady he likes, how do I know if she will like me or if I will like her?" The thought of having to adjust to a stranger moving into one's home and acting like a parent can be pretty terrifying, or at the very least a nuisance; it means having to share space one has gotten used to—closets and drawers, for instance—and time and attention—your time and attention, for instance.

So remember, sympathetically, your children's feelings and fears when you introduce them to your friends. Help them to get to know and to like the people you like. But this doesn't mean pushing your friends at them. Be patient and wait for the children to make the overtures. It isn't easy for children to open their hearts to a person they feel is replacing one of their parents. Their hearts are large enough, however, to make room for a new person if they don't feel that the new one is trying to shove aside their first loyalty, so it helps enormously if they are encouraged to think of a stepparent—potential or actual—as a supplement rather than as a replacement.

I would like to pay a tribute here to a loving and considerate stepmother I know. She is a psychologist by profession and also a good one by instinct. After her stepson had known her for about a year (during which he had given her a pretty rough time, being resentful and unfriendly, but she had kept her cool), he went to his mother one day and said, "Mommy, I hope you won't mind but there's something I'd like you to know. I love my stepmother. Do you mind?" His mother said no, she was glad. And then he added, "You know why I love her? She's never tried to *make* me love her." His mother wasn't jealous; she was happy and relieved to know that his life had been enriched by an additional loving relationship so that now, instead of being "a deprived child living in a broken home," he was lucky enough to feel at home in two homes. But without a lot of tact and understanding and patience on the part of both his father and his stepmother, estrangement rather than enrichment might have resulted from his father's remarriage.

This is not a book on faith and morals except in so far as they impinge on one's functions as a parent, so I am not going to advise any reader on whether or not to join the twentieth century's sexual revolution. I don't think it is my (or even your children's) business what you do in private as long as what you do doesn't damage you or them or your relationship with them. Everyone, even a parent, is entitled to and needs a certain amount of privacy—though little children often don't realize this and have a tendency to burst into bedrooms without knocking (be warned!).

If you feel free enough and strong enough to break old-fashioned rules which most people consider wise and you want to adapt or change these rules in your own life because "circumstances alter cases," be careful not to do it in ways that will hurt anyone. It is good when rigid legalism gives way to intelligent and inventive flexibility (because "the letter killeth but the spirit giveth life"), but making up new rules while playing a game can in some cases lead to confusion and fights rather than to victory. One needs an uncommon amount of common sense to know when and how to break rules wisely. Situation ethics—like a charge account—is liberating and creative in the hands of an honest and sensible person, but dangerous if the user is foolish or selfish. Once again, "know thyself" is one of the most basic and important of all rules.

I do emphatically believe that everyone needs a "love life." To live without love means to be only partly human. The most joyous way to become fully alive is to experience mutual and passionate love with someone who relates to you in important, unique, and intimate ways in a union that broadens and deepens the being of both persons.

When marriage ends or never begins there is a type and degree of human experience which a person lacks: a close, regular, in fact daily, contact and sharing with another person of his or her own age or close to it. The love that one feels for one's children and the friendships one has with people outside one's family can never be a full substitute for this. If you are deprived of it there is no point in denying that you are deprived of something which can be very valuable and wonderful. And if you don't find some way to compensate for that deprivation your personality will be diminished or warped.

There is more than one way, however, to compensate for a loss.

To get rid of the desolation of loneliness some people set about energetically and determinedly looking for instant new spouses—a serious mistake, because a good and lasting loving relationship cannot be built overnight, or with inadequacy as its basis. To try to fall in love just because you feel incomplete by yourself is to delude and, ultimately, to disappoint yourself and your lover. The only valid reason for falling in love is falling in love.

Some people try desperately to find satisfaction in affairs, which range from deeply significant and enduring relationships to exciting but very brief encounters. And some people seek to bury their loneliness in more shallow ways, dashing breathlessly from cocktail party to cocktail party in search of new conversations, new acquaintances, new flirtations, new anything. Sometimes they do it so desperately that they overdo it and end up exhausted instead of refreshed. Hyperactivity is as unhealthy as indolence, and going out every night is just as ineffective as staying home alone every night, as far as uprooting the causes of loneliness is concerned. Scattering yourself in shallow relationships with lots of people is no cure for loneliness, because loneliness isn't caused simply by solitude. What hurts about loneliness is the feeling that you don't matter, at least not to anyone who really matters to you. The cure for it is finding people who do matter to you, and relating to them in meaningful ways, not in one-night stands.

The point is that to be a really happy and unlonely person you must love. Not *be* loved. *Love!* And real love is not something you "fall" into. It's something you create and build.

There is a nice popular song called "You're Nobody Till Somebody Loves You" which has wise lyrics. They don't suggest that you sit around passively waiting until somebody loves you. The song says, "Find yourself somebody to love." Somebody *you* love, not somebody who loves you.

What does this mean for people who do not succeed in finding one special person, one member of the opposite sex, to love? Are they doomed? Of course not! They can do what the widow of Peter Marshall did (many others have done it too but she has articulated it particularly well in her books): spread their love around and find exciting, challenging, and fulfilling new outlets for the energy and warmth which a loving sexual union at its best gives. In other words, they can sublimate their sexual drive and let the love which might have been focused on just one person benefit many people through a sort of radioactive fallout.

The word *sublimate* means to many people "do without and pretend you don't mind," "learn to accept second best and say it's what you wanted all along," "forget what you're missing and think about something else." But that is not what the word means. It means *transcend, make sublime*.

A person who has loved one other person very, very much and very, very specially may never be able to find another individual who can take that one's place, not because he or she has become withdrawn and unloving but because the love given to that person is still and always will be so tremendously real, so permanently alive, even though the person who inspires it is gone, that it simply cannot be transferred to someone else. People are not automatically interchangeable, after all, like nuts and bolts in a machine. When you love a unique person with your whole soul and heart no one else can be an entirely satisfactory understudy for that person because no one else will ever be exactly like that person. You may miss that person to the end of your days.

Even so, this does not mean you must be loveless from now on. Not every novel is *The Brothers Karamazov*, but other books are still very much worth reading. So don't close your heart off from new people, no matter how much it belongs to one person. There are other people also worth knowing and loving. Other people may not have the same things to offer you as that person, but each has something, something unique and valuable. Get to know what it is. Relate warmly to it. Give of yourself to people and allow them to give to you.

Spend yourself giving love—this is one thing you need not budget. Perhaps that love will express itself in beautifully intimate, including sexual, ways. Perhaps not. But don't close off the vulnerable, receptive, giving, warm part of yourself, as if the very thought were impossible or disloyal or sinful.

Now: what can you do if you find yourself having a time-and-emotion-consuming relationship with a new person while you are still housebound and child-centered and you don't want to distress, shock, neglect, or replace your children?

Establish some kind of realistic and just social schedule which permits you to give your children a lot of time and which also gives you free time. Help your children to understand that although they are an extremely important and lovely part of your life they are not and cannot be and should not be the whole show.

Even before you have any special reason to convince them of this, get them used to the fact that some of your time will not be at their disposal. Absent yourself from them now and then. You are trying to raise nice, loving, sharing people—not egotistical tyrants. So do this even when you don't particularly need to, so that they will be able to accept it easily when you do need to. Actually, they will feel prouder of you, happier about you, and freer, if they know you have a life of your own in addition to your life with them, than if you are always hanging around them.

I remember when my youngest daughter said to me once, admiringly, "Linda's mother has such nice boyfriends!" The implication was clear: what's wrong with *my* mother? I also remember when my own mother told my sister and me that she would never, never, never think of marrying again, although she had been divorced for many years and there was an attractive, amorous architect hovering hopefully around our house. We said, "Why not?" I respect her preference and her decision, but I remember how we felt as well as how she felt: we didn't want to be the only people in her life; it was too great a burden, too heavy an obligation, too claustrophic.

So do what you want to do, socially and romantically, as long as you take precautions not to hurt anyone. And don't do what you don't want to do. It's *your* life. If you need or ardently desire the intimate companionship of one loving person of the opposite sex and if such a relationship is available and will help you be a more vigorous, cheerful, creative, affectionate parent, accept your good fortune gratefully. But if you don't, if that aspect of your life is now over, *be at peace* and find other outlets which will enable you to live vigorously, cheerfully, creatively, and affectionately.

If at times you feel lonely and useless, realize how much

lonelier and more useless you would be if you had no children. And to help both you and your children become the full, multidimensional people you were meant to be, extend your family and include in it friends and friends' friends. Give love lovingly and lavishly. *Love ricochets, and the more of it you give the more of it you will receive.*

My little granddaughter Amy learned a lovely song recently in kindergarten:

> Love is something if you give it away
> You end up having more.
>
> Love is like a magic penny.
> Hold it tight and you won't have any.
> But let it go and you'll soon have more,
> Rolling all over the floor!
>
> Yes, love is something if you give it away,
> Give it away, give it away,
> You end up having more!

11

INVOLVING YOURSELF:
Conquering boredom by developing strong interests

Boredom is to loneliness something like an itch compared to an ache. It makes you fidget rather than faint. It is more annoying than tragic. And it's somewhat easier to cure because it will usually disappear in the presence of a distraction, whereas loneliness can settle down inside your soul and remain there even when you are busy. Boredom isn't fatal, despite the expression, "I'm dying of boredom." But it's *boring* and can sour the disposition, so it's a good idea to get rid of it.

Obviously, its antidote is activity. Yet that is not quite enough. A person can work very hard and still be bored by the work. Days filled with nothing but endless housework prove that. You must find things to keep busy at which genuinely interest you.

It really isn't dreadful to have to face the fact that from now on you will be spending much of your time alone, if you are determined not to fritter away all that time brooding aimlessly and instead begin doing those interesting things which people can only do alone, either because they require intense concentration (e.g. learning to paint or draw or sew, studying, memorizing favorite poems, meditating) or are embarrassing to do when other people are there (e.g. beauty regimes or exercises to keep thighs, tummy, and waistline in trim) or are annoying to other people (e.g. singing happily but off-key, or playing your favorite phonograph record for the thousandth time or turning the bathroom into a photographic dark room).

What you need to remember is that being alone need not mean being lonely or bored. Being alone can be a very pleasant intermission between pleasant activities, a refreshing rest period or a helpful time of preparation. There is nothing inherently threatening or sad about it. Think of aloneness in the right way and you can be a spiritual alchemist, turning a privation into a privilege.

If you are not used to spending much time by yourself you will have to practice learning how to do it well—just as surely as someone has to practice the piano in order to learn how to play it well (that, by the way, is a splendid thing to do when you're alone).

Your first instinct may be to sleep or loaf the time away—a very bad idea, conducive to getting lazier and lazier and hence more and more bored. When you are in a desert and can't find any way out, you'll die of thirst if you just lie there. So, instead, collect your tears into a little pool and build yourself a lovely oasis!

Not that every minute you are alone need be spent purposefully. Just plain relaxing by yourself at times is a fine and enjoyable thing to do. Especially if your children are very active and noisy and keep you hopping, it is soul-soothing and soul-stretching to cultivate quiet, leisurely solitude when you have a chance.

At first—particularly if the reason you are alone is a recent divorce or widowhood—you may not have enough pep or enthusiasm to fill your time with any truly ambitious projects. The main thing you need in the beginning is not to push yourself so hard that you get overtired and discouraged, but to ease yourself little by little into the habit of enjoying yourself by yourself. Do little things, self-indulgent things, distracting things that don't demand too much of you. When you have recently been through a bad situation that is no time (if there ever is one) to be puritanical and spartan. When you are trying to learn to feel unsorry for yourself you can indulge yourself a bit without feeling that you are being extravagant or giddy.

Many people who hate being alone get a pet to keep them company or to be a watchdog.
Personally, I would approach this particular solution to solitude with extreme caution, because a single parent is already awfully tied down to the house, having to look after a child or children, and dogs and cats require almost as much attention as children do—and their medical and food bills can be as large as those of a human being. It can be just as difficult to find a baby-sitter for a fish tank or a canary as it is to find one for a baby. So a pet may keep you company (though not human company, which is what you are really trying to compensate for), but at the same time it deprives you still further of freedom, and freedom is what you should be learning to relish and take advantage of.

Children are always begging parents to buy pets, promising fervently that they will take care of them, feed, wash, train, walk, and groom them, but about two weeks after the pets have become members of the household it is usually a parent who gets stuck with the extra chores. It doesn't make much sense to me to try to cure one problem by taking on additional problems.

On the other hand, adding a new member to your private menagerie may be exactly the right thing to do to bring new joy into your life if you are a passionate animal lover: my sister and her husband used to console themselves for every disappointment and celebrate every triumph by buying each other another animal, and not just dogs (though they did that too—they had seven) but guinea pigs, parrots, parakeets, lovebirds, peacocks, ducks, geese, swans, horses, anything that moves! They thoroughly enjoyed doing this, but people differ, and I wouldn't swap my solitude for their food and veterinary bills.

Even if you have a naturally sunny disposition, there are

bound to be a few times when your mood is pale blue if not indigo. Progress goes along in a jagged, back-and-forth motion, never—or almost never—in a straight line upward. So don't get scared or dismayed or mad at yourself when you find you're in a slump long after you thought you had become fully adjusted to your single state. Everyone has some bad days. You're entitled. Be gentle with yourself. Breathe deep, and cultivate patience. This too shall pass!

It is safer and wiser, I think, as well as more considerate, to stay by yourself when attacked by the blues. This is not a time when I would recommend socializing. You are more liable to depress your friends then they are apt to undepress you. So watch TV or turn on the radio or go out to a good movie or art exhibit or concert. Such activities will fill the physical, outer silence that is bothering you, even if they don't completely drown out the inner silence.

Speaking of going to the movies, however, a word of caution: There is one thing which some single and baby-sitterless parents sometimes do which I think is seriously wrong. In their longing for adult diversion they go to a place that is unsuitable for children and take the children along. Perhaps to a bar that is crowded, smoky, noisy, full of couples coupling, drunks wobbling and quarreling and exchanging dirty jokes into the wee hours. Or to a movie which is much too scary, or too sophisticated, or too late at night. This is exploitation of your children. Granted that you might enjoy the bar or the movie. Very understandable. But if you cannot get a sitter, then settle instead for a book, television, radio, or phonograph. (How spoiled we are, come to think of it! Our own parents didn't have anything like the wide range of recreational resources at home that we have.) Keep young children away from places which can frighten or overstimulate them, and keep yourself away from such places if you can't get there without having to leave the children alone. You can go there some other time. In the meantime, if you don't want *"mean* time" to describe the interim, find some other thing to do.

Go to a library and get yourself a good book. Not a book on how to be a better parent or person—being "uplifted" is sometimes less uplifting when you are in a very down mood than something entertaining that is completely unrelated to what is bothering you. Find a very exciting or funny book if your mood is fidgety.

If you are deeply troubled or searching for more meaning to your life, that's something else: in that case, delve into the inexhaustible riches of poetry and philosophy and history and psychology and art. An author can be a truly great friend in need, one who doesn't get upset at the fact that you are not at your scintillating best right now and who will not walk out on you in disgust (or hang around too long).

Or write. You can pour out the full flood of your frustrations, rage, grief, confusion, yearnings on paper, safely, because paper won't hit back at you or argue with you or get depressed by you, whereas a human listener might not be able to take it. Write a journal, or poems, or indignant letters to the editor, or write friends (but don't mail anything until a few days have passed so that you have a chance to read it over and see if it makes any sense or if you have just produced whiny, rambling drivel).

It isn't always necessary to see people in order to keep in regular touch with them. Two very pleasant ways to keep pleasant friendships alive, which many of us forget to cultivate, are *letters and phone calls.*

In recent years I have discovered the joys of the long-distance call. The ads explaining that "long distance is the next best thing to being there" and that if you call on weekends it is not expensive finally got through to me. You can phone California from New York as cheaply as you can phone someone in your own state, if you make a station-to-station, dial-it-yourself call instead of calling person-to-person.

I can't describe the sheer joy I have felt at hearing voices I hadn't heard in years. There is usually a moment of stunned silence at first, but as soon as your old friend or beloved relative discovers that you aren't calling because of anything alarming or practical but just out of sociability or affection, this is usually followed by a great burst of liberation and mutual glee. You probably can't afford to, and may not even want to, talk on and on—except sometimes—but when you do, it is worth the money. It doesn't cost any more than a movie you might go to and not enjoy nearly as much. And even a brief chat with a really good old friend can give your heart a lift that will brighten up a whole week.

Similarly, learning the art of the short letter is valuable. I tend to make the silly mistake of waiting until I have time to compose what I consider a "real" letter before I get around to writing friends. I have to fill the whole first page with apologies and explanations about not writing sooner, and then I have to bring them up-to-date on many months of news—this turns letter writing into a difficult chore. But I have a very lovely and smart and thoughtful grown-up daughter and a few wonderful friends through whose good examples I am trying to learn to master the two- or three-line letter form.

Anne and Noreen and Isobel and Dez and Charlotte and Clay and several other people I know give (and get) enormous pleasure this way—and I hereby thank them publicly for the many times they have brightened my days. If they see something in a magazine or newspaper that's funny or that they know would interest someone, they pop it in the mail. They keep track of birthdays and anniversaries and other special days and remember to write you something special in time to arrive on such days. When they know you are facing a particularly difficult time they dash off a quick note of timely comfort—and the word *timely* is all-important. Procrastinating and sending it three weeks later would be almost meaningless. They remember to let you know they love you and are thinking of you when you really need to know it.

Whenever you have read about one of your friends in the paper (they have been promoted, or they've moved, or one of their relatives has gotten married or has died, or someone you both know has done something newsworthy) or if you see an editorial you know they would agree with or a cartoon they might have missed which you think is very clever, sending this off with a brief note, even just one line, will delight the receiver —and almost always will bring you a dividend in the form of a return note, phone call, or even a visit. Even if it doesn't, knowing you have given pleasure is a good feeling.

It isn't necessary, actually, to have even that much of an excuse to write a short chatty letter. People enjoy hearing from each other unexpectedly and for no particular reason, and most of them tend to answer back. The mail you get in return can be very heartwarming. It's a big relief to find a personal letter in among the piles of bills, advertisements, and requests for charity when you open the mailbox.

One lonely widow I know of has gone to unusual lengths to develop a thriving correspondence. Every week she writes to prisoners whose names she got from a social worker. She has never met these men but she takes an interest in their problems and befriends them from a distance, and they write her back gratefully and entertainingly. "I know I exist," she says, "when that mail comes. I no longer feel invisible."

One thing that I believe in doing when I find myself bored and/or lonesome but also a bit lazy is simply getting up and going outdoors. Anywhere. Either to a favorite spot, or somewhere I've never been before. Having a specific destination and purpose may add interest to a walk but just ambling along pretty or busy streets, looking in store windows and houses, exploring parts of town you haven't seen before, or best of all admiring a magnificent sunset or a charming garden or a handsome view is an extremely pleasant way to spend time. It gets you out of your own quarters and gives you something more intriguing to look at than those four square walls which sometimes seem to close in on you. And it's invigorating exercise, as good for your figure and blood circulation as for your spirits.

Some women have a special problem. They think the Eleventh Commandment is "Thou shalt not go out anywhere without an escort." They won't go for a walk or set foot in a restaurant or accept an invitation to a party or go to the theater unless they are accompanied, preferably by a person of the masculine gender. They have exaggerated fears of being mugged or raped or getting lost, and besides, they think it is a serious disgrace to be seen alone.

The first few times you go out alone, when you are a new single parent, are the hardest. You do feel strange. You are very conscious of the person who is not there. The first time you walk alone into a restaurant you may think everyone is staring at you, murmuring under their breath, "I wonder why that person who just came in has no dinner companion—must be a dreadful drip!" Of course no one there is doing any such thing. That is sheer conceit on your part. As one wag put it to me, we would worry much less about what people think about us if we realized how rarely they do. You are not nearly as interesting to the other people in the restaurant as the menu and their own companions. So forget that problem when you feel like going out. Take a good book or magazine along as a dinner companion, order something you like (preferably something you don't know how to cook), and enjoy yourself!

If I am going to spend an afternoon reading a book or writing letters I often take my things outside to a park or a sidewalk café, to read or write over a leisurely cup of coffee or a cocktail, instead of staying home. Having other people around, even though they are strangers, can make you feel less cut off from the rest of the human race, and the fact that they are strangers means you don't have to put on an extra-cheery face or make conversation when you don't feel like it. When you do feel like it you may make some nice new friends. This must be done, of course, with discretion, but many parents have made firm lifelong friends of the parents of children their own children have played with in a playground or park. Some mothers complain about having to accompany their young to the park, thinking of it as a boring task because "there's nothing to do there," but a park isn't boring if you're friendly. And even when you are not feeling friendly, trees and grass and flowers and birds and open skies are lovely company.

Take advantage of all the resources your community offers. There are probably many more than you realize until you start looking for them systematically.

When I was a little girl I had a wonderful governess one year, Mrs. Holmes, a widow who had adored her husband but who loved life even more and who, though she missed him, didn't know how to be unhappy. She used to take me to all kinds of places, to give variety to our daily routine, instead of taking me always to the same part of the same park. On rainy days we visited churches, museums, libraries, shops, railroad stations, even banks, factories, offices, fire stations, police precincts, hospitals. We dropped in on posh hotels and sat in their luxurious lobbies, pretending we were newly arrived in town, picking up all available sight-seeing literature and observing the handsome clothes or amusing quirks of all the elegant or funny-looking people rushing around us. On sunny days we visited monuments and parks and explored highways and byways. We window-shopped, we took long bus rides and subway rides and strolls to different sections of town.

As a result of her inspiring guidance I learned how many things there are to do and to see in a city, and I developed imagination and the habit of insatiable curiosity—because the more you exercise either the more of both you acquire. A great deal of pleasure in life comes from the simple practice of learning to observe things and people closely and appreciatively.

There really doesn't seem to me much excuse in this multimedia world to have extremely long periods of boredom. Of course there are, inevitably, occasional dull moments or days. Sometimes one doesn't feel well enough to go out and do anything interesting, so time hangs heavy. But if you find this happening to you more often than not, then something is wrong with you and your attitude rather than with life itself.

Keep your eyes and ears and heart wide open. As Robert Louis Stevenson said, "The world is so full of a number of things, I'm sure we should all be as happy as kings." Many kings, RLS to the contrary, are far from happy, but perhaps that's because they have become too fixated on a few things and on the wrong things: power, politics, war, money, elaborate ceremony. The fact remains that there are so many wonderful things in this world, to relish and use to the hilt during the few years that we have the unspeakable privilege of living here, that we can be happy if we really take the trouble to notice them and use them and *want* to be happy. If some of the beautiful, funny, interesting things and people in the world don't intrigue you there must be others that will if you search them out and give them a chance. Look for whatever it is that will fascinate you, whether it's taking up a sport, a game, an art, acquiring a new skill, or admiring the skills of others as they are presented in museums, theaters, concert halls, and books.

And don't think of these things as ways of "killing time." They are quite the opposite. They are ways of bringing time alive, using time to add new life to your life.

Do museums bore you? Do you think it would be a "drag" to drag yourself around one? Maybe that means it's a long time since you were in one. You may have memories of being taken years ago by a schoolteacher on too long an expedition, so that your feet hurt, and of being annoyed because you were told "hush" and "don't touch" every time you started to get enthusiastic about anything, so you haven't been back since. But both museums and libraries have changed a lot in recent years. They are less stuffy and formal than they used to be, and their displays are more varied. They are full of beautiful things to see, and tape recorders and attractive booklets and pleasant guides are available to help you understand what you are seeing and thus get more out of it, and their monthly schedules are crammed with more activities than your own schedule will allow you to take advantage of.

If museums and libraries do bore you, it may be because you don't know enough about art, or science, or history. Contrary to the popular cliché, "I don't know much about art but I know what I like," usually people who don't know much about art (or some other subject) do *not* know what they like, and they don't like very much, because they haven't been exposed to enough things or made sufficient effort to understand them. If this is true of you, then go to some lectures at a library or museum and learn more about something, to see if you can find out why other people like it and maybe even get to like it yourself. Dare yourself to become more informed and therefore less bored.

Lectures are an excellent free-of-charge recreational resource. Many museums, libraries, churches, community centers, and educational institutions run them regularly. You may feel that, now that you are past school age, you're too old to go and sit in front of a lecturer. But there is no longer any such thing as "school age." With all the new opportunities for leisure we have acquired in the twentieth century—and for all the serious sins of our century, its wars and crises, we should give it credit for the time-saving and other inventions that have made leisure a possession of the average person for the first time in history— the concept of informal and lifelong education has gained momentum, so no one looks askance today at the sight of a grown-up taking a course in a school.

A very pleasant surprise is in store for you once you grit your teeth and decide to go to a lecture for the first time since you left high school or college. Most lecturers are *not* bores or they wouldn't get paid to give lectures. The reason they have been hired is because somebody has found their comments interesting and worth hearing. They are people with something to say and you will also have more to say, and to think about, after you have let them have their say to you. You will know more about current events, art, books, travel, philosophy, psychology, whatever you would like to know more about. We can't all become globe-trotters or full-time scholars, but it is possible, and fun, for us to learn unusual and amusing facts about lovely places, people, and things to broaden our outlook.

You may have to goad yourself into doing this kind of thing at first, simply because you know it's "good for you" rather than because you really think you would enjoy it—the way your mother made you eat carrots or shrimp or oysters or onions or salad when you were an inexperienced and unadventurous eater (and now you like all or some of them so much you can hardly believe you had to acquire the taste). It's worth forcing yourself. When you learn new things you enrich your own conversation so that you are a more attractive and therefore happier person than you were when you started. Your social, as well as your interior, life will improve when you expose yourself to more people and ideas, because one of the best ways to become an interest*ing* person is to become an interest*ed* one.

Be active, not passive. The world is full of wonderful things but it will not come uninvited to our door to meet and entertain us, bringing its riches along. We have to seek it out and respond actively to it. We have to give something of ourselves to situations and relationships in order to get something for ourselves from them . . . and we have to get something for ourselves in order to be able to have more to give. This is one of those lovely unvicious circles we can set in motion to benefit ourselves, if we will give it a little push to start it rolling.

Some people take up hobbies in order to develop interests which have more sustained continuity than an occasional lecture or concert. That's a suggestion that makes a few people squirm self-consciously almost as much as being told to go to a psychiatrist would. They say, "Oh, for heaven's sake, I don't want to become one of those silly pathetic characters who go in for endless bridge games or stamp collecting or artsy-craftsy puttering just to fill up empty days." Well, there is absolutely nothing laughable or pathetic about learning to become good at something, especially if it is something that brings enjoyment and beauty into your life. There are many activities that are increasingly absorbing the longer you do them, and there are many things it is entertaining and useful to learn. There are especially many things which it is extremely beneficial for a *parent* to learn.

If we would like to develop certain talents and interests in our children—social, aesthetic, scientific, athletic, or whatever —there is no better way to do so than by cultivating those talents and interests in ourselves. We can study photography, drawing, painting, sculpture, dancing, singing, the piano or guitar or recorder, sewing, weaving, knitting, crocheting, embroidery. We can take up bridge, chess, golf, tennis, bowling, swimming, hiking, camping, skiing, ice skating, etc., etc., etc. In many towns there are museums or clubs or community centers that hold parent-and-child classes in various crafts and that arrange family excursions to interesting places. Participating in these can be a delightful way to strengthen family bonds at the same time that it develops new interests and skills. There are many projects we can undertake jointly with our children, which are every bit as amusing and educational for us as for the children, once we have surmounted our initial inertia, indifference, laziness, shyness, and pride.

Share some of your interests with your children, and adopt some of theirs for your own too. Do you hate the way they dance or the type of music they like? Learn more about it and you may find out why they like it. And then, reciprocally, introduce them to some of the things you like. You'll all end up more intelligent, and closer emotionally.

Part of the respect you owe every child means that you mustn't try to twist their interests, tastes, abilities, and personalities into a direction you like, to the exclusion of their own personal choices. You should give them opportunities to learn about things you think are important and interesting, but you should also respect their preferences, as they should respect yours. If your child's other parent was an athlete (or artist, or whatever) and you yourself couldn't be less interested in sports (or art, or whatever) but your child shows great interest and ability in sports (or art, or whatever), don't insist that he or she play that down and concentrate instead on things that interest you more. Realize this attraction and talent may be part of the child's basic natural makeup and that each of us—this can't be emphasized too often—has the right to be *who and what* we are.

There is one laudable, and always available, type of activity which is for many people a sure cure for boredom: good works. As I mentioned earlier, one of the best ways to help yourself is to help other people. And in these troubled times I doubt that there is a single community in the world so fortunate that it has no need for people who can offer services to its needy members: old people, handicapped people, poor people, neglected children. There are so many worthwhile causes and organizations that are in constant need of more helpers: UNICEF, your church, the Red Cross, the Scouts, the Sierra Club, the League of Women Voters, the PTA. And so many individuals too. Part-time and full-time jobs are waiting for volunteers at schools and in hospitals, in old people's homes, in preschool day-care centers, and in orphanages—almost anywhere you look.

If you are qualified, you could teach English to foreigners or tutor children who have math or reading difficulties or be a nurse's aid or a teacher's assistant. You could help out in a library, or you could be a recreation leader at a playground or day-care center. You could read for the blind or to children in hospital wards. Or do errands for, or just chat with, housebound old or sick people (a social welfare agency or church rectory can put you in touch with them).

Useful volunteer work is a marvelous thing to do when we are trying to reach beyond ourselves and make our lives more gratifying. Before regarding it as a cure-all for loneliness, however, there are several important things to consider.

It may not be such a great idea to undertake this kind of work when first learning to cope with the problems of single parenthood.

For one thing, your own children—particularly if they are still little—already provide large scope for your do-good instincts. They really need your close and sustained attention, at least in the beginning. They need you around more than children with two parents would. It is terribly important for children who have lost one parent to feel safe and secure and important with the remaining parent. I am certainly not saying that you must stay with them constantly and wait on them, hang on their every word, jump to satisfy their every desire, in short overindulge them. A single parent must be reminded and reminded to guard against this tendency carefully. But being around enough to be reliable and supportive, and being a creative, imaginative, entertaining, and enjoyable parent, rather than merely a conscientious provider of bread and board, is the best "good work" a single parent can perform.

Secondly, in the beginning you may not emotionally be up to volunteer work that puts you in close contact with people who have severe problems. You already have enough problems of your own to attend to, without taking on even more shattering ones. A really vigorous case of the blues may increase instead of diminish if you try too hard to be too "good," and when you are way down you won't be much comfort to other people anyway. It may be unwise to surround yourself with other sorrowful people when you are trying to get over a sorrow of your own. You may not be strong and cheerful enough to be a real help to them, and you could actually hurt them instead of helping.

Thirdly, don't start what you don't intend to, or can't, keep up. Don't commit yourself to a demanding schedule when you don't yet know how much free time you are really going to have available. Don't volunteer to do work at a hospital or school unless you intend to take the job seriously and be reliable about it. Your motive in offering your services should not be to help yourself pass the time now and then when you have nothing more interesting to do; it should be to help others, and that means you must be conscientious and dependable, or you're a phony. It would be cruel to assign yourself a job like visiting a sick or lonesome old lady every week until she began to count on it, and then let her down because you got tired of doing it or got too busy. Similarly, it wouldn't be fair to establish a "Big Brother" relationship with a delinquent or neglected or handicapped youngster (one of the most wonderful things which a person who is good at parenting can do) and then, once the youngster has become emotionally attached to you, disappear; giving him such a blow might leave him much worse off than he was when you offered to help him.

On the other hand, if you do have enough time—when your children are away or in school—to help other people, and if you have enough energy and emotional stamina to be a real help to others, and if you would *like* doing something like that (instead of feeling like a martyr about it), then there is no better way to get away from your own problems and to convince yourself that you are a valuable person. Once again, what is important is that you really know yourself well enough to know (1) what you are good at and (2) what you really enjoy doing. If you *are* good at helping people, you're lucky—and so is your community.

Even if you are not equipped emotionally to do demanding social work, there may be other activities you could become involved in. If you are interested in politics, you might enjoy offering your services to a neighborhood political organization. You might become a useful assistant at a library or community center. Or join a discussion club or a local amateur theater group, or a church choir, or become active in an alumni association. Whatever you do, if you do it regularly and intently you will get more out of it than if you go about it halfheartedly.

Even people who don't need to work in order to earn money need to do some kind of regular work, I think. "All work and no play makes Jack a dull boy," but all play and no work makes people even duller. Any woman who is not married and whose children are in school all day should find a regular and absorbing outside job, paid if she needs money, unpaid if she doesn't, because activity outside the home will make her a more interesting and contented person when she is inside it. An outside job widens her world, fills her time more usefully than the endless housework which, following Parkinson's law, will fill up all of her hours if she lets it, while giving her nothing exciting to talk or think about. Needing to have money is by no means the only reason to work. The wholesome discipline which a regular responsibility provides and the additional interests it fills your mind with are also important reasons.

And when you are depressed, getting a new job or a strong and steady interest which involves you on a regular basis can be as therapeutic as (and a lot cheaper than!) going to a psychiatrist.

Thousands of socially vital institutions literally could not exist were it not for the work done by willing and hard-working volunteers. This is particularly, notably true in the fields of education and hospital work, but it is also true of many other types of work which are needed to keep communities running. Some of this work pays and some of it doesn't. But whether it does or not it can be useful, stimulating, and rewarding.

There are many instances where work started on a voluntary basis, either out of a spirit of social service or because of a personal interest, and later grew into a paying job even though that was not the doer's original intention. Part-time hobbies can become full-time careers.

Take any job you have, unpaid or paid, seriously, and do it *well*. You may get rewarded with praise, you may get rewarded with money as well as praise, but one thing is sure: *you will get rewarded.*

12

PROTECTING YOURSELF:
Coping with financial problems

For a few single parents money is no problem. Some widows have been left adequate amounts of life insurance by thoughtful and farsighted husbands. Some divorcees receive adequate alimony payments from generous (or begrudging but affluent) ex-husbands. Some ex-husbands are fortunate enough to have such good jobs that they earn enough money to take care of all their own needs and those of their children, even though they may also have to provide alimony to former mates. And a few people were born with silver spoons in their mouths. These lucky people can skip this chapter.

Most single parents, however, have financial problems that range from mildly worrisome to alarming. Most alimony covers only partial expenses and only about 20 percent of widows are left adequately provided for, even with Social Security benefits included, and they often have a long wait while courts are settling an estate, during which they are living precariously in a financial limbo.

From now on, your money is going to have to s-t-r-e-t-c-h.

If a woman had a paying job while she was married her income was doubtless a supplementary one. A two-parent family's main source of financial security is, in most cases, the husband's earnings, not the wife's. Even in the few cases where women earn as much as or more than their husbands, marriage still means there are two incomes in the family—unless the husband is a student or artist the wife is proudly supporting so he can "do his own thing" or he is so indisposed physically or psychologically that he brings in very little money indeed and the wife is the actual breadwinner, but that is most unusual. So no matter how prosperous an ex-wife has been or now is, the fact remains almost certainly that she must live on money which would once have gone much farther than it now does.

A woman who has been completely dependent financially on her husband, who has never earned any money at all, is now going to have to start paying much more attention to finances than she has ever had to before.

And any ex-husband who pays alimony to an ex-wife is now going to have to help maintain more than one household: his and hers.

In other words, almost every single parent has to learn to budget and spend money more carefully than ever before. Like many other things, this isn't quite the unbearable fate it may seem to be at first thought, once you have started doing it and getting the swing of it.

When you list your assets and expenses, the unbalanced balance sheet you see before you may be a pretty dismaying sight. But cheer up: among the assets you have which you haven't listed on paper are your arms, legs, eyes, ears, brains, and stout heart, and the fact that you now have one less person in your house to feed, clothe, and entertain than you would have if you were married. On the other hand, you do have many unavoidable expenses, unfortunately and undeniably: taxes, rent, food, clothing, school bills, medical and dental bills, transportation, telephone, gas, electricity.

It is truly depressing to have to list all the items for which we all need money. I think that most of us hate to budget, not so much because we are too undisciplined to like being systematic and limiting our extravagant desires, but because when we stop to survey all our financial needs in one great panoramic swoop they seem so enormous that we really wonder how on earth we have managed thus far to escape bankruptcy, ruin, and starvation, and how much longer we will be able to continue doing so. This is such a scary thought that we would rather forget all about money and turn quickly to a more pleasant subject.

To live within a limited income is one of those things which, when you contemplate it coldly in the harsh light of day, seems virtually impossible. It's a bit like those startling facts people sometimes give out about the amount of adrenaline required to run away from a charging elephant or the number of calories that are used up in the act of copulation—if we really thought seriously about either of those facts at the moment when it was necessary or desirable for us to perform, and we stopped to worry about how we were going to acquire that amount of energy or stimulation, we probably wouldn't be able to do what is required. But such situations fortunately take care of themselves because we just go ahead without pausing to analyze the difficulties—like the bees who keep on flying, not realizing that according to the principles of aerodynamics they are too fat in proportion to their wingspread to be able to fly. Many of us are this way about money. We survey all our assets and expenses and realize we can't possibly manage—yet somehow, in gallant defiance of all the laws of probability and economics, we do manage, month after month, year after year.

Even though the balance sheet seems so unbalanced, it is a good idea to look it over from time to time, to let ourselves know the worst. Then the only financial surprises we will have will be pleasant ones.

What are some of the financial sleight-of-hand tricks we can learn to help us get by?

We learn to absorb, even blithely ignore, a certain amount of unavoidable worry that nags us but which doesn't render us powerless or permanently gloomy.

We learn to feel grateful instead of insulted when a generous relative or friend gives us or our children some secondhand but thoroughly usable clothing or toys or furniture.

We learn which bills it is truly essential to pay on the dot and which can be safely postponed a month or two . . . which costs are inevitable and which are optional.

We learn to do many things for ourselves which make it unnecessary to spend money we haven't got. We learn to walk where we used to take buses or taxis (and this is good for our health and our figures, as well as for our budgets). We learn to patronize libraries instead of buying all the books and magazines and recordings we want to read or hear. We watch TV at home instead of going out to the movies and the theater as often as we used to. We learn to fix our own hair instead of depending on barbers or hairdressers, and to wash and iron our own clothes instead of sending them out to a laundry. If we're very smart we also learn to sew and to make clothes for a few dollars that would cost twice or three times as much if we bought them in a store. And instead of feeling glum and grim about how spartan we are being, we feel happy and proud of ourselves for being so much more competent and resourceful than we used to be.

We also learn to take advantage of bargains and special sales. This isn't such an irksome thing to have to do either, once we get in the habit. Most of us get considerable glee out of feeling we have cleverly outwitted a shop owner or manufacturer by obtaining an item at an unusually low cost.

By planning purchases ahead we can synchronize our shopping with merchandisers' schedules, waiting until January to buy new sheets even though our old sheets got ripped in November, for instance. There are clearance sales when stores go out of business or when they are temporarily overstocked, and we keep an eye out for these, but most sales are scheduled at predictable times which we learn to anticipate.

There are almost always great bargains to be found in storewide sales on Washington's Birthday, the Fourth of July, Columbus Day, Veterans Day, and Election Day—if you can stand clawing your way through the mobs of shoppers who have the same idea you have. There are also more peaceful, month-long sales of marked-down items at different times of year. In case you have never bothered to familiarize yourself with the yearly schedule which most merchandisers follow, here are the times when most prices are reduced by 10 to 50 percent:

Bargain Calendar
air conditioners—February and August
appliances (small)—January and February
automobiles (new)—September
automobiles (used)—February, November, and December
bedding—February and August
books—January
building materials and lumber—June
camping supplies and sports equipment—August
children's clothing—July and December
china and glassware—January, February, and September
coats (women's)—April, August, November, and December
coats (men's)—January and August
curtains and slip covers—February, July, and August
furniture, housewares, and lamps—January, February, July, August, and September
fuel oil—July
furs—January, February, August, and October
garden furniture—July
gardening supplies—August and September
gift items—the week after Christmas
handbags—May
hardware—August and September
hats (men's)—January and July
hats (women's)—March (after Easter) and July
infants' wear—January, March, and April
jewelry—the week after Christmas
linens and blankets—January and May
lingerie—January and May

men's clothing—April
piece goods—June, September, and November
radios and stereos—January, February, and July
refrigerators—January, February, and July
rugs—January, February, July, and August
school supplies and back-to-school clothes—August and October
screens and storm windows—June
shoes—January and July
silverware—February
sportswear—January, February, and July
spring clothes—March (after Easter)
stoves—April and November
suits (men's and boys')—April, August, and December
summer clothes—July (after the fourth) and August
television sets—May and June
tires—May and August
toys—December (after Christmas), January, and February
washing machines and dryers—January, February, March, and April
winter clothing—December and February

We also watch food bills very carefully, learning to buy the most economical (which doesn't mean the worst) cuts of meat and to make meatless meals (which can be delicious and nutritious) more often than we used to do, and we stay away more than we used to from restaurants and bars. We learn to be delighted with ourselves for our remarkable ingenuity with leftovers. "Waste not, want not" is a slogan you may have learned in your childhood, and when you apply it to food, becoming inventive enough to whip up delectable concoctions out of practically nothing, it's a boost to the ego as well as to the budget. And it can be done—I know. Perhaps this is a boastful digression, but if so forgive me:

A few years ago my teen-age daughter became concerned with the new ethic—ecology and the simple life and nonviolence

—and decided she should be a vegetarian. I worried about her wasting away since, as I told her, she was going to be in an unusually difficult situation—as a vegetarian who loathed most vegetables. Bacon, chicken, steaks, and hamburgers had been her mainstays for years. But I was determined (being very fond of her) that she should not die of malnutrition, at least not while she was still living with me, so I summoned up every bit of brain and energy I possess to think up menus she would like. And guess what happened? She thrived, I became an imaginative cook for the first time in my life, our meals became more varied and delicious, and our food bills went down—even while inflation was making food prices leap up.

This shouldn't be so surprising. After all, many of the gourmet meals for which the French, Spanish, Armenians, Hungarians, Japanese, Chinese, and other cultures are justly famous originated when housewives had to be frugal. That's why they invented all those gorgeous sauces and seasonings and side dishes and fancy, decorative ways of serving food—to disguise the fact that they were using leftovers and inexpensive cuts of meat, to stretch budgets, and still keep eaters happy.

Bouillabaise, goulash, paella, cacciatore, sukiyaki, teriyaki, stews, casseroles, Spanish omelettes, souffles, crepes suzettes, curries and rice dishes, turkey divan, arroz con pollo, stuffed squash, stuffed cabbage, stuffed peppers, meatballs and meat loaf and pot pies, salads, hors d'oeuvres, smorgasbord, vegetable soups, chowders, apple brown betty, bread pudding, fruit cup, and frothy whipped desserts—the list could go on and on—are all delicious and filling ways to stretch leftovers economically, using little snippets of meat or fish or vegetables or fruit, tidbits sliced and diced and spiced in lovely combinations and swimming in tasty, varied sauces. Yummmmmmmmm.

If we are weight watchers and calorie counters as well as pennypinchers we have a problem, because the more economical food is usually the more fattening. The great food stretchers and enhancers are flour, breadcrumbs, butter, gravy, and cream. And the great filler-uppers that are inexpensive are macaroni, noodles, spaghetti, baked beans, rice, potatoes, breads, biscuits, dumplings, pancakes, waffles—all starch, all fattening. Fortunately, however, modern scientific ingenuity is coming up every day with new low-calorie high-protein versions of many such things, and anyway we can afford occasional splurges. Budgeting calories is like budgeting money: it's the overall expenditure you have to watch carefully, not each individual item. If you go wild at one meal with high-calorie ingredients, your calorie budget need not get overloaded. You can compensate at the next few meals by eating mostly bunny food, and even that is delicious, as all bunnies know.

Figure watchers and budgeters even learn that you can skip a meal now and then and not merely survive—it's good for you. You can go without lunch or just have tea and toast, or coffee and grapefruit, or bouillon and crackers, thus saving money that a lavish and wholly unneccessary spread would have cost you. I am certainly not suggesting that you should starve yourself in order to balance your food budget, but occasional cutting down or fasting is not starving. In almost every modern's life there are large areas of waste (and of waist) and when you become a single parent it behooves you to eliminate or at least reduce these by becoming more efficient, more observant, more selective about where your food money goes—because where it goes is not always becoming, let alone healthful!

There are some economies that are not economical.
Some people always buy the greatest "bargain" and therefore get stuck with shoddy merchandise which breaks quickly and which they have to replace. Thus they end up spending more in the end than if they had bought a higher-priced item in the beginning.

Other people pride themselves on never knowing or caring what anything costs (or worse, they only value things that are highly expensive, like star sapphires and Rolls Royces), and they are thrilled when they have been absurdly extravagant; they figure they'll find the money somewhere (somewhere often being a foolishly fond relative or friend). They seem to consider it proof of how cultured they are if they are unwilling to buy any but the most expensive item among various alternatives, and they kid themselves into thinking they selected it because it's a "better buy." Actually, their taste may be so insecure that they don't have the courage to admit they see no real difference between the two-dollar and ten-dollar versions of the same thing, like the Emperor and his courtiers who didn't dare admit they couldn't see the Emperor's invisible (because nonexistent) new clothes. They think a higher price must automatically mean better quality. The beneficiary of their timidity, ignorance, affectation, and vanity is the manufacturer who issues a high-priced line to appeal to snobs and a lower-priced line to appeal to realists: witness Elizabeth Arden's expensive cosmetics and Elizabeth Post's inexpensive ones which, I understand, are identical except for labeling and packaging. If you really want to know which items are the best buys, buy the monthly magazine and the annual paperback book, *Consumer Reports*; they are not beholden to any advertisers, and they test competitive items and tell you factually what is better or worse about them.

Some people think they have been clever and virtuous by saving money when they haven't in fact saved any at all—like the cartoon wife who comes home and tells her husband elatedly that she has just saved him $500 by buying a mink coat that was marked down from $2,000 to $1,500. It doesn't occur to her that she could have saved a great deal more money by being content with a cloth coat, or even more by making last year's coat serve her for one more year.

This kind of financial Marie Antoinetteism is as foolish as exaggerated parsimony is. Once again, the large and spacious area between outlandish extremes is the place where most of us choose to live and where most of us are fully capable of functioning happily.

Another type of false economy, in my view, is to put off purchasing something you really need, which would save you money if you had it. For instance, if you have an old iron which is scorching all your clothes and linens, it would be much more sensible to buy a new iron than to keep using the old and defective one—even if you have to buy the new one on time and therefore must spend a few more dollars for it than you would spend if you waited until you could afford to buy it outright. In the meantime you will be saving money on un-ruined dresses or shirts or sheets, instead of having to replace them, so you will save more than the cost of the iron.

In inflationary times (and actually every time since money was invented has been inflationary; Samuel Pepys, in the seventeenth century, complained in his diary that the price of theater tickets in London had gone up from a half-penny to a penny or from threepence to sixpence, I don't remember which) it is particularly wise to buy now and pay later. Even with a finance charge added on, since the purchasing power of your dollar is constantly shrinking, you may end up paying less in the future than you would now, in terms of your total spending power. Your dollar will be worth less than the seventy-five cents or whatever it is worth now in five more years, but your pop-up toaster will still be popping up toast. A useful possession is worth more than the piece of paper you buy it with.

It is annoying to have to keep thinking about what things cost, and my idea of one of the greatest delights life could offer me would be to be able to go into good restaurants and look only at the left side of the menu, or to go to a store and buy something merely because I wanted it, without having to look at the price tag before deciding. I cannot stand comparison shopping. If I see a dress I really like, when I need a new one, and it is becoming and not outrageously expensive, I will buy it and enjoy it without worrying about not having checked with every other shop in town to see if perhaps one of them had a dress that would have been an even better buy. I also refuse to drag myself from supermarket to supermarket to find out if I can pick up a can of soup somewhere for eleven instead of twelve cents.

Some women travel far afield in quest of a store which has

greater bargains than its equivalent in their own neighborhood —and they forget to calculate the cost of carfare in the total price of what they buy. My mother used to do this at Macy's. She would come in from New Jersey to shop there, instead of patronizing a local shop, and she was always overjoyed because she got a slight discount on the books she bought at Macy's. But she never remembered to include transportation costs in their total price, although her train and taxi fares more than canceled out the discounts. That's fine if you enjoy traveling around on trains, ferries, subways and buses, taxis and trolleys, as she did; but if so, recognize that you are spending money on a diversion, not saving any money. You may still be demonstrating financial wizardry, however, because the discount is helping to pay for your recreation.

Time should be budgeted as well as money. One reason so many women tend to budget in a niggling, detailed, penny-wise and pound-foolish way is that they completely forget to budget their time. They don't realize what men know, that time is worth money.

Of course, it's understandable that most women forget this economic fact, because for such a large part of their lives they work without receiving any paychecks or even tips. Economists and insurance companies have occasionally computed the financial worth of wives and mothers and have demonstrated that if they were paid for every bed they make, every meal they cook, every item they wash and iron or mend, every errand they do, and so forth, hardly any husband could ever afford a wife. Chase Manhattan Bank did a study several years ago which concluded that the average American housewife works at least 99.6 hours a week (in contrast to the average 40-hour work week of people who "work") and that the tasks she performs are worth over $10,000 a year. Another, more recent, study estimated that housewifery encompasses at least twelve occupations, which are valued on the open market at a minimum of $257.53 a week—and that adds up to $14,391.56 a year! One of the several reasons that housework has so little prestige and is so disliked by many women is that it receives no monetary reward commensurate with the number of hours that have to be spent on it, so when women start thinking about the financial value of their time they get pretty resentful—as any issue of *Ms. Magazine* will prove. Better to suppress all thought of time-as-money when you have to spend long hours working hard for no pay.

Yet even if you don't realize or believe that a specific amount of your time is (or ought to be) worth a specific amount of money, you should still take time into account when managing your money. Remember that time has its own built-in budget: there are only twenty-four hours in a day. Therefore, if you spend an hour trotting from store to store in search of minuscule bargains, whether that hour is worth anything to you in monetary terms or is merely a never-to-be-repeated opportunity-provider, it might pay you to ask yourself if there was something you could have been doing during that hour that would have been more productive and constructive, as well as more fun.

A budget should be flexible, not rigid. It should be a helpful tool, not a slave driver. An approximation, not something to be followed as literally as a timetable. A set of guidelines rather than unbending, unvarying rules.

I do not believe in budgeting down to the very last dime or penny. This makes budgeting so irksome that you are apt to give it up altogether, in disgust and despair. It is quite true that pennies added together do turn into dollars, and if you habitually buy things telling yourself they only cost "about a dollar and a half" when actually they cost $1.97 you are soon going to be in financial trouble without having any idea of how you got there, but it is boring and time-wasting to keep track of every penny you spend, and it's unnecessary. Use the rounding-off method the income tax people recommend: ignore pennies that are less than fifty cents but add another dollar when listing items over fifty cents (thus listing a $1.97 purchase as a $2.00 one and a $1.47 purchase as a $1.00 one)—they will average out.

Look at the *total* picture instead of becoming fanatical about any one item. Figure out what your daily, weekly, or monthly resources are and then move with happy freedom and imagination within that general framework, instead of thinking "I must never, never, never spend more than such-and-such for such-and-such."

I mentioned calories a minute ago, and the comparison with pennies holds. There is no reason for calorie counters not to indulge once in a while in a malted milk or chocolate cake if they feel their lives are blighted without the occasional presence of that kind of treat. On days when they have a malted or a piece of cake they must realize they have used up a lot of calories on that one item and then go extra easy on others, but they can still manage to stay within a sensible and healthful total calorie count for the day or week. Similarly, you can stay within a moderate budget and still have a spree now and then, if you keep your wits about you. Just realize that each splurge means that some other purchase must be postponed or eliminated.

Some "nonessentials" are essential! Just as all work and no play makes Jack a dull boy, a life with nothing in it but necessities would make Jack an unspeakably gloomy, unfortunate boy. A few "unnecessary" things are absolutely necessary for happiness—so provide for some in your budget.

It is false economy (and psychology) to think "I can't afford this thing I want so much because I must spend all my money, as well as all my time and energy, on my poor suffering children who are now deprived of their birthright, namely two parents." As I said earlier in connection with social life, you have needs as much as your children do, and if you don't meet yours you won't be able to meet theirs. Furthermore, one of their needs is a happy parent (I'm sure I have said that before too), and if you don't provide that you will hurt them far more than by spending a little money on yourself. I think every single parent should budget for pleasure just as carefully as for rent and food. (One good way to make this possible, if you don't have enough money to be able to hire sitters regularly, is to arrange a sitter-exchange cooperative with some friends or neighbors; instead of paying each other in money you swap times together.)

I remember one period when I was feeling low and my remedy was to subscribe to a florist's service. Each week I received at my door a stunning, huge, mixed bouquet. Sometimes the flowers lasted so long that I had several weeks' worth at a time. My living room looked like a star's dressing room on opening night. My children and I loved it! It is impossible to be in a room glowing with colorful flowers and feel gloomy—at least I think so. Some people might have considered this a silly extravagance at a time when I was having to watch money carefully, but I certainly didn't. I gladly made other economies instead, to enable me to live for a while in my own private botanical garden. Flowers are not *necessary,* but having them around did more to buoy my spirits than "sensible" use of my money could have.

Once again I realize that every generalization needs to be qualified. The advice to budget for pleasure obviously cannot be followed in every case because some people's incomes are so severely limited that they literally have no room at all in their budgets to provide for *any* extras. But if you had the money to buy this book you are probably not in that dire a situation—though, come to think of it, you could have picked it up from a free public library or gotten it from a friend. If so, that is an example of another reassuring fact: *There are many things we can get for ourselves that don't cost any money at all!*

It is certainly not as easy to get along without money nowadays as it was in the days of barter, but we don't always need nearly as much as we think we do. In any reasonably large town there are exhibits, concerts, museums, special events held in parks and schools and hotels and banks and stores and town halls, parades, fairs, private gatherings and happenings—all kinds of pleasurable activities and places which can provide delightful recreation without our spending a cent. Keep alert for announcements of such things and take full advantage of them.

In the country people are even less dependent on money than in urban areas. There are so many enjoyable things to do and see outdoors during every season of the year that life need not be joyless, even when we are flat broke.

Obviously, however, money is a very nice thing to have. Money can't buy happiness but it sure helps.

Another thing that helps is using credit—with common sense, with gratitude, and without guilt.

I know that some people seem to be temperamentally incapable of possessing charge accounts or credit cards. As soon as they have one they overbuy and find themselves heavily in debt and, eventually, in law courts. But to a rational person these are blessings, and can even save you money.

With credit cards you can buy things you need when you need them, or when they are on sale, instead of having to do without them for a long time because you have no cash. Credit cards make it possible to operate more freely and still stay safely within a total budget. They make it easier to budget because you can provide that each month you are going to pay Mastercharge (or some other credit firm, American Express, or whatever) fifty dollars, let's say, and this can take care of all of your purchases even during months when you have extra expenses coming up which might otherwise throw your budget out of whack. You also have receipts which give you a clear, accurate, and detailed record of what you have spent, so you can see just how you're doing. Every month go over the receipts and note where (if) you have been too extravagant or where you have been unnecessarily stingy, and you can get a better view of your overall situation, I think, than when you have been spending cash and can't remember where on earth it all went.

Another important factor is that using credit means you don't have to carry around as much cash as you would otherwise.

Carrying lots of cash is dangerous; you can get held up, and you can lose it. I see no reason to take either risk. Of course your credit card could get lost or stolen too, but unlike loose cash it can be insured ahead of time so that the loss is not a disaster. So I pay for gas, clothes, appliances, vacations, school bills, all large purchases, with credit cards, using them with a clear conscience and with admiration for the clever people who thought them up as a way of helping me manage and stretch my money. If they are getting rich off of me, that's all right with me. They deserve to. And, after all, there is no finance charge at all if I pay my bill in full when I get it, only when I *need* to postpone it.

Of course credit must be used with sensible precautions, as must any type of borrowing. Don't borrow from finance companies which charge exhorbitant rates of interest. It is easy to find out which those are. Borrowing from a bank (better still, if you can, a credit union) is always more economical than borrowing from a lending company, and borrowing from a reliable lending company is inevitably much safer and less expensive than borrowing from a fly-by-night outfit. And never borrow more than you can comfortably manage to repay—you *do* have to repay the money you borrow, after all!

Having something in the way of security—a car, home, or regular income—as a back-up is, of course, essential in order for you to be allowed to borrow or use credit. Sometimes this is a real problem. Divorcees and other single women sometimes find that companies are reluctant to extend credit to them. One of the women's lib organizations—NOW—is now working on this problem. It's a very worthy cause. Any woman who needs help with her financial worries might join NOW and help them help her and her sisters in their fight to get stores and legislators to end this discrimination.

One of the nicest things about credit is that it builds upon itself. Used sensibly it can be an extremely useful household aid because once you have established credit at a bank or shop by paying promptly for charged items it is that much easier for you to get credit at another place, making it easier and easier for you to manage your finances.

But there is one way of getting credit which I think should never be used except in a life-and-death emergency—and I would hesitate even then. Getting a co-signer to back up a loan is, I think, too great an imposition on friendship. Even with the best intentions and prospects of paying the bill back without the slightest difficulty, it would worry me that my friend might get stuck. Therefore a person with no tangible assets that a bank or credit company will accept as collateral, and with no regular income, is wisest not to try to use credit at all. In that case my only advice is to get busy and change that situation as fast as possible.

Saving sensibly is as important as spending sensibly.

It is essential to manage our money in such a way that we put aside a certain amount for the future. The specific amount will vary according to our temperament, assets, and obligations, but *something* must be put aside for extra-large expenses that we know are coming up and for possible emergencies, medical and otherwise. Even on a very small income you should put away a few dollars each week or month. Just pretend your income is smaller by that amount, and forget about what's accumulating in the savings bank until you have a big medical bill or your children need braces or are going to college.

Some people, particularly if they have never been used to handling money, are unable to see even as far as a week ahead! If they are paid by the month their money is invariably gone by the middle of the month. If they are paid by the week, they are broke by Wednesday. They are constantly being taken by surprise by next month's phone bill, electricity bill, even by the rent, and have to run around scrounging from friends and living in fear of having the phone taken out, the electricity cut off, or of being evicted.

Granted that there are occasions when one gets in an unavoidable jam, on the whole there is little excuse for not being able to pay for regular and predictable items. If you are on a salary or have any other source of regular income, you know exactly how much money you can count on each month and it is a matter of quite simple arithmetic to see how much of it must be set aside, not to be touched for anything except fixed needs. If your basic unavoidable expenses leave nothing over, or exceed your income, then obviously it's time to move to a less expensive home fast and take other drastic measures, but if the figures make any sense at all on paper then it is ridiculous to act wide-eyed with amazement each month when the regular bills come in. When I talk of spending money flexibly I mean the money you have *after* you have put aside whatever you require for basics.

If you have an irregular, completely unpredictable income *and* unpredictable but unavoidable expenses, that's a different and very special problem, of course. The unpredictable is, by definition, unpredictable. This is why you have to put aside some money when you have it, in order to have it there when unpredictable needs arise. In good weather you must remember, and provide for, the possibility of rainy days.

Some people, however, save so much money for rainy days that they never have any to help them enjoy sunny days. Saving can become a neurotic, miserly compulsion rather than a sensible precaution. To save so much that you have nothing left over to spend is as foolish as doing the opposite. So, after you have managed to get yourself a comfortable financial cushion, sit on it and relax. That's what a cushion is for. Enjoy the money you have left—spend it before inflation makes it worth only half or a third of its present value.

How much is enough? The rule of thumb that most financial advisors recommend is to have enough money available in one form or another—in savings banks, insurance policies and/or bonds that have cash value, mutual funds, and other relatively safe securities—to tide you over a six months' period. In most cases that would be enough to keep your family afloat during an emergency, while you recovered from an illness or looked for a new job. Work toward that amount—and when you reach it, halt! Don't keep on saving more and more in a quest for security that keeps becoming more elusive the more you accumulate because you are never satisfied and don't feel safe no matter how much you have put away.

A six months' cushion won't be enough if you ever become permanently invalided or totally disabled, or if you get one of those awful illnesses that involve a year in a hospital and enormous doctors' bills—but nothing would be. If something like that happens to you it could wipe out six years of savings as easily as six months, and there would be nothing you could do about it. You'll just have to go on relief a little sooner than you would if you had a larger bank account. Even extremely wealthy people are not immune from that kind of apocalyptic disaster. So don't ruin your life today by trying to pay in advance for ruin tomorrow. You will probably never be either a millionaire or a pauper, so a nice, sensible, in-between amount of money is all you realistically need to (or can) set aside.

It is our daily bread, not an eternal supply, that we are supposed to pray for. To provide oneself with an entire lifetime of security ahead of time is impossible. Single parenthood should have taught you by now that the future is full of surprises. You almost certainly did not expect ten or fifteen years ago that you would today be a single parent. Equally, you cannot possibly know today what you will be doing ten or fifteen years from now. So you cannot anticipate all of your future expenses.

The myth that anyone can do this is something insurance companies like to foster, because this gets us to give them so much money that they can get rich even if we can't. If we obeyed all of their admonitions literally we would be in the poorhouse trying to stay out of there. We'd have to spend so much money on insurance that we might just as well go ahead and have some of the financial emergencies the insurance is meant to protect us from, because it wouldn't cost us any more to meet some of them than it would to try to avoid them all. Don't buy indefinite amounts of life insurance, health insurance, hospital insurance, accident insurance, fire insurance, burglary insurance, automobile insurance, liability insurance, cyclone insurance (what about insurance insurance, in case the insurance company goes out of business?). Each of these is something it may be important to have a certain amount of, but if you are looking for total protection against *everything* all you are ever going to find is a mirage.

If your finances are so precarious that they are literally "uncreditable" and your budget is so tight that there is no money at all to set aside for savings and to spend on small treats like movies, toys, magazines, and a little sheer nonsense now and then, find out how you can alter that situation as quickly as possible—by moving, or by taking a job, or, if you already have a job, by taking on a supplementary job on weekends or one evening a week, or by figuring out how to make yourself so esteemed by your boss that you get a raise, or by looking for a *better* job.

Don't spend precious time in futile fretting. Find some way to bring more money into your life, via an imperfect but temporary arrangement if necessary while working out a long-range goal and strategy. But don't delay.

As one of the posters that are so popular these days truthfully says: Today is the first day of the rest of your life. You have twenty-four hours to live!

Don't waste time *or* money. Spend them both—well!

13

SUPPORTING YOURSELF:
Getting—and holding—a job

Unless you are so lucky that you have inherited wealth, the chances are that in order to enjoy living you must do something to earn a living. Also, even if you are already earning a living, the chances are that you could and would enjoy living more if you earned a better living.

How can you add to your income?

If the first answer that pops into your head is "play the stock market" you had better have (1) a strong love of gambling; (2) a large savings account on tap, so that if you lose money you won't mind; (3) a fairly sophisticated knowledge of business and finance; (4) a trustworthy financial advisor. Almost everyone knows that, by and large, stocks increase in value slightly faster than the rise in the cost of living, so that investors are usually able to beat, or at least keep up with, inflation better than noninvestors are. But everyone also knows that stocks can go down as well as up, so buying them is not a good way to get rich quick or to ensure staying comfortably well-off unless you already have enough money so that you can afford to take risks. In other words, the rich can get richer by investing in the market, but the poor don't dare.

A paying job, doing work at which you are skilled, provides much better security than most "securities" do.

People who have never acquired any marketable skills or who have received only partial or highly specialized training for which there is not now much demand (like a Ph.D. in Latin or Greek) can get pretty frustrated and worried when they have to support a family. Some women have concentrated all their energies on creating a home for their families, so that if the day comes when they need to get a paying job they don't have the faintest idea of how to go about it. And some men have worked so exclusively in one particular field that if the day comes when that field is closed to them because of changes in the world's economic or political structures, they have no idea of what else they could do.

No one is to blame for having been shortsighted if they honestly thought they were doing "the right thing" and it turned out not to be, but blamelessness, alas, does not enable one to avoid the consequences of a mistake. So if this has happened to you, learn from this mistake not to let your children make the same one. Encourage them to acquire more than one interest and to develop more than one skill. Overspecialization is mentally narrowing and can be financially disastrous.

However, let's say that, in your case, this has happened, either because you were lazy or badly advised in the past. It is now too late to do anything about what has happened or should have happened or could have happened, and you cannot afford to spend your present or future wringing your hands over past foolishness. Start right away to make up for lost time.

You may need to go out and look for some job that doesn't require any special skills; and/or you may need to get some training which will qualify you for a job you would like better (and which would pay better) than an unskilled job; and/or you may need to study your personal traits to find out which, if any, could be transformed into a financial asset even though you have never hitherto thought of it as one.

SUPPORTING YOURSELF | 233

Income-producing work can sometimes be done right at home. There are a number of inspiring examples of women who found themselves stuck at home but who triumphed—not in spite of, but as a result of, this apparent limitation. The famous, delicious, and nutritious Pepperidge Farm bread was originally the creation of a widow who found herself in financial need. The only thing she knew how to do was cook—so she proceeded to turn her one skill into a huge financial asset. There are sauces, soups, salad dressings, pickles, chutneys, jams, jellies, breads, muffins, cookies, candies, cakes, and pies on the market today which have brought handsome incomes to other women who also found themselves in this predicament.

The multi-million-dollar diaper service industry, to which all of today's mothers are so beholden, also started this way. A young widow found herself trapped at home with preschool children to take care of and therefore no way to go out and earn a living, so she decided to sound out her neighbors to see if any of them would be willing to pay her to wash their babies' diapers, since she was home anyway washing her own babies' diapers and had a washing machine. A great many mothers were overjoyed to learn that someone was willing to wash their babies' diapers for them. Word got around quickly and she was in a short time so inundated with dirty diapers that she had to hire assistants. The demand for her services kept growing and soon she was launched into Big Business. She made a lot of money—as did many other enterprising people, both men and women, who in other parts of the country got the same idea around the same time. It was "an idea whose time had come."

The now very popular and prosperous telephone-answering services were also begun by people who had to earn a living from their homes. Men and women who have a telephone but no way of getting outdoors—because they are invalids, or elderly, or the mothers of very small children—now earn regular money for themselves this way.

Another possibility: Many people who know how to type run

a typing service at home, getting customers by placing ads in local papers. This can be a fairly lucrative home-based operation if you live in a university town where lots of student theses and scholarly articles and books are written.

Still another possibility: Maybe you could open a baby- or child-sitting service in your home, since you already have a supply of toys and books, crayons and building blocks. If you like children and would like to have more playmates for your own children, take out an ad in the local paper and see if there aren't several busy mothers who will be delighted at the opportunity to pay you for watching their children along with yours for several hours, mornings or afternoons or both, every week.

Giving piano or guitar or singing or dancing or language lessons is another set of possibilities for some people. Sewing—dressmaking and tailoring and mending—is another home-based activity which might be turned to profit if you are good at it.

Maybe you can think of some other needed service which no one else has yet thought of, which could make you rich or at least comfortable. It needn't be original as long as it's useful and well done. Senator Charles Percy supported himself through college by providing a convenient, quick, reliable, inexpensive laundry and dry-cleaning service that included pickups and deliveries for his fellow schoolmates. He started his freshman year as one of the poorest boys on campus and by his senior year was one of the wealthiest—and when a Chicago businessman heard about what he had done he was so impressed with his enterprise and efficiency that he offered him a job in his company, in which successive promotions eventually led to his becoming a millionaire! How about that for an inspiring example?

There are some thriving mail-order businesses which are operated from home base. People manufacture and sell their own products (arts and crafts, sewing materials, food delicacies, and so forth) or ally themselves with publishers of books or magazines, manufacturers of cosmetics or hosiery, wholesalers of stationery and greeting cards and other gift items. They conduct profitable retail businesses without having to step outside their homes. The investment needed to start off is often surprisingly small. Many companies give their merchandise on consignment, which means that you don't have to lay out more than a small initial down payment, and then after you have sold some merchandise you simply give them a small percentage of your earnings.

This is, of course, a more chancy way to earn a living than holding down a salaried job. Your income is apt to have seasonal fluctuations, involving much overtime work at peak seasons and pretty slim pickings at others. However, if you really cannot find a way to get out of your house, and you need to bring some money into the house, you could at least try such a thing for a while to see if it pays you.

If you are in need of regular money that comes in predictably in fairly large amounts, this type of thing may not be your best prospect. *An outside job (full- or part-time) for a solvent corporation is a more consistent income producer.*

If you are the mother of preschoolers you may hate the thought of leaving them during the day and may find it hard to get reliable people to take care of them while you are absent, but there are more and more good day-care centers these days for the children of working mothers. If there is none conveniently located for you, perhaps you and some friends who also have small children can organize a cooperative one, with each of you helping out at the center one day a week. Some companies are willing to adjust working hours so that employees can manage an arrangement like that. Also, many teen-age baby-sitters are willing and able to help out after school hours, if you find a job that has afternoon and/or evening hours. Contact a school or social service organization or employment agency for information.

If you have very young children still at home and you can't or don't want to leave them all day, you will be glad to know that the part-time job market has grown in recent years. Many firms are willing to employ people just for the morning, afternoon, or evening—and night work, when the children are asleep and sitters are available, has the advantage, usually, of paying double, at overtime rates. Hours can often be worked out at mutual convenience, if you get a job in a restaurant or a store. And many jobs that pay by the hour permit employees to stay home on days or weeks when their school-age children have holidays.

Some large companies have even begun to do what is widely done in some other countries: set up crèches where employees can leave their children under trained supervision during working hours. In cases like this, your children may end up even better off without you than they now are with you (in this case you will probably have a new problem, not financial but emotional: jealousy).

What kind of outside job can a person get without previous training or experience?

If you are young and attractive you can probably get a job without previous working experience fairly easily—as a clerk, receptionist, attendant, or usher somewhere. If you are not young and pretty but middle-aged and droopy, it won't be quite that easy, although older people are still very welcome in many jobs if they are intelligent, friendly, and efficient. More and more companies these days are willing to hire people, including older ones, who have had almost no training, if their *attitudes* are right. The once insisted-upon skills of shorthand and rapid typing are no longer always demanded of secretaries, for instance; in many businesses there is such a continuing need for secretarial help that, reluctantly but realistically, executives will now employ people of reasonable intelligence and goodwill even when they are not fully qualified technically.

Don't consider it beneath your dignity, when you really need a job, to take one which involves running errands or making meals or doing housework. These things are not beneath your dignity when you do them for your own family, so isn't it really a rather silly affectation to think they are demeaning when you do them for other people? Dignity is a quality a person possesses, or lacks, within himself or herself. It is not dependent on the way in which one earns a living. One can be a charming waiter or a good cook, a skillful gardener, a reliable chauffeur, a thoughtful companion to an invalid or elderly or handicapped person, a cherished nanny, a pleasant maid in a motel or hotel, an efficient friendly hospital attendant, an invaluable all-round general assistant, an efficient and honest repairman, a capable superintendent of an apartment house (getting your rent free), a courteous doorman or elevator man, an energetic messenger or garbage man, a pleasant cleaning woman—a nice *anything*—and in none of these posts does one lose an iota of dignity if one does the work well and cheerfully. The concept, much too widespread in our culture, that service work is inherently degrading is utterly ridiculous. Any mother or father really ought to know better.

Housework got its currently bad reputation because so many housewives treated their servants so abominably that the servants got to prefer the most arduous or monotonous factory work, *any* kind of work, to working in someone's house. This doesn't speak well for housewives but it partially explains why there is now such a shortage of houseworkers that anyone willing to make beds or cook meals or dust furniture can almost always find jobs. Housework pays above minimum wage (except when a housewife does it for herself!). And ever since a Norwegian nanny married a Rockefeller and one of Jackie Kennedy's cooks wrote a best-selling book, it has been obvious that even women of above-average intelligence and glamor can be nursemaids and servants. A recent example is Betty Hutton, formerly an adored movie star, now a cook in a church rectory —who claims she's much happier now than when she had the world at her dancing feet.

Many aspects of housework and maintenance work have become professionalized in our time: dressmakers, tailors, seamstresses, cooks, caterers, bartenders, window washers, carpenters, repairmen, and cleaners now work on salary in separate business establishments, specializing in one aspect of what used to be lumped together under the general category of housekeeping or "service." When the work is specialized it somehow is considered to have a higher status than when it is part of an unspecialized "servant's" tasks.

There really are many possibilities for work that pays, even in a period of economic recession, if one makes up one's mind to accept the fact that one must *work*. The work available may not be what you would freely have chosen if you were not in a hurry to establish yourself on a sound financial footing, but whether you make a temporary or permanent association there are many, many things that most reasonably competent people can do to earn money. Here are a few more examples, in case you still need to be convinced:

Without any previous training or work experience you might be able to get hired as a waitress or waiter, or as a hostess or counter girl or busboy or bartender in a nearby restaurant, or you might get work as a salesclerk in a shop near your home. There are definite skills required in such jobs, and some leading restaurants and shops will not take on anyone who has had no previous work in a comparable establishment, but many others are less fussy and are willing to give on-the-job training. The telephone company and local supermarkets are two other possibilities. All you need to know how to do is to speak clearly and courteously on a phone, or how to count and add. They will teach you the rest. Banks, retail shops, and factories also often provide brief training courses (two or three weeks long) for new employees.

If you know how to drive a car you might inquire about getting a job driving a taxi or bus or teaching driving at a driver's ed school. No doubt that is "hack work" but it sometimes pays very well. Women as well as men are driving taxis and buses these days. In some cities the demand for drivers is so great that you can name your own hours. Many people (especially schoolteachers and actors) supplement their regular salaries by driving cabs on evenings, weekends, and/or holidays.

Other places where people with no previous job experience can sometimes find work, especially if they enjoy being around children and are good at it, are schools and community centers. Public schools have a nasty way of requiring education degrees and licenses, and of course it helps enormously if, when you were in college, you had enough forethought to major in psychology or education, but in many private schools it is not essential to have a teaching certificate or any other specific academic qualifications—not because private schools have lower standards but because they have different ones. They are more interested in your personality and your rapport with children and general intelligence than in your pedagogical training.

If you are not qualified to be a teacher there are supplementary jobs around many educational institutions. You might be a teacher's assistant, a recreation leader, a clerical worker associated with a school, a chauffeur running the school bus, or a school cook or lunchroom attendant. Lots of these posts are filled by volunteers or by mothers in return for reduced or free tuition for their children (and that's not a bad idea, either, if you have the time), but some of them are salaried jobs.

Camp counseling doesn't usually pay more than room and board, but even so that is a possibility to remember if you would like to provide a beautiful place for you and your children to stay during the summer. A camp or resort job is well worth thinking of, at least as a temporary one-shot possibility. As for wintertime, many boarding schools, colleges, and other institutions (hospitals, nursing homes, rehabilitation centers, etc.) provide room and board in addition to a small salary to people who are good with children and/or at housework—not simply maids and housekeepers and grounds attendants but supervisors ("house parents") are in considerable demand in many areas. This kind of position is one which many widows and ex-wives have found makes it possible for them to live in an extremely attractive, even luxurious, atmosphere, in a pleasant community among bright young people, which is as good for their children as it is for themselves.

Sometimes, however, the best answer to the question, "How can you get a job that doesn't require training?" is: "Don't." If you are not in urgent need of money, the smartest thing to do is (1) to think about what kind of job you would really like the best, instead of taking a stop-gap that may soon have you bored and restless, and then (2) to go out and get the kind of training you need for that type of job.

Among the most reliable income-producing jobs that are almost always available in every town for qualified people are hospital jobs and secretarial jobs. Don't try to become a registered nurse right way; their training requires investing several years, but take a nurses' aid or practical nursing course. Or take a secretarial course—not a Katie Gibbs one that involves full-time study for two years, but a crash course. If you have a normal IQ and apply yourself seriously, you can learn enough typing and shorthand to be a passable secretary in a few months.

What should you do if you get a job and then hate it? Obviously, if you can afford to, walk out of it and get another. But if you hate that one too and leave and get another, and then hate that one too, the chances are that your discontent is the fault of your attitude, not of the jobs.

Whatever kind of job you have, cultivate a constructive attitude. One of the most important ingredients of success both in job holding and job hunting is the determination to do whatever is necessary (and a little extra) eagerly, not complainingly or halfheartedly. Don't be late every morning and a clock-watcher every afternoon, and spend half your days in the john or taking coffee breaks or making personal phone calls, if you want your boss to like you enough to keep you, let alone promote you or recommend you later to someone else for a better job.

In order to provide bread and butter for your family's table you may have to endure an extremely dull job for a while—working on a factory assembly line, for instance. (It's nice to know, if it should come to that, that most big manufacturers have learned how much more efficient happy workers are than unhappy ones, so they try to make up for boring work by providing compensations: attractive lounges, recreation rooms with ping pong and billiard tables, frequent coffee breaks, music while you work, generous vacations and insurance policies and pensions, etc.)

Another thing that it pays (literally) to know is that the more boring work is, the better it may pay. I know a boy who spent a summer enjoying himself during the day and working nights checking Coke bottles as they came off the assembly line to see if they were all filled to a uniform level (I bet it never occurred to you when you bought soft drinks that anyone has to do that!). Because he did it at night he got double pay, and at the end of the summer he had a bigger bank account than his mother, who was a high-paid magazine editor.

If you have a dull job but really need it and cannot afford to give it up, hang in there bravely, trying to enjoy the people you work with even if you can't enjoy the work, and stash your money away as rapidly as possible in order to speed the day when you can leave and move on to something else. In the very mean meantime consider the possibility of taking on an *extra* job that is entirely different, on weekends or one evening a week —not only to make your savings pile up faster but to give yourself a needed change of pace. You may think this would be too tiring, but a change of activity is often more restful than rest is. Many of us who think we are too tired to undertake more hard work are in truth merely so bored that we are drained. If we did something interesting which demanded great energy of us, suddenly the energy would be there. So if you are tied to a boring job, an unboring part-time supplementary job might help to brighten your outlook.

Another thing to do is to challenge yourself to find something interesting in what bores you. If you know enough about why and how things are what they are, you can almost always discover something interesting about them. Also, almost all people enjoy doing anything they are really very good at and hate doing things they are not good at. Therefore my slogan is:

Harder is easier. Work harder and the job will seem easier. Trying to get by on a job with a minimum of attention can be utterly exhausting. It takes a tremendous amount of energy to pull yourself through a boring day! But when you are willing to spend some of your natural energy digging into the work instead of resisting it and protesting against it, the day will speed by twice as fast as it would otherwise.

If you need to take a special course to qualify for a job you know you would enjoy much more than your current one, take advantage of the few free hours you have to take that course. If you are tied up all day long you may be able to take night courses, or a home correspondence course. Follow your interests in picking courses. How about one in photography or journalism or interior decoration or horticulture? If you love to garden, why not get yourself qualified for a career in landscape gardening or, less ambitiously, for a job in a florist's shop?

And when you have a job, know clearly why you have it and therefore don't complain endlessly about its inevitable limitations. *All jobs have annoying and difficult aspects. To dwell on these simply increases the boredom, annoyance, and aversion one feels.*

When you are doing a job you really dislike, simply for the paycheck, keep your eyes focused sharply on that check. Realize this is why you are doing it, and if this is the case, save as much of your salary each week as you possibly can, so you can reach a point where you can afford to quit and look for something better to replace it. Until then, do the work as uncomplainingly as you can—because *you* will suffer more from your complaints than anyone else will, and why suffer more than necessary? Life provides enough suffering unasked, without our deliberately accentuating it.

I said "quit it" because usually it is very hard to job-hunt while holding down a full-time job. There just aren't enough hours in the day. Many people have successfully used lunch hours or Saturdays to track down and land better jobs while employed full-time, but this is almost as hard as stuffing yourself with two Thanksgiving dinners on the same day. However, you still don't need to feel permanently trapped, even if you are at present in a job which is so fatiguing and demanding that it doesn't leave you any time for job hunting. Just save your money like mad until you can walk away a free person—and better luck next time!

Attitude is usually more important than previous training, both in holding down and in acquiring a job. If, somehow, you can get yourself to radiate confidence and goodwill, you can even find job hunting an interesting job—a sort of suspenseful treasure hunt. It gets you inside some fascinating places you would probably never otherwise have any opportunity to visit, and you meet many extremely interesting people.

What makes job hunting so harrowing to some people is that they approach it in fear and trembling, as if they were beggars about to be kicked, feeling so sure they aren't going to get the job they want that they guarantee that they won't. They enter each office with a hangdog expression, or with the kind of stiff fixed nervous smile that people used to put on their faces in the days when cameras worked so slowly you had to hold your expression five minutes. Or they try so hard to act more confident than they feel so that they appear aggressive and arrogant rather than relaxed and pleasant.

Of course, it is much easier to know that charm and confidence are qualities you should radiate than it is to succeed in radiating them, but if you can persuade yourself not to feel fearful, and not to feel guilty, about the fact that you are looking for a job, and if you can recall what your assets are and manage to reveal them in a good light, displaying your best points to advantage and slyly concealing your weakest ones (the way you used to do when you first went out dating and turned on all your charms), you can find job hunting not merely unharrowing but actually fun.

When you are job hunting, don't look on yourself as a nuisance or a charity case. If you do, that is how you will come across. Don't be belligerent or over-cocky either. Don't assume that because you need a job someone has the duty to give it to you. Examine your interests and talents realistically, to see where they would usefully fit into the demands of that particular job—if they wouldn't, admit it and be glad you won't get the job.

Be businesslike. Make appointments through secretaries—and for goodness' sake don't snub the secretaries and act as if you think you are wasting your time if you don't see the top boss; secretaries who like you can be useful allies and spies for you, and those who get mad at you can ruin your chances with their boss. Be courteous. Be reliable. Come on time to an appointment. Write thank-you letters and reminders afterward. Don't be craven but do be appreciative of the time people give you. Speak up clearly about why the job appeals to you and why you think you could handle it well, but don't go on and on, chattering aimlessly. (Some unemployed people get talking jags whenever they meet a new person). Your interviewer is probably very busy, so don't take up so much of his time that he gets annoyed with you. Be serious, yet relaxed; warm, but not coy; enthusiastic, but not gushy; smiling, but not giggly; friendly, but not presumptuous; intelligent, but not pompous. In short, use all the social skills you have acquired through your years of growing and socializing.

Also, get your friends to help you. Don't be afraid to "use" friends as business contacts. Everyone in the world who has gotten anywhere has made use of personal contacts at times. There is a big difference between consulting people sensibly and exploiting them unfairly and no reason on earth why you should hesitate to let people you know, who could possibly give you a helpful lead, realize you are looking for a job. Discuss your interests, skills, and limitations with them, frankly and objectively, and see if they have anything useful to suggest. Unwillingness to accept advice and other forms of help—as I said when speaking of self-reliance—is not merely foolish, it's a form of ingratitude.

It is part of that phony "I can manage all by myself" syndrome which is really arrogance masquerading as independence. If you are too hung-up to be able to accept help for your own sake, accept it for the sake of your children; then, instead of feeling parasitical and opportunistic, you can feel very virtuous. Besides, it's true. Your children need the money you're going to earn.

Once you have a good job, you have another problem at home that you will have to cope with. How do you juggle outside work and partnerless parenthood so that neither of them suffers from neglect?

Sometimes a working mother dashes home from her job feeling so guilty about having been away all day that she is in a frenzy for the next few hours, overindulging her family both as companion and slave, waiting on everyone hand and foot, playing with them to the point of exhaustion. Even when her children are naughty she fondles and cuddles them and fails to reprove them, because she dotes on them so much that she thinks their brattiness is "cute" or hardly notices it, or else excuses it because she is afraid their misbehavior is caused by the fact that the poor little things were so lonesome for her and therefore she owes it to them to be extra understanding and tolerant.

Overcompensating for a sense of guilt is as unwise pedagogically as it is uncalled for ethically. First of all, realize that you should not feel guilty about the fact that you have to earn a living. Either feel matter-of-fact about it or feel proud that you are resourceful enough to do what has to be done. Second, realize that the quality of the time you spend with your children is far more important than the quantity. Third, realize that the quality will deteriorate dangerously if you allow your children to be rude and thoughtless and allow yourself to become the kind of person that people are rude and thoughtless to.

If you don't let yourself and your children slip into these bad habits you will find, very likely, that part-time motherhood is more fun for both you and the children than full-time motherhood—because instead of being around each other so much that you get sick of each other and therefore cross, you will all be so glad to see each other when you come home that the time you spend together will be joyous.

For part-time parenthood to work, you have to make sure that your children are well provided for when you're not there, even when they are no longer babies. Psychiatrists and social workers hear many sad tales about the pathetic so-called "door key children" who come home each day from school and let themselves into an empty house, who feel and are neglected. Unless you have a maid or grandmother on hand, spend part of your salary on sitter money. Help a high school girl or boy earn some welcome money by hiring one to come to your house each day after school to be with your children until you get home, helping them with their homework, fixing them juice and a snack, listening to their jokes and keeping them company. This is an extra expense but a necessary one; you have to spend money to earn money. But remember that the government lets you deduct from your income tax as much as $400 a month for daytime child care necessitated by your working.

It is even worse, of course, to leave very small preschool children alone unattended than to leave school-age children alone —in fact, it is not merely worse, it is inexcusable. Even though you wouldn't think of doing it for long stretches of time, you might think of doing it briefly. Many a mother has gone out on a short errand or visit to a neighbor and has come back to find her house or apartment robbed or on fire. This happens far more often than one would like to believe.

Children can get themselves into trouble at incredible speed when they are little. They can turn on the stove and cause gas to escape and start a fire by accident, or they can spill hot food or scalding water on themselves and get severely burned. They can fall and hurt themselves badly, falling out of bed, downstairs, or even out a window. They can get into fights in which they seriously injure themselves or each other. They can lock themselves in closets and become terrified, or even smother. They can roll over in their sleep and entangle themselves in clothing or blankets, or they can play with plastic bags and suffocate in a matter of minutes. They can run outdoors when they shouldn't and get lost or run over or kidnapped.

All of these things sound melodramatic and highly unlikely, but they do happen (every single month three hundred babies in the United States are killed in home accidents), and they only have to happen once. When they do, all the times you took a chance and nothing happened will be no comfort. Read any newspaper regularly and you will one day read a story about a mother who thought such a thing could never happen to her children, and who is now much wiser and much, much, much sadder. *Make it an absolutely solemn, unbreakable rule never to leave small children alone.*

This is sometimes a very difficult rule for a single parent to follow, particularly one who works outside the home. When you have been away all day and come home at night, after putting the children to bed you want to run down to the laundry room in the apartment house basement, because that's the only time you have to do the laundry, or you feel you have to run out to a corner store to pick up something you need. You are sure the children will be perfectly all right because they are safe in bed asleep. Yes, but they may wake up with a nightmare—and suffer no more injury than a thorough emotional shock when they discover nobody is there. And worse things could happen. A burglar could come in, or the child could walk in his sleep, or wake up and wander outside in semi sleep. It is simply not safe, *ever,* to leave tiny children alone. Take them with you to the laundry room or to the store, even though it would be so much quicker and easier for you to go there without having them along, running around and getting in your way.

What happens when you find yourself out of something you need in the evening and you feel that you *have* to go out to the corner store? You tell yourself that it's only a few doors away and you will be back in two minutes. But, again, *don't*—unless you are fortunate enough to have a friendly next-door neighbor you can call, saying, "Would you mind sitting in my living room for five minutes while I run down to the store?" If you have one of those treasures around you are very lucky, and it doesn't hurt now and then to take advantage of luck. But be careful, in that case, not to do it too often or you will press your luck and be resented. Try to work out some kind of systematic reciprocal arrangement, doing as many favors for your neighbor as your neighbor does for you. Maybe you can do her laundry along with yours, or pick things up at the store for her while you're out. That attitude will produce a happy state of affairs for both of you.

But if there is no one nearby whom you can ask to help you out, then you must simply resign yourself to the fact that you are neighborless as well as husbandless or wifeless and consequently cannot leave your children. This can't be said too forcefully.

Parenthood does involve a few sacrifices, after all, and single parenthood at times involves many. I have stressed throughout this book the need to look out for your own interests, because so many single parents tend to go overboard in the opposite direction, but nothing I have said was meant to imply that you should look out for your own interests *instead of* your children's. You must look out for yourself *and* for your children. Don't make sacrifices that are unnecessary, but do make those that are, with good grace.

When are children old enough so they do not always need an older person with them? That varies greatly with the individual child, depending on how reliable, intelligent, and self-sufficient he or she is. You have to know your children well and learn from observation and from gradual loosening of the reins just how much leeway is safe. You must notice when they become capable of learning new skills and of accepting the responsibilities that go with them. Teach them how to cross the street carefully—stopping and looking in both directions, then walking, not running—with you right there beside them at first and then stepping aside, farther and farther out of the picture. Teach them how to use the phone correctly, how to handle appliances safely. Entrust them with errands that are more and more complicated after they have done simple ones well. Never let them think it's "smart" to do things sloppily or incorrectly. And when they become capable of assuming bigger and bigger responsibilities, it is as important for their development that you let them do these things independently as it was earlier to protect them. A mother is a launching pad; it is her function to provide a safe setting from which her children can eventually move off on their own. Her job is to provide such good training that she eventually makes her job obsolete.

As a single parent you simply have to learn to become more observant, as well as more efficient and thoughtful and analytical than many other people have to be. You have to become a skillful juggler. Just as you must plan your social life ahead, to avoid having too many holes in it, and plan your finances ahead to avoid having too many holes in your pocketbook, and plan ahead to prevent and provide for emergencies, you also have to plan ahead in order to take care of little things like household purchases and errands. You have to plan and organize your time. You have to simplify and streamline your housework and your outside tasks.

But never mind. With practice you become more and more efficient. What has to be done can be done. And what can be done can be done well. And what is done well gives the doer pleasure. Life may become more and more demanding for you but at exactly the same rate it will become more and more interesting and gratifying. The more efficient you get about managing both time and money the more things you will find you are able to do. You will have less time to do things in and yet more time to enjoy yourself, because you will learn to take advantage of time that other people waste (and that you too would be wasting if you hadn't become so efficient), so you will get more out of life than most other people do or than you would otherwise.

Time used actively is far, far more enjoyable than empty hours dragging slowly along while you are idle and aimless. Your days and evenings, when you are a working single parent, will be crammed with activity, and you will be so tired at night, most nights, that you will fall asleep quickly and sleep soundly, and therefore wake up the next morning full of pep for another day also crammed with action!

One last point: remember, when planning your time, to plan for periods of relaxation and enjoyment as well as for all the work you have to do. It's just as important to set aside some of your time to be spent on pleasure as it is to set aside some of your money for this.

When thinking of the need to "earn a living" too many people forget that key word *living*. They are so busy earning one that they forget to live one.

Work hard on your job while you are on the job, and get your housework done on weekends as efficiently (which means not only well but also quickly) as you can. But when you come home each afternoon from your job, try to leave all problems connected with the job locked up in your desk or locker, and play just as hard as you have worked—sometimes by yourself, sometimes with your friends, and *lots* of the time with your children.

14
EXTENDING YOURSELF:
Bridging the generation gap

If you and your children are frequently at loggerheads and the generation gap sometimes seems to widen to Grand Canyon size, it may comfort you to remember a remark Mark Twain once made. He had been on the outs with his father during adolescence and considered his father an old fuddy-duddy who didn't know anything about anything. Then a few years passed, as they inevitably do, and he began to understand the reasons for some of his father's attitudes and even, surprise, to agree with some of them and to respect his father. He expressed the change this way: "It's really quite remarkable how much my father learned between the years when I was eighteen and twenty-one!"

Children and parents can be in bitter conflict one year and be the most congenial of friends the next. Today we talk about the generation gap as if we had invented it, but it has always existed to some extent. If it hadn't we would all be living in caves, because no adventurous young people would ever have left their parents' home to try a new way of life. There have always been some things youngsters wanted to do which their parents deplored or forbade, and some things they did not want to do which their parents commanded or demanded. When the youngsters disagreed and disobeyed parents used to punish them, often with terrifying severity, but this didn't necessarily end all disagreements. Many children simply learned to disagree and disobey secretly.

Even in a close marriage between two very compatible people differences arise. When a man and woman become "one flesh" they do not become one soul. Each of two lovers remains a distinct person. As Kahlil Gibran said, "Let there be spaces in your togetherness—trees grow not in each other's shadow." Well, if differences cannot be avoided between people of the same generation who love each other, it is not strange that they are unpreventable among people of different generations. Again quoting Gibran, "Your children are not your children. They belong to the world of tomorrow, which you cannot visit even in your dreams."

It is a mistake to deplore these differences. Without them the world would be a much duller place than it is, and there would be no progress. We want our children to amount to something, don't we? The way they will is the way we ourselves have done so (if we have), by forming standards and values and opinions to live by regardless of, though greatly influenced by, those which have been passed on down to them, adding new perceptions to those they have received. Children are meant to be themselves, not mere replicas of their forebears. And they have a right to be, as we also have.

It's good that tastes and interests vary. If they didn't, as the proverb says, every man would want the same wife. It therefore is not necessary or advisable to feel like ringing the fire alarm or calling the police every time someone in a family wants to do something the others don't like. There is no need for you to permit your children to do things which seriously offend or worry you, but don't take offense or start worrying every single time they like or do things you don't like and wouldn't do. Isn't freedom one of the things you believe in? Personal preferences differ regarding friends, books, music, hair styles, and clothing (ah yes, these days there's the rub!). If you want to live where everyone dresses alike move to China.

EXTENDING YOURSELF | 253

Several years ago there was a hit tune called "Kids" in which a parent asked, "What's the matter with kids today? Why can't they be like we were, perfect in every way?" This is the generations-old complaint of many typical parents. And it is as unrealistic and as unjust today as it was when and if your parents said it about you. If you really have learned to know yourself and have grasped and accepted the idea that you are not now and never have been and never will be perfect, you will not get upset when you find imperfections in your children either. You will have tolerance, patience, compassion, and realistic expectations.

An American Indian adage on the subject of tolerance says, "Let me not criticize my brother until I have walked a mile in his moccasins." This good advice ought to be even easier for us to apply to our children than to our "brothers" because we *have* walked in our children's moccasins (or the equivalent: sneakers or sandals) if we will but remember. Once upon a time we ourselves were small children (99 percent ignorant). Then we were transitional (99 percent bewildered). Now we are "grown-up" presumably (about 90 percent ignorant and bewildered still, but about different, somewhat more complex, and, we think, more important things). But the small children and the adolescents we once were are still alive and kicking inside us, and three-dimensional self-knowledge takes account of past-present-and-future, which means recognizing, recalling, understanding, and integrating all these phases of ourselves.

Many children justly complain (you probably did it too, about your own parents) that "my parents have forgotten what it's like to be young—they don't understand me." And many bitter arguments between the generations, disputes which cause deep wounds and break up families, are caused by that forgetfulness.

Years before the term *teen-ager* was invented there was a generation of "oh you kids" who horrified their parents by drinking illegal bathtub gin in flasks and swallowing goldfish and performing the undignified Charleston and the Black Bottom, to the accompaniment of raucous "vulgar" ragtime music in illegal speakeasies. A few generations before that there was another generation which horrified its parents by dancing the waltz; we may consider this a graceful, sedate dance, but people raised on the minuet thought the waltz was the most immoral thing that had ever been invented, because the dancers put their arms around each other.

When the girls and boys of the twenties outgrew their short flapper skirts and bulky raccoon coats, threw away their flasks and became respectable mothers and fathers, many of them completely forgot how "fast" they had been in their youth and were utterly aghast when their children came along with variations on the theme: "bobby soxers" began "trucking" and doing the Lindy to noisy swing music in nightclubs, swooning over crooners, wearing zoot suits (or if they were girls wearing bright lipstick that their mothers associated only with floozies) and smoking cigarettes and participating in panty raids.

And when that generation, in turn, grew up and calmed down, it also forgot what it had felt like to be "wild" and had hysterics when its own children began wearing love beads and miniskirts and hot pants and sandals (or, at present writing but subject to change at a moment's notice, dirty blue jeans and bare feet or nothing at all if they are "streakers"), writhing and wriggling in the various successors to the twist (I can't keep track of the variations, having been a bunny-hopper myself rather than a teeny-bopper) in discotheques, "making out" in co-ed college dorms (instead of "spooning" in the rumble seats of roadsters like their grandparents, or "necking" in the back row of movie theaters like their parents), smoking pot, and occasionally, perhaps most bewildering of all, burning incense while meditating in the lotus position and listening reverently to rock and roll music.

Fashions in student life change as dramatically as fashions in clothes and music. There are eras when a huge number of students horrify their parents by becoming "pinkos" or "reds" or "leftists" or "militants." And there are periods when they quiet down and parents and teachers start worrying because they are too apathetic.

The student activists who demonstrated in droves for racial justice and against the Vietnam war and other social ills of their day were often rude, noisy, disruptive, and unreasonable in their zeal, but they were no more terrifying to their parents than their forerunners, the Socialists and Communists of the thirties or the anarchists and free-thinkers of the twenties, had been to theirs. Foul language has escalated unpleasantly in recent years, but such things are culturally relative. "Shit" has little more deep significance and shock value today than "hell" had when I was a teen-ager or than "oh fudge!" had when my mother was. My grandparents were as scandalized by "darn" (in fact, by any slang) as my mother was by "damn" and as you are by ———.

Today's young women's libbers are belligerent and noisy, but so were the suffragettes who chained themselves to posts in front of government buildings hoping to get arrested, or the Prohibitionists who went around with hatchets chopping down doors and breaking windows. The Beatles and their hard rock successors are really no more musically vile than nasal Rudy Vallee or slurring Bing Crosby or note-scooping Frank Sinatra or sobbing Johnny Ray or gyrating Elvis Presley seemed to each older generation when they first came on the scene. Boys' long hair and beards may not appeal to you but they should be far less upsetting to you (your great-grandfather and Abe Lincoln and Jesus Christ, after all, also wore them) than girls' short hair was to Irene Castle's contemporaries when she first set a now-worldwide style by bobbing hers (since *no* lady had ever been that shorn before).

I am not defending the clothing or behavior or musical taste of today's (or yesterday's or tomorrow's) teen-agers. I am simply saying that my generation's innovations and my mother's generation's views were no more acceptable to parents then than today's are today. I think that every youngster growing up in a free society makes some crazy experiments during the period of transition between childhood and adulthood. I started to say "and maturity" but maturity is something it really takes an entire lifetime to attain; it does not get handed to us the day we get our voter's registration card or our first driver's license or our first paycheck and officially become adults.

Some of the experiments that adventurous growing people make while they are trying to discover what they like and dislike about the world and about themselves are extremely risky, and parents should certainly do their level best to help teen-agers avoid making mistakes which will produce lasting, irreversible harm. But we have a far better chance of being able to do so if we understand why they feel the need to experiment or even to revolt, and if we preserve some sense of humor and sense of proportion (usually the same thing), allowing them a certain number of safe safety valves, than we do if we criticize or forbid everything they do that we dislike.

Being "tolerant" and "understanding" does not mean allowing everything, as some permissive and simplistic parents seem to think. It doesn't mean surrendering to the anything-goes philosophy. A sharp, clear line must be drawn, for the sake of the younger generation's welfare, between what is merely distasteful or silly and what is really dangerous or immoral or illegal.

Bernard Shaw once said he believed in strict old-fashioned Catholicism—although he himself was a free-wheeling Protestant—because he thought everyone needs something strong to rebel against! His point, which he made jokingly, was a serious one. It was that each generation has the need to feel that it is more adventurous, more innovative, more intelligent than the previous one, and that therefore, each new generation, as it is coming into its own, needs to assert itself by defying and changing some of the conventions of the previous generation.

If the older generation is very strict, so that a boy gets paddled for taking one puff on a cigar, he can exercise this psychological need to rebel very safely. He does "his thing" and gets punished for it and feels angry and defiant and makes up his mind to exercise his right to be himself by taking another puff just as soon as he gets another chance. But that's as far as it has to go. He has been able to gain the feeling of daringness and independence, which he needs if he is to succeed in the world, at a pretty low price: a cigar or two.

If, on the other hand, parents have no standards and enforce no rules at all, if they try to be so totally understanding that they allow a child to do absolutely anything the child can think of to do—first a few cigarettes at a too-early age, then more and more of them; then liquor at a prelegal age, and then more and more of it; and then pot, and then hard drugs; first late hours, then very late hours, unsupervised; and then "sleeping around," and then "shacking up"—youngsters have to go terribly far to get the feeling that they have gone *too* far. They may go so far they end up with VD or in jail for life.

I am not advocating taking your children behind the woodshed (assuming you can find one anywhere these days) and beating the daylights out of them if you catch them at a minor crime. But I am saying that we don't do our children any true service if we allow them to feel safe about doing things that are not safe. We know more than they do about a few things, and we should give them the benefit of our knowledge, which sometimes means not allowing them to do something they consider harmless or smart.

You can understand why your children have different preferences from yours and why they think certain old laws or conventions are stupid, without letting them think it's sophisticated and okay to hurt themselves or others. Find *safe* ways for them to express and assert themselves (let him grow his hair down to the floor if necessary; let her wear granny dresses no self-respecting granny would be caught dead in). Be somewhat lenient about minor infractions of minor rules but firm where safety—moral, legal or physical—is involved. Explain why and let the argument end there. There's nothing to discuss. You won't convince them you are making sense until years later, but that doesn't matter. What matters is their safety. Be definite and apply strong sanctions if necessary, though it probably won't be necessary if what you say is clear and consistent and definite.

It's lovely, by the way, when children find ways to rebel that are constructive instead of destructive. My own children have asserted their superiority to me and my generation by refusing to be so "dumb" as to get "hooked" on cigarettes. Their scornful comments when I smoke make me feel depraved but at least I have the satisfaction of knowing that *they* are not.

A remark which I think it is very helpful to remember is one which the British philosopher John Locke directed at parents several centuries ago: *"Never trouble yourself over faults in your children which time alone will cure."* So much abrasive and abusive nagging goes on in families, making "home sour home" an unpleasant place to live (and, when it does its worst, causing children to run away), in attempts to correct children's traits and attitudes. If we indulged in a little more "benign neglect," looking the other way when they did certain things which we cannot approve of, instead of jumping on them each time, they would outgrow some of the things we dislike more quickly and painlessly than they do when we keep criticizing them. Pope John also had a very good rule: "Praise most things; overlook many things; correct a few things."

Teen-agers are often troubled and troubling during the identity crisis they experience as they change from children into adults. The bizarre (to older people) clothing and hair styles so many of them insist on wearing these days are deliberate efforts to establish a recognizable identity distinct from and independent of the one they feel adults are trying to impose on them (unfortunately, in their efforts to discover their own independent identity many of them lose it by imitating each other even more slavishly and unquestioningly than anyone ever imitated a parent).

A single parent has to be extra careful not to become a deadly nag, because his or her voice is the only parental voice the children hear, and as I've said before, there is a tendency for unshared authority to become tyrannical. ("Power corrupts; absolute power corrupts absolutely.") The fact that you feel personally and solely responsible for your children's future may, if you're not careful and self-observant, make you so overanxious that you overplay your role.

When children are going through an unpleasant stage, the more you attack them for it the more stubbornly they will instinctively defend themselves against your attacks. Look back at your own life, during comparable stages, and gain some insight into the process by which you gradually evolved into the person you now are. You will realize that no stage is permanent and that it is the people you admire the most, people who are nice to you, who have the greatest influence over you in guiding you from one stage to the next. Some traits and habits do become fixed over the years, which is why serious character flaws (unlike fashionable fads) must not be ignored or condoned, but even with these, self-knowledge will help you discover the best tactics to use in trying to eliminate them.

Think of how you react when a basic aspect of your personality (or one which you temporarily think is basic) is angrily attacked, or when a conviction which you hold strongly is ridiculed. Don't you immediately feel defensive, angry, and hurt by your opponent, rather than humbly apologetic?

If you don't like to be nagged or insulted or bossed constantly or belittled or threatened, what makes you think your children feel any differently about it when you do those things to them? They don't. They will not be inspired to self-improvement by your "picking on them" nearly as much as they will if (1) they genuinely like and admire you and therefore want to please you, which is only possible if you are pleasant to live with and just to them, and (2) you truly love them and show them so in ways they can feel and want to repay. Loving someone doesn't mean being overindulgent or blind to their faults. It means trying to be understanding and considerate and appreciative of their good qualities and of their difficulties and helping them to fulfill themselves, not because this will reflect glory on you but because it is what will make them happy.

In order to get along peacefully with each other it is obviously necessary to learn to put up with our differences, but if we aspire to more than mere coexistence and absence of hot war we must do more than just tolerate each other. We must try—genuinely—to respect, appreciate, and understand each other. And we can't do that unless we really get to know each other—not totally, since that is never possible, but as well as we can. Even incomplete knowledge, when it is genuine knowledge, is useful.

People can live together for years and remain strangers, because of lack of communication. A frightening recent study of "happily married" couples found that the average couple spends only twenty-seven and a half minutes per week talking to each other! Many parents never sit down to relax and chat with their children in genuine back-and-forth conversation, or "meaningful dialogue" to use today's "in" term. They talk *at* their children or *down to* their children and *about* their children but not *with* them. They correct them, scold them, bark at them, give them phone messages and orders, tell them to pick up their socks and to put on their sweaters, to go outdoors or to come indoors, to get up or to go to bed, to eat faster or slower or less or more—but they don't really enter into an "I-thou" relationship. And then they have the nerve to wonder why their children don't confide in them, why they are so inconsiderate, so disobedient, so hostile. The children in turn wonder why their parents are so uninterested in them, so cold, so critical, so unsympathetic, and so "square."

There are also parents who talk *too* much . . . yak-yak-yak-yak-yak . . . and who never stop long enough to let their children get a word in edgewise. Communication, to be effective, has to go in two directions; parents must listen as well as talk to their children. An Arab proverb says God gave us two ears and only one mouth to show us that we should listen twice as much as we talk!

The title song of a very successful and moving musical show, based on the soul-searching writings of ghetto children, was taken from the heart-felt cry of one such child: "I am the ME nobody knows!"

In so many ways, every one of us is. You have felt this way yourself.

Nobody can ever be *fully* known by anyone else because no two people are ever exactly alike. That large mysterious core inside each one of us is inaccessible and private. God does not manufacture people on an assembly line or with a cookie cutter or carbon paper or a Xerox machine. There are no duplicates in creation (not even identical twins are wholly identical—ask one).

This is the most baffling and frustrating fact of life, but also, I think, the most fascinating. We all long for contact and communication and want to unite with someone we wholly understand and cherish who reciprocally and equally understands and values us. Our uniqueness therefore makes a certain amount of suffering, existential loneliness, unavoidable. But it also makes mutual fascination possible since there is always more to be learned both about ourselves and about others. And the more we learn the more we understand, and the more we understand the more we are capable of learning. It's another one of those marvelous chain reactions that can make life more and more fascinating once we start moving in the right direction.

If all of us were alike, mutual respect and communication would certainly be a great deal easier to achieve than they are (though much less interesting), but since that is not the case, what to do? The essential first step is to respect people, both ourselves and others. I must respect my me-ness and your you-ness, and so must you, and we must each respect every child's his-ness and her-ness. Even when the differences between you and your children are perplexing and irksome and large, each of you is entitled to fundamental respect and courtesy as a human being. If behavior is seriously wrong by your standards, and needs correcting, you can still respect the person who is misbehaving while not respecting the behavior. As Christian moralists put it: hate the sin but love the sinner. That unfathomable essence that makes you you and someone else someone else is holy ground, the most special and valuable thing about each of you. Don't violate it.

So many times when we criticize our children (particularly if we do it in front of other people) their feeling is that "you're always putting me down." Their immediate reaction is anger rather than contrition. Try to make them, as well as yourself, aware that you are putting *it*, the behavior, down, not them. The words you use, the explanations you give, the tone of your voice, the timing of your criticism, the opportunity you offer them to make amends and save face—all of these are important in preserving this vital distinction.

Explore the many ways in which you are alike, despite all differences both obvious and subtle. Don't forget to react with pleasure when they say and do things you like, so that they won't think the only way they can get your attention is by misbehaving or arguing. Look at things from their point of view as well as from your own, and try to find out what they like (and why) and what they don't like (and why), and let them know about and share what you like too.

Whenever you really get to know anyone well you discover many more areas of similarity and contact than are apparent when you are not close. So value and enjoy whatever you share in common, not instead of but in addition to valuing the uniqueness of each of you, and use the common ground as a basis for further close and frequent and deep communication.

Constant and reliable affection and understanding are the keys to good discipline—and good discipline is the key to successful achievement. I once watched a beautiful performance in England by some sheepdogs, in which they demonstrated their amazing skill at rounding up sheep scattered over many miles. I saw the eager speed with which they sprinted off when they received the signal to go, and how clever they were at finding all the wanderers and the solicitude with which they attended to each little stray, and then, having rounded them up, how joyously they wagged their tails as they rushed back to their master with their charges, and how he laughed and patted and hugged them while they licked him like an especially tasty lollypop. And I was fascinated to hear the shepherd's explanation of how he trained his dogs. He said four things were essential:

1. *patience*—instructions must be clear and repeated without irritation again and again and again, because learning something well takes a lot of time.
2. *gentleness*—you must speak in a calm and gentle voice, not a harsh or excitable one.
3. *praise*—all good behavior, both obedience and initiative, must be praised whenever it is done so that the doer will know he has done the right thing and will enjoy doing the right thing.
4. *consistency*—each of the first three things must be done *always*, or instead of teaching what you are trying to teach you will cause confusion.

Punishment has no part in the training. Punishment, he explained, would make the dog resentful or nervous. He could only be a happy and good dog if he loved you and trusted you completely, and he could only do that if you showed him what love is, by your unfailing patience and justice and affection.

Another time I saw a filmed demonstration of how seeing-eye dogs are trained, and the message was similar. One blind man was not allowed to have a dog because he, not the dog, failed his training course (owners of seeing-eye dogs get trained along with the dogs, an advantage parents and children don't have!). The man just couldn't remember to pat the dog every time the dog had helped him cross a street or rescued him from a danger, and the commentator explained that this inconsistency of reaction would eventually cause the dog to become so confused about what he was supposed to do that he would become unable to guide the man safely. The dogs *must* be rewarded *each* time they act correctly.

Incidentally, important as it is to acknowledge achievements, it has been found to be a mistake to *over*reward. The best reward is not a special treat afterward but the pleasure received by doing something well, knowing you are, and knowing that someone you love knows it and appreciates it.

If we make an extrinsic reward more important than the achievement itself the learner becomes less and less interested in what he is doing and more and more interested in what he is going to get out of it. He becomes so anxious to finish the activity, so that he can get the reward, that he no longer enjoys the activity in itself.

This useful pedagogical discovery I picked up not in a book on education or child care but in a delightful book about chimpanzees. The biologist Desmond Morris had put a group of chimps in an artist's studio to see if they could be taught to paint. Some of them loved holding a brush and stirring the paint and slapping it onto canvas. He let them do it as long as they were doing that but stopped them as soon as they began running around or throwing the paint at each other instead of at the easels. At this point he would take the equipment away and reward each chimp that had done a picture, with a banana—no punishment was given to those who had goofed off, but reward was given to those who had used the materials correctly. Gradually they all got the idea that if they put paint on the canvas they would get a banana. They began working more and more assiduously. For a while this improved their paintings but after a while it had the opposite effect. They worked faster and faster and more and more carelessly, tossing the paint any-which-way in their hurry to get a banana. Some would gobble the banana and dash back to the easel, throw a little more paint at it, run back to get another banana, and so forth, paying less and less attention to their pictures.

Only one chimp—named Congo—kept on painting. A true

artist, he enjoyed praise and he enjoyed bananas but he equally enjoyed the process of choosing colors, dipping his brush very carefully into them and very deliberately stroking a piece of canvas, swirling the colors in different patterns, making bold horizontal, vertical, and diagonal stripes and great sweeping circles, standing back to look thoughtfully at his work, and then adding little finishing touches. His ultimate reward, it is interesting to note, was international celebrity: he had two one-man shows, one in a London gallery and one in New York, which were taken seriously and admired by art critics!

You may feel I am denigrating human children by advocating teaching methods developed for dogs and chimpanzees. I certainly don't mean to. I realize human children have a far higher intellectual capacity than dogs and chimpanzees. Nonetheless, each of these times when I heard about the way in which these bright, active, happy animals were trained I couldn't help wincing in embarrassment. I wonder how great our children would be if we parents were as consistently patient and kind and intelligent in teaching them as these men are to their animals!

One mistake that single parents may be tempted to make in trying to correct a child's faults is to attribute them to the parent who isn't there. If you see a trait in your child which you dislike and which you know was a weakness of the other parent—a vicious temper or irresponsibility or anything else you dislike—naturally you will shudder and think, "Oh dear, he's going to turn out just like his father (or mother)!" But don't tell the child this or you may make your fears come true. You may convince him he is predestined to act that way and give him a fatal case of fatalism.

Correct the fault when it occurs (promptly and decisively, not going on and on about it); make it very clear that you dislike that kind of behavior—while at the same time making it clear that you don't dislike *him*—but don't make cracks about the fact that your wicked or weak ex-spouse acted the same way.

"Stop acting just like your father (or mother)" is an unfortunate remark that slips out of too many parents from time to time. Even married people are apt to say to each other when a child misbehaves, "Look at what your child just did," as if suddenly the child is no longer theirs, while they proudly take credit for "my" child's cleverness or goodness. This bias is all the more unfair when the other parent isn't around to give you back your own medicine.

There is no real reason to fear that an absent parent's influence will be stronger than your own. Since you are the only grown-up they live with, your children know no other adult's views as well as they know yours. For better or worse, therefore, you are the most influential person in their lives. Your influence is more obvious and thorough when they are little than in later years when schoolteachers and peers go a long way toward supplementing or nullifying it, but your attitudes are those that your children encounter daily and therefore regard as the norm.

I recently came across a list compiled by that prolific writer Anonymous, entitled *A Short Course in Human Relations*. It was a list of words, not aimed at parents but at business people. However, it is applicable to parent-child relations, because parents—as surely as any employer or advertiser or politician—are in the business of persuading. We want to convince our children to do the things that we believe will make them happy people, and treating them with courtesy and consideration will make them more receptive to our views than all the force, threats, punishment, or yelling in the world.

Here is the list of recommended words:

The 6 most important words: "I admit I made a mistake."
The 5 most important words: "You did a good job."
The 4 most important words: "What is your opinion?"
The 3 most important words: "If you please."
The 2 most important words: "Thank you."
The 1 most important word: "We."

Perhaps I have spoken too much in this chapter about problems and children's faults and discipline. The main way to bridge the generation gap is to emphasize the love you have for your youngsters, not the differences you have with them. They are people, not just children, and they are interesting people. Many families have the idea that you have to be polite to friends but needn't bother to be with your own family, that friends are people you choose to know but relatives are just people you happen to know and from whom you will escape as soon as you have the chance.

The old saying "Charity begins at home" has been in disfavor in recent years because it was so often interpreted as "charity begins at home and goes no farther." People have rightly come to realize that it must not *end* at home but must be extended far beyond the home and even beyond next-door neighbors, to people of other classes and races and nations. Some of us now seem to be in danger of going too far in the other direction, thinking "charity begins overseas" and need never be practiced at home.

There is no reason to be "either/or" about charity (and I trust you know that I am using the word to mean love, not alms). We should practice it at home *and* abroad, abroad *and* at home.

If you love people, it isn't hard to reach across a gap, whether that gap is large or small, across an ocean or a generation.

15

OPENING YOURSELF:
Facing the future without fear

The trouble with life is that we have to live it going forward but we only understand it looking backward. That remark by Kierkegaard is one of the wise observations I've picked up along the way which helps to explain things. And here is another one: There are no rules about stepping out into the new because nobody has ever been there before.

That is what is ahead of us: *unknown newness.* We are moving along on a conveyor belt which is carrying us forward inexorably, no matter how much we may at moments want to rest or get off or go backward, through areas we cannot always see clearly, toward a destination we cannot guess at with accuracy.

Even when what you are looking forward to is pleasant, the unknown is a little frightening simply because it is unknown. And how can you help being afraid when you know that some of the things you are going to run into up ahead are going to cause you difficulties and make you sad, and you have already felt the full force of difficulties and sadness, enough to last you a lifetime?

This book is nearly finished but some of the problems discussed in it are not yet over and never will be. Some will end soon, some a little later, some never, and some may be replaced by even more complex and difficult-to-solve problems. As the years go by many new concerns will replace those that occupy you now, and new situations will arise. Even without gazing into a crystal ball, we can see what some of these will be. There will be changes in your relationships with your children, as the children grow older and, eventually, away from you. Problems associated with your own increased age will also arise. Deaths of good friends. Failing health. Illness. Finally, your own death.

If these things were all you had to look forward to from now on you might well want to jump right off that conveyor belt. But we never know, really, what is up ahead. We never know for sure what is going to happen to us next. To think that everything in the future is going to be worse than everything we have have known in the past is to have an extremely limited imagination. Things in the future will be *different* from what they are now, but not all of them will be worse.

What are some of the particular problems which the future may hold for single parents?

If you are divorced, the parent who does not live with your children may continue, through conscientiousness or true devotion, to stay very close to your children. This may cause a few problems, and may relieve a few. That obviously depends on what kind of a person that parent is. In some cases, the absent parent will drift away. This too will cause some new problems and alleviate a few. There also may be a new marriage in the future (his or hers, or yours) which will bring with it both new complications and new opportunities.

If your ex-spouse becomes the spouse of someone else, you will have to cope with your feelings about your children's attachment to their new stepparent and perhaps, later, about their relationship with half-brothers and half-sisters. It is a strange, almost spooky, feeling to realize that your own children are becoming extremely close to someone you don't know and are usually not allowed to know. You will wonder if this is the kind of person you want to have influencing your children—and part of you will hope so and part of you may not, because you may be jealous.

Don't be. Jealousy is an idiotic emotion, uncalled for and self-destroying. The fact that someone else is nice and loved never takes a single thing away from you if you are also nice. But let jealousy lodge itself inside your soul and you will not be nice and therefore will not be loved, and that will be your fault, not the fault of the person you are jealous of. Be glad if your children have more than one or two adults in their life whom they can love and be loved by. Human hearts are large enough, or should be, to include more than one love, as every mother who has more than one child knows (a mother's lap is finite; love is not).

When your children go to visit their other family—the one you don't share with them—don't feel deserted. Rejoice in the fact that you now have some free time without having to pay a baby-sitter for it! Do something you enjoy that you can't do with the children.

And when they return, don't pry inquisitively into what they did while they were away, worrying about the fact that they may have had a better time there than they have when they're at home. They probably did. They were guests and got company treatment. But if you force them to tell you so, you will embarrass both them and yourself, and what will you have gained? If you really love them you should hope that they did have a very good time. If they want to tell you what they did, look interested, not wistful, while they describe how much more beautiful the other house is than yours, or how much better the meals are there than at home—children have never been known for tact! But a grown-up should be able to take this sort of thing in stride.

If they don't tell you much about it, never mind; it's really none of your business. It's the quality of the time that *you spend* with your children that is your concern, not what they do with their other parent, assuming that he or she isn't a monster who is trying to poison their minds; if that is really the case, you can get a lawyer or the family court to do something about it, but if it isn't then don't act as if it is.

Often, over the years, parents who don't live with their children become more and more remote, even eventually losing contact with them. They may move away, or become so absorbed in a demanding career or a new family that they neglect the children you had together. It is sad and hurtful when this happens, and if it happens to your children try to make up for it to them in some way. Try not to be bitter about it or to let them feel bitter. Explain that the indifference or neglect is no reflection on them; it is simply because life carries people off in different directions. Try to surround your children with friends who are loving, especially friends of the same sex as the disappearing parent so that they can learn how to relate naturally and easily to people of that sex. Try to fill their lives with such healthy interests and happy relationships that this one big hole in their lives won't expand and make them feel empty inside. It *is* a hardship, a blow—but people can survive hardships and blows. That's something you have discovered by now!

If you are a widow or widower, one of the things that will wound you as the years pass will be that your children will gradually forget their dead parent. If you loved him or her very, very much this will hurt you, even shock you. But childhood memories inevitably fade in time and they cannot be kept alive indefinitely by artificial respiration.

How long and how vividly should you try to keep the memory of a dead parent alive? Not only how long should you, but how long can you? And *how* can you?

The answer depends, of course, in part, on the children's age at the time when the death occurred. If they were very little they will forget dismayingly quickly. You can still help them to know about the person, but what they will remember is what you have told them, not what originally happened.

Don't make your children feel guilty or stupid when they

begin to forget. They aren't forgetting on purpose. They can't help it.

There are certain things you can do to keep early memories alive—photographs help, and anecdotes, and souvenirs. *Not* endless visits to the grave. These will remind the children of death and corpses, but not of a lovely, once very-much-alive person. Try to continue speaking of the dead parent naturally when doing so fits into the conversation—without sorrow, without dragging the subject in when it isn't relevant, without sticky sentimentality, and without harping on it. Occasionally tell funny or dramatic stories about the past. Remind them of little quirks that make the person a colorful and unique individual instead of a vague shadowy figure. Tell them facts they will find interesting, especially things they can respect, in which they can take legitimate pride.

But don't go on and on until you're a bore—and don't look pained if the children fidget. Don't overdo pride-inculcating, or sermonizing. Remember that a child who grows up under the shadow of a superhuman dead parent can became (1) very unrealistic about what to expect of other people and (2) extremely discouraged about himself because he knows he is not equally superhuman.

In short, in trying to keep a memory alive be sure you keep it *alive,* not mummified, neither overdoing praise nor, in trying to avoid that, overdoing criticism. Let your children know about a real human being, not a retouched photograph or plaster statue. Sometimes it may take considerable sleuthing to find faults to criticize, if your own attitude is worshipful. But it is worth the search, so that your children will know about the person you loved instead of a lifeless stereotype or an idealization that never existed in the flesh.

If you give the impression—especially if it's not merely an impression but a fact—that every time you speak of this person you have lost you get sad all over again, your children may conclude that every time you see *them* you feel a little sad, because they are constant living reminders to you of your once intimate relationship with this mysterious person they don't know. Poor Jean Jacques Rousseau, who made such a mess of his own private life (making his faithful mistress miserable for years by refusing to marry her and sending their many babies off to orphanages to be raised, without even looking at them), was tortured all through his childhood by the fact that his father practically never spoke to him without reminding him that his mother had died giving him birth. Because the father had adored his wife he hated the sight of the son who had, utterly unintentionally, caused her death, and the fact that the son was never allowed to forget this warped his personality permanently.

You are placing much too heavy a burden on small shoulders if you convince your children that their dead parent was such a genius or hero or saint that there is practically no hope of their ever living up in any way to his or her sacred memory. So try to be balanced, rational, moderate, and realistic in your appraisals and comments. Try to let your children grow up with pleasant but not idolatrous impressions of their dead parent as well as with good feelings about their own qualities. Another future possibility is that the day may arrive when a new person comes along who takes the dead person's place in your life. Don't feel "disloyal" or "unfaithful," if this happens. Don't think you should feel guilty for making a new attachment. Life does move on, and we are meant to move on with it. I know a widow who never removed the wedding ring her first husband had given her, even when she remarried many years later; she insisted on wearing both rings, which must have been a bit rough on Husband Number Two (but he was such a nice man that he understood and sympathized with how she felt, and his reward came on their tenth anniversary when she finally removed the first ring).

People who have been happily married are usually more eager to marry again than are people who have been unhappily married, so a widowed person who remarries is not betraying the dead but paying a compliment.

When your children finally grow up and go away from you, what then? Will you, if you are still unmarried, face a rerun of the terrible loneliness and sense of uselessness that you felt after your divorce or the death of your spouse? Will you feel that there is now nothing to do but to curl up and wait for the undertaker?

Not if you have paid any attention to, and believed, any of the points made in this book. You will by then have become so interested in so many people and things that a little extra free time will be welcome. Your children's departure will provide you with even more opportunities for happy and successful living than you have had before, not with fewer. And you will feel such satisfaction at the fact that your children are off on their own, as they are meant to be, and that you have helped them become independent, that you will be glad to be on your own too. And the more independent you are, the more full your own life is of your own interests, the more they will be glad to see you when they do. Coming home for holidays, or inviting you to their house for weekends or vacations, will not be an irksome filial duty they will have to be heroic to perform; they will actually want to see you.

What about growing old? Perhaps you feel that you can handle the problems you are facing now, or at least learn to one day, and that you could also handle even greater problems with a little more practice, if only you knew that you would always have as much energy and good health as you now have. But you know that as the years go by you will get more frail, more forgetful, and some of your friends will die, so your loneliness will increase and your health will deteriorate and your ability to earn a living will diminish. If you think far enough ahead into the future you can get really and truly scared.

I am not yet in my eighties so I cannot reassure anyone about the joys of being an octogenarian (except by referring them back to chapter 5), but I can reassure anyone younger than I am about the fact that joys can increase with the years. When I was in my teens I thought nothing could be so marvelous—the whole world was before me, and I had such good friends, and I was learning so much, doing so much that everyone younger than I was seemed unfortunate. I felt the same way in my twenties, but even more so; I wondered how I could ever have thought I was enjoying my teens, since the twenties were so much better. And in my thirties I wondered why everyone in their twenties didn't realize that they were still wet behind the ears. I don't intend to say what advanced age I have now reached, but I will say that every year opens up more possibilities and they keep getting better and better. There have been a few years I wouldn't want to relive, but the basic thrust of life, I have found, is not only forward motion but upward.

As you know by now, I am a proverb collector, and one I like very much is: "Whoever thinks all fruit ripens in the spring may know a lot about strawberries but knows nothing whatever about grapes." Lilacs are gorgeous in the spring; chrysanthemums are equally gorgeous in the fall; some things, like grass and floribunda roses, are beautiful all summer long; other things, like apple trees and mountain ranges and the ocean and the sky, are beautiful at every season. Beauty and joy are not dependent on a calendar, so throw in your lot with perennials and pine trees instead of with day lilies. Take advantage of the fact that human beings, unlike plants, have the fantastic freedom to choose when and how constantly they will bloom.

In America most people equate both happiness and beauty with youth. They forget that young people may have acne and teeth that need straightening, which embarrass them dreadfully, and that they have agonizing fears of inadequacy—sexual, social, and intellectual—caused by lack of experience, and that they have an even longer future to be scared of than older people do. But youth and beauty are not a matter of age nearly as much as of attitude. Surely you have known some youthful, beautiful, old people and some stodgy, unenergetic, prematurely old, young people. Youthfulness and charm are caused by vivacity, curiosity, ambition, eagerness, openness, friendliness—and those are things one can keep all one's life, if one chooses to. As Jack Benny said on one of his many thirty-ninth birthdays, "Age is a case of mind over matter. If you don't mind it doesn't matter."

As we get older most of us get double chins and paunches and are not as beautiful as our youngsters are—on the outside, anyway. But look at it another way: our youngsters are not as knowledgeable as we are. So which age group really has the greatest advantage, the greatest reason to rejoice in its state? Wine improves with age—why shouldn't people?

Yes, we have more aches and pains than we used to have—but we also have more patience to enable us to put up with them.

Yes, we have less energy than we used to have—but we also have more efficiency so that we don't need as much energy.

Yes, we have more problems than we used to have—but we also have more understanding about how to cope with problems.

Yes, we have more wrinkles than we once had—but life has taught us to be less vain than we once were, so we don't mind them as much as we would have when we were younger (and we can call them "character lines" and get to like them).

I don't mean to sound euphoric or manic about all the wonderful possibilities life has in store. Of course there are, and will be, certain times when things go wrong and get you down. No one is *always* in top form and no one's life is always the best it ever has been—the best is the best, not the average. There will be times when problems bunch up on you and seem to be more than you can handle. There will be times when sorrows will outweigh joys and failures will loom larger than successes. There will be times when you get mad at your children or yourself or other people, and times when you will feel as if you have forgotten or have been mistaken about everything you ever thought you had learned, and that every optimistic remark anyone ever made is sentimental nonsense. But here comes another repetition: these moods won't last; things change. And as you get older you will realize this more and more clearly, as a result of experience, and it will therefore become easier and easier for you to ride out the rough times.

Unfortunately, repetition is unavoidable when one is examining emotional attitudes and problems, and so is inconsistency— at least apparent inconsistency. So many times in this book, when I have been speculating about what single parents should or should not do, I have said "do this" but "don't *over*do it" and "*also* do this." At one point one says something like "be self-reliant" and at another "be sure to ask for help when you need it." Or "examine your past mistakes in order to learn from them" and then, in the next breath, "leave the past behind; it's *now* that matters."

This is because one is always trying to strike a sensible balance, "the golden mean" between opposite extremes. Yet even that is not always desirable! Not *all* extremes are to be avoided. For instance, you can never give your children too much love. You can all too easily give the wrong kind, too much attention or too much indulgence, but you can never give too much real *love*. You also can never acquire too much self-knowledge. You can become too self-absorbed, too self-centered, too selfish, but real understanding of yourself can never be excessive.

To achieve a perfect balance at all times is humanly impossible, however. Even a skillful tightrope walker wobbles precariously at moments. Yet we still have to keep trying to achieve balance—and that sounds like still another apparently inconsistent remark, saying one should strive for something unattainable. But as someone (was it Browning?) said, "Our reach must exceed our grasp." When we strive to do our best we will not succeed all the time but we will do better, more often, than if we had not tried. And doing (and being) a little bit better than we did (and were) before is worthwhile and should satisfy us. There's still another inconsistency! "Satisfy" is the wrong word, because it seems to imply that we will want to stop there, when we should want to make still further progress.

A Danish poet-wit, Piet Hein, put the problem this way in a delightful book of short aphoristic poems called *Grooks*:

> The road to wisdom? Well, it's plain,
> And simple to express:
> Err
> And err
> And err again
> But less
> And less
> And less.

Good advice is not only inconsistent and repetitious but also frequently trite. So many things that are true are obvious! So many breathtaking discoveries and original perceptions turn out to be merely adaptations and updatings or paraphrases of things that other people have often said before.

Truth is very rarely original. Much wisdom is stolen goods. There are many wise people in the world and many wise people who were in it once and who have left their wisdom behind to benefit the rest of us.

We do not *invent* truth; we *discover* it. It has been there all the time, and many other people discovered it before we did. But each of us has to discover the truth for himself, at the point when he needs it and is capable of comprehending it. A psychologist I know told me that truth is never useful to anyone until it collides with an experience. When people need a truth and realize they do, they look for it—and there it is! Waiting for them. Already known by someone else, but only now available to them.

Of all the important things I think I have learned so far in my fairly long life, one of the most important is that all through life we have to keep on learning and *un*learning and *re*learning what we thought we already knew. *We have to keep on keeping* *on*. We have to keep telling ourselves the same things in many different ways at many different times because even when we know somthing it takes a long, long time to realize all of its implications and applications. But every time we unlearn or relearn something we are learning more about it and seeing it in greater depth. Like the patina on a battered but valuable antique, the wisdom in an old cliche may shine more brightly each time we dust it off and repolish it.

There is another problem, though. We learn many things when it is almost too late to apply the knowledge. "Man only sees the handwriting on the wall when his back is up against it," Pete Seeger says. We learn to shift gears smoothly, and someone comes along and invents automatic transmission so that shifting gears is unnecessary. We learn how to diaper a baby quickly and neatly, and the baby outgrows diapers. We learn how to cope with "the terrible twos" and our child turns three and becomes a charmer. Not only is our knowledge acquired too late, but we can rarely sit back and bask in it—because always some new problem, which we don't know how to handle, promptly appears out of nowhere.

We resemble babies learning to crawl. No sooner do they find out how to zip around a room efficiently on hands and knees than they discover the possibility and desirability of walking upright, and then they have to go through the whole laborious process again of experimenting, longing, trying, failing, getting frustrated, struggling over and over, in order to acquire a new skill. And once they have mastered that, are they (or is the life force) satisfied? Not at all. They decide they want to learn how to run, and to climb, and to swim. It is our nature never to be able to stop, always to be driven to learn more and more and more. Tree branches have to reach out and spread or die, and so do we.

But this endless process is not futile. An athlete who pole vaults or skis or plays baseball or climbs mountains is doing things that exhilarate and delight him every bit as much as the baby is thrilled to learn how to climb out of his crib and maneuver himself across a room. If the baby had been commanded to stop learning once he had mastered these skills *that* would have been frustrating, but having to keep on learning is *fulfilling.* Human beings are made and meant to keep learning, just as much as the sun is meant to keep shining and fish are meant to keep on swimming.

A new problem is therefore not really something to deplore; it's a sure sign that one is making progress. And the rewards received for continuing to make progress are enormous. Our horizon keeps expanding, the light keeps getting brighter, the air keeps getting more invigorating. The problems may keep getting harder but the ability to cope with problems also keeps increasing, in direct proportion.

Happiness and success are worth whatever they cost us to achieve them because they are priceless. Have I just contradicted myself again by bringing in words like "happiness" and "success" right after saying no one can ever hope to escape problems and can never learn to cope with them until it is time to be faced with another even more difficult one? I don't think so, because I have made another very important discovery in my life: *Happiness and problems can peacefully coexist.* Success and frustration, happiness and confusion can be experienced simultaneously.

Neither happiness nor success is a static or permanent state of affairs, an accomplishment which is attained once and for all and then fixed in position. As long as we are alive, since we and the world we live in are both constantly changing, we are in perpetual motion (and perpetual emotion). Happiness and success are relative and variable states, and our conceptions of them keep changing along with their characteristics.

This does not mean that they don't exist. It does mean that they are part of a vast dynamic process. They are broad areas open to the wind and the rain as well as to sunshine. They are subject to continual alteration. But that too is nothing to weep about. In fact, it's something to cheer about, because—since they always contain unexpected qualities—we are spared the satiety that would kill desire, the stagnation and boredom that would destroy happiness.

While you keep on keeping on, don't overlook or underrate the power of religion to increase your happiness and power to cope.

Karl Marx regarded religion as "the opium of the people" because it makes "the masses" more docile and willing to put up with hardships and injustice than they would be without it. But if religion is to be compared to a drug, I would liken it to health-restoring medicine or to health-protecting vitamins or to an invigorating stimulant rather than to a tranquilizer or soporific or anesthetic. It may, to be sure, make you more willing and more able to endure hardships and injustices than you would be without it (surely, though, that's an advantage it gives you, not a disadvantage, something to praise it for rather than something to condemn it for), but it also can *challenge* and *inspire* and *compel* you to be more outgoing and more creative, less supine rather than more so. The belief that goodness is ultimately rewarded does not imply, to me, that one is meant to put up uncomplainingly with evil. It means that we are meant to provide ourselves with the spiritual power that will give us the courage and integrity and perseverance we need so that we can conquer and transcend evil, replacing it with good.

People who lack religious faith usually feel superior to the "superstitious" and "naive" people who possess it. I disagree. I think they are showing themselves to be less curious, less speculative, less observant, less grateful, less trusting, less *whole* than people who realize that there is more to human life than getting up in the morning and filling sixteen hours with transitory activities and then going back to sleep.

When newly divorced or widowed, religious faith is temporarily severely shaken—as a tree is by a hurricane. There is a period when one is apt to be so disillusioned or discouraged that pious phrases such as "God knows best" (which I think is true) and "everything happens for the best" (which I think is true far more often than we realize) stick in the throat, and if someone says them to you they have a hollow ring. You are convinced that you have quite clear evidence that God doesn't care about you or your children and is obviously not in firm control of things, at least not on a personal enough level to help you.

This is why I have not talked earlier in this book about turning to God for help in your troubles. When someone is starving his need for physical food is greater at the moment than his need for spiritual food, until something nourishing has been put in his stomach. Piety as an accompaniment and a supplement to practical help is very comforting to many people, but as a *substitute* for practical help, when one is struggling with a serious here-and-now problem, it is apt to seem phony and pretentious and even irrelevant—not because it really is, but because one's perception of its value is temporarily dimmed.

After a while, however, if one is observant and has tested it, religious faith may actually be strengthened by the doubts and challenges to it that one has had to overcome. When your situation has straightened out and you have regained your balance and can begin to make sense of all the bewildering things that have happened to you, you will be surprised to find how many of your former values have survived the interruption. You used to accept many things unquestioningly; then you were forced to question them; now you are capable of understanding them and accepting them less superficially, less simplistically, less naively, than before. You will discover (I think) that there does seem to be such a thing as Providence after all. Something awful has happened to you and you have not merely weathered it but have emerged stronger and better than ever. And then, the next time around, the blows you receive will not be as great, or even if they are, your ability to withstand blows will be so much greater that they won't feel as great, because you will realize from personal experience—the only kind of knowledge that is fully convincing—that there may be some very good reasons for and compensations for the blows.

As a result of my own journey from belief to skepticism and back again, I think I have made some valuable discoveries.
First of all, while in the pit of cynicism and confusion, we should try to keep our mouths shut! Lots of the things we feel like saying at such times, like those said in the heat of anger, are nonsense, and if we say them we will be sorry later. And if we are parents and have been sounding off in front of our children about how rotten the whole world is and how unreliable everyone is and how nothing ever makes any sense, these views, which express a very real but a temporary mood as far as we are concerned, may be taken seriously as a fixed point of view by our impressionable children. We may plant permanently in them attitudes of despair and cynicism and hostility, and if we do we won't like the kind of people they will turn into. Despair is a dangerous weapon and like all dangerous weapons it must be kept out of the reach of children!

Second, we must enlarge our perspective beyond the present moment and beyond ourselves. Many things that don't work out for us exactly the way we want or when we want may still be working out in the right way in the long run. When we ask God for things he sometimes answers "No" instead of "Yes" and sometimes he says "Not now but later," so we mustn't conclude too quickly that prayers aren't answered. We must learn to wait for their fulfillment. It takes a very long time for an acorn to grow into an oak tree, and a very long time to realize our most important dreams. But it is by continuing to try to actualize those dreams that we may be able eventually to make them come true, whereas if we toss our highest hopes away we can never achieve what we want most to achieve. So it's worth holding on to ideals that are worth holding on to, and to keep on dreaming dreams that are worth dreaming—even if no one else does. If they are larger than we are (and if they're worth having, they have to be—an ideal smaller than we are would hardly be an ideal ideal!) then we can be happy working toward them even if we never see them realized.

Moses never reached the promised land—but he helped other people get there. Christ died ridiculed and despised—but he has had a greater influence on mankind than any other person who ever lived. Martin Luther King died without seeing his dream of racial brotherhood realized, but he *will* overcome someday! Johnny Appleseed had no idea how many apple trees would spring up where he scattered seeds by the roadside, but apple trees have been beautifying (and nourishing) all of America ever since. So if we keep holding fast to our dreams and ideals we can make them valuable forces in many other people's lives and help other people achieve them even if we don't. A strong enough belief and determination on one person's part can make many wonderful things happen that would not happen otherwise. The history of every important invention and discovery has been the same: one person had the guts to hold on to and stand up for what he knew was true, even when nobody else cared about it or when everyone thought he was crazy.

So don't be afraid to be yourself and to believe what you believe, whether or not others do. Even if you think everyone else on earth is opportunistic and dishonest and selfish (an idiotic exaggeration) that does not mean you have to join them. That would be like throwing away your own vitamin pills because you think everyone else has a vitamin deficiency.

And don't be afraid of getting hurt. By locking up the door of your heart to protect yourself from all pain you close yourself off to life's deepest and most beautiful experiences. People could never fly an airplane or sail a boat or ride a horse or climb a mountain or swim or do anything else enjoyable if they were always afraid they might get hurt. No one could ever even cook a meal if he was too afraid of fire. Anything worth doing—above all, living and loving—involves risk. So keep on taking risks, gambling on life and love, even when the odds seem stacked against you. If you don't like the way things are at the moment at least keep on liking the way you think they *could* be, instead of deciding not to like anything at all anymore. By remembering and continuing to live by your values, instead of accepting the lowest common denominator as your guide, you may be able to change the way things are into a nearer approximation of your ideals, but you will be issuing yourself a guarantee that the best will never happen to you if you give up hoping. Some people in your life may have deeply disillusioned you and betrayed you, but don't conclude that you should imitate their behavior, or that everyone else will too. People are not all alike.

There is a poster that says what I am trying to say much more succinctly and eloquently than I can:

> *Believe in the sun even when it is not shining.*
> *Believe in love even when it is absent.*
> *Believe in God even when he is silent.*

Obviously I don't know what your conception of God is; I can only speak for my own. But I am certain that he is *there*—always—though not always accessible to us, not because he closes himself off from us but because we close ourselves off from him. He is like air—able to supply the oxygen we need in order to live—but we sometimes hold our breath. He is like light—able to supply what we need in order to see—but we sometimes shut our eyes. He is like food—able to supply what we need in order to grow and stay strong—but we can close our mouths and refuse to eat. He is like a rock to stand on—but we can jump off.

He is not a pushy, doting, protective, indulgent baby-sitter who keeps us out of trouble and gives us whatever we want. He is more like an intelligent, far-sighted, ambitious-for-us parent who allows us to make our own experiments and even serious mistakes so that we can learn from them, and I think he uses our mistakes to force us to learn things which, if he spoon-fed us everything we needed in advance, we would never bother to learn.

In short, I think he creates, guides, and inspires us but then undictatorially expects us to make our own way. We can relate to his powerful, permanent, and loving spirit if we want to, but there is a precondition we must accept if we want his help. We can only communicate with him through faith, hope, and love. And it is not unreasonable that we need these qualities before we can receive his help. The best teacher in the world could not teach anything to a student who refused to listen to him or to do his assignments. The best therapist in the world couldn't be any help to a patient who had no faith in him or in therapy. The best cook in the world couldn't feed someone who refused to touch food. So we need to keep ourselves wide open, alert, appreciative, responsive to his guidance—even when it's hard to.

God's ways are not our ways. The evils he permits often baffle and scandalize us. But trying to discover what his ways are, and why they are what they are, and what we are meant to do about them, trying to learn to relate to him more and more closely, and to converge our ways with his, is the most stimulating, fascinating, inspiring, and finally the most deeply satisfying thing that anyone can do during a lifetime.

And if you ever succeed in developing a strong enough abiding sense of the presence of God, you will have such fresh, invigorating air to breathe, such a solid rock to stand on, such nourishing food to strengthen you, such a brilliant, undying flame to light your way even through darkness, that no personal problems will have the power to annihilate your deep-down joy. How can you ever feel really lonely or altogether worthless if you are truly and continuously conscious of God's living, loving presence—with you, in you, beside you, under you, over you, behind you, in front of you? And how can you ever feel utterly defeated, no matter what obstacles confront you, if you can grasp the intuition Saint Teresa of Avila possessed when she was asked once how she managed to accomplish so much in spite of the opposition of many powerful people. Her reply was, "Alone I couldn't. I'm only one person. But Teresa and God together constitute a majority!"

Many people today talk about "mind-blowing" and "consciousness-raising" experiences, and some of the ways in which a few people are trying to heighten their consciousness are more mind-destroying than mind-expanding. Yet they are right to want to expand their consciousness and to sense that it can be done. Many people do get genuine, thrilling glimpses of their oneness with one another and the oneness of everything with the All, an awareness of how everything and everyone in the entire universe is intimately united and interrelated, from the nearest pebble or leaf to the farthest star, from the tiniest electronic particle to the great unending vastnesses beyond the cosmos, and when one achieves this sense of unity with the creative power that initiates and supports everything that exists, one's own individual concerns seem to dissolve like tiny dewdrops glistening and then evaporating in the warm, bright rays of the morning sun.

"Put your hand in the hand of the man who stilled the waters," as the folk song says: he came that we might all be one and that we might have life and have it more abundantly.

Make up your mind to be happy. You are not a piece of furniture that has to stay where it is put and that can do nothing on its own. You are not a tree that has no choice but to stand wherever it has been planted. You are not a cloud that must weep when it gets filled with water. You are a human being, with the marvelous power to decide what you want to do and how you want to feel about the things that you do. Decide to enjoy them.

Happiness is not lying around somewhere waiting for you to stumble across it and pick it up. It is something inside you, waiting for you to develop it. It is something you must *create* for yourself.

Many people think of problems and happiness, or of duty and happiness, as opposites in perpetual conflict. The Bible, however, uses the same word—blessed—to mean both good *and* happy. Spiritual teachers have proclaimed over and over again the "good news" that the goal of life is eternal (that is, unending) happiness, but it sometimes seems as if they don't mean it. Pious gloom-spreaders sometimes twist God's good news into strange and unpleasant shapes and become "multipliers of burdens" even though Christ said they shouldn't be, and so many strict, burdensome rules have been invented to keep people on "the straight and narrow path" that the Kingdom of Heaven (translation: true happiness) which is "within you" has been shoved farther and farther away, until it often seems as if the only happy Christian is a dead Christian. Some "good" people have strapped themselves into psychological and moral straitjackets and they struggle along in this "valley of tears" so grimly that solemnity at best and anguished suffering at worst seem to be their goal in life. Self-denial, self-sacrifice, self-punishment, breast-beating, even self-loathing are proclaimed from some pulpits as desirable attitudes for followers of a man who said he came into the world so that we all might have life and have it more abundantly! The radiant joy which theologians consider a sign of true holiness has not been a conspicuous characteristic of people who worship the cross more than they imitate the spirit of the man who carried it.

But unhappiness is *not* blessedness. It is not virtuous. It's ingratitude. It's wastefulness. It's lack of imagination. It's sloth. It's a failure to appreciate the many truly marvelous things there are in this amazing world. It seems to me extremely bad manners directed against an extremely generous creator. People who make happiness, instead of God, into a god are not, however, in any better position than the people who think they have a holy obligation to be miserable. Happiness eludes them as much as it eludes the self-made martyr—because happiness is not something that can be had for the asking. Happiness cannot be obtained just by wanting it. It almost always comes to us as a by-product of something else, as a reward for something else, sneaking up on us when we are not expecting or looking for it, in disguise. If we insist on having it, it runs away from us. But if we give up looking for it and do other things instead, we find it while we are looking for something else.

People who try to live a good, active life, helping other people, being very interested in many things, being too busy to look for happiness, are the people who create it for themselves.

Cultivate anxiety and you can spoil any pleasure, no matter how many life gives you. If that is the kind of person you are, there is one comfort: tense and anxious people die sooner than other people do, so you will be relieved of your misery sooner than you might be. But it is surely better to get rid of your anxieties, tensions, and stresses than of your life. Say *no* to them.

George Bernard Shaw once said that his goal in life was to be thoroughly worn out before being discarded on the scrap heap. With this attitude, he lived a lot longer, and more actively, and more productively, than most people do. Don't be afraid to use yourself up. Remember that muscles which are exercised don't become flabby. Windows which are opened regularly don't get stuck so that you can't open them. Machinery which is used hard and often doesn't rust. So stay active and stay curious and you'll stay alive as long as you're alive. Don't do things halfheartedly; it's bad for the heart.

The antidote to stagnation and decay is to give yourself freely and fully to whatever you are doing. The only lasting way to enrich yourself is to spend yourself. The only true way to love yourself is to love others. The more you give the more you get. You know, this is really a rather nice universe after all, for all its defects, because that's a very nice way to have things arranged!

God does not give us the courage today to fight tomorrow's battles; he only gives us the courage to fight tomorrow's battles tomorrow. But he will give us today what we need for today, if we don't turn our backs on him and clench our fists so tight that he can't hand it to us.

There are many things that we still don't know, but that's

an invitation to learn them, not a reason to despair. A crossword puzzle is incomplete, full of blanks; they are there to be filled in, and it's fun to fill them in. Life, too, is full of unknown empty spaces—and it's wonderful filling them in.

On the subject of life's difficulties, Henry Van Dyke wrote: "No doubt a world in which matter never got out of place and became dirt, in which iron had no flaws and wood no cracks, in which gardens had no weeds and food grew ready cooked, in which clothes never wore out and washing was as easy as the soapmakers' advertisements describe it, in which rules had no exceptions and things never went wrong, would be a much easier place to live in. But for purposes of training and development it would be worth nothing at all. It is the resistance that puts us on our mettle; it is the conquest of the reluctant stuff that educates the worker. I wish you enough difficulties to keep you well and make you strong and skillful."

We can learn to accept difficulties and uncertainty. To feel secure without having or expecting total security. To step into the unknown unhesitantly.

This is really not too hard to do once we have done it often enough to learn that most of the things we fear are not nearly as dreadful once they actually occur as they seemed while we were apprehensively anticipating them.

If, at the present time, you are very unhappy, you will probably think I am talking rubbish. But the very fact that you are able to read this book, even if you think it is nonsense, at least attests to the fact that you are still alive. Alive in spite of the fact that some pretty disastrous things have happened to you.

If your husband or wife has died or your marriage has broken up or you have had an illegitimate baby, you are someone who has managed to survive one of the most difficult experiences you could possibly have. So even if you have not yet learned anything else, you have at least learned that you can survive a major crisis. And that is no small thing to learn about yourself. It is the type of knowledge which may not be pleasant to acquire but which is pleasant to possess. It is good to know your own strength. And no strength is stronger than that which grows out of and surmounts weakness.

A person who thinks he is capable of taming lions, but who has never actually had to face a real roaring lion, has faith in himself that may be illusory. It is built on opinion and hope rather than on fact. But a person who knows he can tame a lion because he has actually tamed one has a kind of self-confidence and self-esteem that will make it even easier for him to tame the next lion he meets.

So whatever disasters your life may have brought you in the past, you now have one enormous advantage over people who have never been through a disaster: *you know that you possess a degree of genuine strength.* And that knowledge is a very solid foundation on which to build a future.

You may not actually *feel* as strong as I say you *are*. A person who has just confronted a lion may feel rather trembly and exhausted, weak in the knees. But the fact remains that you have succeeded in getting through the first part of one of the hardest tests life is ever going to give you. So, instead of sympathy, you deserve congratulations!

Single parenthood, in some ways, combines the disadvantages of both matrimony and the single life. A single parent has unavoidable familial duties and worries (financial obligations, limited free time and privacy, parental responsibilities, etc.) along with a certain amount of loneliness due to the lack of any live-in adult companionship.

However, that is only one way—the negative and destructive way—to look at it. It would be equally true to say that single parenthood combines the advantages of both states of life: the gratifications of parenthood along with the comparative freedom of singleness.

So it's all in the way you look at it . . . like whether or not you consider a glass of water half-full or half-empty.

Whether something is a curse or a blessing, a disadvantage or an advantage, a stumbling block or a stepping stone, depends very much on how we approach it. Viewed fearfully, every challenge is a problem. Viewed hopefully, every problem is a challenge. And every challenge involves dangers but also many marvelous, unexpected, creative, happiness-providing new opportunities.

So stay open . . . let the sun shine in and let the wind blow and let the rain rain! When there's a chilly spell, protect yourself with a raincoat, umbrella, boots, sweater, gloves and scarf, but don't spend your days huddled inside a closed room—or heart.

Many older people bundle up so heavily against the elements that they can't move with any freedom. They are so careful to avoid drafts that they never get a chance to breathe deeply of health-giving fresh air. They're afraid bright light will hurt their eyes, so they stay cooped up, with the curtains and shutters drawn, in a perpetually dark world, while the interesting, active world they have withdrawn from passes them by. They worry about failing eyesight, hardening of the arteries and stiffness of the joints, when what is really sad is that their enthusiasm for life is failing, their hearts are hardening and their viewpoint is stiffening.

Don't be afraid to take risks—sometimes it's better to be sorry than safe. Don't regard temporary setbacks or disappointments as permanent failures or tragedies. Be flexible instead of fearful, relaxed instead of rigid.

In short, even if sometimes someone else cheats you, don't cheat yourself. That's all you'll accomplish if you let life be wasted on you. As long as you're alive, stay alive: aware, appreciative, adventurous, receptive, responsive, *loving*.

Warm, outgoing, generous, supportive, patient, persevering, creative love is not merely the key to and secret of successful parenthood. It is the very foundation and essence of eternal happiness.